CONTEMPORARY NATIVE AMERICAN LITERATURE

BAAS Paperbacks

Series Editors: Simon Newman, Sir Denis Brogan Chair in American Studies at the University of Glasgow; and Carol R. Smith, Senior Lecturer in English and American Studies at the University of Winchester.

Contemporary Native American Literature

REBECCA TILLETT

EDINBURGH UNIVERSITY PRESS

© Rebecca Tillett, 2007

Edinburgh University Press Ltd
22 George Square, Edinburgh

Typeset in Fournier by
Koinonia, Manchester, and
printed and bound in Great Britain by
Athenaeum Press Ltd, Gateshead

A CIP Record for this book is available from the British Library

ISBN 978 0 7486 2149 1 (paperback)

Contents

CHAPTER I

Introduction

This book provides an introduction to contemporary Native American literature, focusing throughout on the complex and problematic socio-political status of contemporary Native Americans as colonised peoples within a colonial state. Contemporary Native American literature emerges directly from this imperial relationship, and from the engagement of Native peoples with the legacy of the federal–Indian relationship within a country that is, paradoxically, both colonial and post-colonial. Native writing also emerges from dual literary traditions: from the interactions of individual writers both with the Euro-American literary heritage and with traditional Indian forms of literature, including oral storytelling.

The complexities of the topic are immediately apparent in the very terminology used: the term 'Native American' refers widely to any indigenous community or individual of the Americas, and is the subject of dissent among many Native peoples. Similarly, 'American Indian' is also a disputed term, and the reason for dissent derives from the fact that these are terms not only of identification, but also of 'classification', complete with the numerous problematic 'scientific' connotations of the term. In this sense, they are colonial names that have been imposed upon Native peoples, often eliding Native languages and expressions. This book negotiates this terminological minefield by employing the common tactic of using terms such as 'Native American', 'American Indian' and 'indigenous' interchangeably. I fully recognise that this approach tends to homogenise highly diverse cultural groups within a single generic term, and I have tried to compensate for this by referring to and discussing the individual tribal affiliations of each writer and the variation of worldviews that are expressed.

Given the complex politics, individual writers and their works are fully situated within a detailed socio-cultural context including Indian–white relations, popular Euro-American perceptions and contemporary Native political realities. These contexts are particularly useful as many Native writers express a range of concerns directly related to, for example, the enactment of specific federal Indian policies, and their profound impact upon Indian communities. However, equal care has been taken to foreground Native strategies of resistance to ongoing colonisation, for example the ways that many Indian writers engage both with Euro-American literary traditions and with a range of indigenous oral storytelling traditions and techniques, as a means by which indigenous cultures can be celebrated and, most importantly, continued Indian agency demonstrated.

Gerald Vizenor very pertinently asks of the emergence of Native writing, '[w]hat did it mean to be the first generation to hear the stories of the past, bear the horrors of the moment and write to the future?'.[1] It is within this historical and political context that this book traces the emergence and development of Native writing from the late eighteenth century to the present day, with a constant emphasis upon the political implications of bearing witness to the historical 'moment' in order to 'write to', and thus actively create, an emphatically Indian 'future'. This book therefore considers not only the significance of a series of important historical moments within federal–Indian relations and federal Indian policy, but also the range of literary and political strategies evident and/or developing within Native writings that, from the earliest publications, assert Indian agency by 'writing back' to the colonising force. Given the persistent critique by Native writers of federal–Indian relations and thus, ultimately, of Euro-American–Indian social relations, the attraction of Native writings and writers for an Euro-American audience remains paradoxical, yet clearly draws upon the simultaneous fascination and repulsion that Native cultures have historically held for European and Euro-American societies, and which has become normalised within discourse on the 'Indian Problem'.

To highlight this complex cultural relationship, this book employs case studies of individual writers and key texts in order to assess the impact of important literary innovations and of prize-winning works. Additionally, this approach allows an analysis of the ways in which key Native writers, of fiction and non-fiction, have responded to important political events and issues: for example, the power of institutions (the Christian church, academic disciplines such as anthropology, and the legal and educational systems) over Native peoples; the impact and ramifications of momentous events such as the Wounded Knee Massacre

(1890); the prevalence of persistent and damaging forms of racism, both social and institutional (analysed in Native fiction as early as 1854); and the damaging cultural effects of a range of federal Indian policies that have attempted to redefine the very structure and identity of Native communities and individuals. Central to many Native writings is a recognition that the federal/Euro-American assimilation process requires the complete eradication of Native cultures, and the relationship between Native writers/texts and Euro-American audiences is, therefore, highly complex.

However, an ongoing Euro-American attraction to and interest in Indian writings and cultures provides a wide audience for a range of Native political and literary strategies. In this context, many Native writings can be interpreted as part of a long tradition of negotiation and mediation between cultures, and as interventions into established and implicitly racist Euro-American discourses that employ the conventions of Manifest Destiny to identify traditional Native cultures as redundant in a 'modern' world. This book analyses these negotiations and mediations, especially the acts of cultural 'translation' that make Native worldviews both visible and accessible to the non-Native reader. A repeated feature of the act of cultural translation is the representation of the profound effects of the historic Euro-American–Indian relationship: the cultural dis-location articulated by writers as diverse as Samson Occom (1772), John Rollin Ridge (1854), D'Arcy McNickle (1936), and N. Scott Momaday (1968). Indeed, the ultimate form of cultural dis-location, the precarious socio-cultural status represented by 'mixed blood', remains so politically significant that it persistently appears in Native fiction from Mourning Dove's *Cogewea the Half-Blood* (1927) to Leslie Marmon Silko's *Ceremony* (1977) and Sherman Alexie's *Indian Killer* (1996).

Fundamental to the cultural translations of Native literature is a range of significant literary strategies and tropes that emphasise the importance of Indian cultural ideas and the continued relevance of traditional Indian values and worldviews. Perhaps the single most significant cultural concept is the oral storytelling tradition, which has been emphasised by recent Native writings that attempt to translate the oral storytelling process into the written word, and to explain the significance of story and the power of spoken words to Native cultures. If, as Jana Sequoya suggests, cultures can be interpreted as 'ways of having stories',[2] then cultures are also ways of *telling* stories. For Native peoples, therefore, the stakes are high, with cultural stories representing the 'social, political, and economic *conditions of possibility for Indian identity* within the ... national context'.[3] Native literature is thus intrinsically political.

Many Native writers re-present important Native cultural stories as an illustration of the oral tradition: for instance, the ongoing cultural relevance of sacred stories emphasised by the re-tellings of writers such as Leslie Marmon Silko, Simon Ortiz and Luci Tapahonso. Yet, significantly, a variety of diverse writers – including Anna Lee Walters, Louis Owens, Gerald Vizenor and Sherman Alexie – also engage subversively and ironically with the 'Indian' stereotypes created by Euro-America. This deliberate and emphatic use of humour can clearly be identified as an extension of traditional Trickster discourse, where humour not only challenges and subverts imposed stereotypes and Euro-American cultural assumptions, but also highlights and makes memorable a range of serious political issues.

This emphasis upon the political, and especially upon the ways in which literary politics are presented, is the perhaps most significant focus of this book. A range of political literary strategies and concerns are assessed, including the individual and communal engagements with federal policies and tribal politics that are evident within the Native texts under consideration. On occasion, there is a clear engagement with specific external political movements that impact upon Native Studies, and examples include the intersections with Third World feminism evident in many works by Native women, or the telling absence at the close of the twentieth century of discussions of contemporary Native masculinity and its relationship to Native rights. Indeed, from its first appearance, the most notable aspect of Native writing has been its ability to present deeply complex and often highly unpalatable political truths to Euro-American readers. As a result, Native writings have persistently demanded a reader response that is active, and perhaps even activist. This articulation is most emphatically and succinctly summarised by the contemporary Cherokee writer Jimmie Durham, who asks

> ... how can I write, carry on intellectual or cultural investigations, when our [Indian] situation demands activism? ... Reader, as you read, I want you to have similar doubts and recognise a similar need for activism, at a time and in circumstances that should be intolerable to all of us.[4]

This book considers the complex and varied articulations of these literary demands.

Notes

1. Gerald Vizenor (1994), p. 51.
2. Jana Sequoya (1993), p. 460.
3. Ibid. p. 453, emphasis added.
4. Jimmie Durham (1993), p. 243.

CHAPTER 2

The Emergence and Development of Native American Literature

A Fascination with All Things 'Indian'

With the arrival of European settlers in the New World, there developed a fascination throughout Europe with all things 'native'. This was demonstrated both through the consumption of Indian culture as entertainment through 'travel narratives' that described Indian social practices; and through concerted efforts to Christianise indigenous communities through missionary activity and the creation of an Indian education system. Thus, very early in America's settlement, copious publications emerged that were aimed at an increasingly curious European audience, and discussed Native American cultures often in direct contrast or comparison to European 'civilisation', either as popular entertainment or as an experiment in religion and/or education.

Some of the earliest settler publications illustrate the often simultaneous attraction and dread with which the Europeans viewed America's indigenous peoples.[1] Thomas Harriot's 'A Brief and True Report of the New Found Land of Virginia' (1588) is in effect an ethnography of the Native population, describing their lifestyle and customs. Badly clothed, badly armed, and of limited cultural, intellectual and physical development, Harriot concludes that 'in respect of us [the English settlers], they are a poor people'.[2] As Governor of Plymouth Colony, William Bradford describes the dangers offered by the 'stout and warlike' Pequot who 'slew sundry' settlers.[3] Such descriptions catered for a growing European market for New World 'travelogues', and Bradford assuages any fears of potential settlers by reporting that the Pequot were subsequently 'fry[ed] in the fire' of English victory.[4]

The popularity of this type of narrative, with its sense of titillation for far-removed European readers, is perhaps most evident within Mary Rowlandson's narrative of her captivity (1682), which became a 'bestseller' in seventeenth-century Europe. Rowlandson's tales of her experiences emphasised the physical, spiritual and sexual dangers in which she found herself. While Rowlandson is quick to note that 'not one of them [the Indians] ever offered … the least abuse of unchastity to me',[5] it is possible that the undertone of sexual danger played a key role in assuring the popularity of the text. Rowlandson's text is also important for its emphasis upon Christian endurance and depiction of Native peoples in emphatically religious terms: her captors are a 'company of hell-hounds' engaged in 'devilish cruelty'.[6] While Rowlandson's attitude is common, the alternative was a more philanthropic and religious/spiritual approach to Indian assimilation. Roger Williams' project to provide 'keys' (1643) to indigenous languages was a declared attempt not only at better communication (a desire to 'spread civility'), but also at promoting a wider understanding of Native culture as something other than inherently sinful.[7] Although Williams himself was not an advocate of assimilation, his text is significant for its subsequent use in highlighting the positive benefits of Indian religious conversion and social assimilation, and for enabling Christian missionary activity.

These two attitudes – Indians as sources of fascination and/or as souls to be saved – became quickly ingrained and normalised both within popular culture and within discourse on the 'Indian Problem'. Consequently, a combination of the two can be detected throughout the nineteenth century and the Indian Wars in the concerns of federal Indian policy, and in philanthropic projects such as Indian education. Thomas Jefferson's letter to Meriwether Lewis (1803), giving detailed instructions for the Lewis and Clark Expedition's approach to the Native Americans they would encounter, clearly outlines a list of ethnographic data that should be collected, including 'peculiarities in their laws, customs, & dispositions'.[8] Significantly, details of 'the state of morality, religion & information' are requested for the subsequent benefit 'of those who endeavour to civilize & instruct them'.[9] This paradoxical combination of hostility and philanthropy is perhaps most evident in the principles of the Carlisle Indian School, founded in 1879 in former army barracks in Pennsylvania by Captain Richard Pratt, a veteran of the Indian Wars. An extension of Pratt's experiments of the early 1870s in acculturating Indian prisoners of war in his charge at the notorious Fort Marion prison in Florida, Carlisle was run in accordance with military principles and Pratt publicly stated that his educational policy was to 'kill the Indian, and save the man'.

It is in response not only to European settlement but also to these types of entrenched popular attitudes that many Native American authors begin to write, often – like slave narratives of the nineteenth century – with the published word used as a means by which a dialogue with white society could be established. Many of the early writings can be read as responses to ongoing social problems, such as racism, violence and land theft (for example, John Rollin Ridge's 1854 novel *The Life and Adventures of Joaquín Murieta*); the increasingly precarious social status of the 'mixed blood' Indian (discussed in Mourning Dove's 1927 novel *Cogewea*, among many others); or the alienating experiences of Native children forcibly removed from their families to attend 'Indian schools' such as Carlisle (for example, Luther Standing Bear's reminiscences in *Land of the Spotted Eagle* (1933)). Native writers also often responded directly to specific and sometimes traumatic national or local events (the Wounded Knee Massacre of 1890 is the final focus of S. Alice Callahan's 1891 novel *Wynema*); to the ramifications of implementing federal policies such as the 1887 Dawes General Allotment Act (discussed by John Joseph Mathews in his 1934 novel *Sundown*); or to the ongoing power wielded by the Christian church and American legal system over reservation communities (evident in D'Arcy McNickle's 1936 novel *The Surrounded*).

In this sense, much Native American writing clearly embodies and expresses the concerns of indigenous Americans as colonised peoples: for example, the effects of displacement, language loss, enforced Christian conversion, enforced education and the loss of sovereignty, to name but a few. Equally evident are the economic, legal, social and political conditions of colonisation, and Indian responses to them. Nonetheless, the use of 'postcolonial' theory within Native Studies remains contentious: while postcolonialists have long identified literature as one of the means by which colonised peoples respond to their colonisers, there has generally been a marked (and remarked) tendency to disregard Native Studies entirely.[10] One distinct problem seems to be that the concept of the 'post-colonial' is usually taken to apply to post-Revolution American society, which is clearly problematic in terms of the colonisation to which America's Native peoples are still subject. Paradoxically, contemporary American society is therefore both colonial *and* postcolonial, and the application of postcolonial theory to Native Studies should be understood as a process by which the responses of colonised groups can be assessed. In this context, many Native writings exhibit a range of strategies of resistance and also foreground not only indigenous cultures but specific storytelling traditions and techniques. These are presented as an alternative to Euro-American literary techniques and expectations, and as a form of active resistance to imperial worldviews, but also as a discussion and celebration of Native cultural ideas and values. Most importantly, the writings discussed in this study highlight the continued agency of Native peoples in their interactions with the colonial power. Accordingly, the following readings will both assess specific Native writings as negotiations with, and resistances to, the forces of colonisation, and also explore Native writings more fully within their own cultural contexts.

Early Native Writings: the 'Christian Indians' of Connecticut, 1772–1836

Given the emphatically Christian context of American settlement, it is both inevitable and ironic that the first published Native text in English (1772) should be a Christian sermon. Its author, the Mohegan Samson Occom (1723–92), had converted to Christianity at the age of sixteen or seventeen, during the religious revival (the 'Great Awakening') that swept Connecticut in the 1730s and 40s. Occom subsequently attended a private Christian school run by the evangelical preacher Eleazar Wheelock. Becoming an ordained minister in 1759, Occom also recruited further Indian students for Wheelock, and undertook a two-year fundraising tour of England in the mid-1760s, where he testified unsuccessfully on behalf of the Mohegan in a land claims case in London. Wheelock's failure to support the case, and his decision to use the monies raised in England to found Dartmouth College rather than the Indian Charity School for which it was collected, fed Occom's disillusionment with Euro-American culture. In 1774, Occom negotiated a tract of land – Brothertown – in central New York for a community of Christian Indians, where he remained as a teacher and spiritual leader until his death in 1792.

Occom's writings emerged directly from his own personal circumstances and interactions with white settler society. Occom's status as a Christian Indian, and his work among his fellow Mohegan as a Christian missionary, ensured that his role – and to some extent his identity – was one of constant negotiation and mediation. His writing inevitably reflects this liminal socio-cultural status. Occom's text, *Sermon Preached By Samson Occom ... at the Execution of Moses Paul, an Indian* (1772), was attractive for a white audience due in part to the general popularity of execution sermons (which had become something of a New England tradition); and in part to an ongoing fascination with Indian lives and the concept of Indian 'savagery': Moses Paul was a Christian convert who had murdered a respected white citizen while under the influence of alcohol. Thus pervasive popular Indian stereotypes, and entrenched ideas of Native Americans as biologically 'savage' and ultimately irredeemable, were satisfied: the event was a unique opportunity to assess 'the moral capacities and disabilities of the Indians'.[11]

Occom's *Sermon* is notable primarily for the care with which he negotiates the varied, often conflicting, concerns of his multiple audiences, all of whom are individually addressed. While Occom's speech is inevitably compromised by the inherent imbalances of power within the colonial relationship, he nonetheless offers a tentative response to problems within Indian–white relations. Although he condemns Paul's crime and an increasing reliance upon alcohol within Indian communities, he is also careful to point out to his white listeners that 'vice and immorality … are abounding every where amongst *all* nations'.[12] More emphatically, rejecting popular ideas of biological inferiority, Occom insists upon racial equality in the eyes of God: 'Negroes, Indians, English, or whatever nation soever; all that die in their sins must go to hell together'.[13] As A. LaVonne Brown Ruoff notes, Occom's text is significant because it 'convey[s] the implicit message that human nature, not race, makes us susceptible to temptation'.[14] Given the drunken nature of the crime coupled with the disreputable history of alcohol provision to Indians by settlers,[15] it is significant that Occom's subsequent argument is aimed at the additional crimes resulting from white abuses of unequal power relations: Indians 'have been cheated over and over again, and … have lost … [their] substance by drunkenness', and Biblical sources are identified that 'denounc[e] men … who put their bottles to their neighbours [*sic*] mouth to make them drunk'.[16]

While Occom's message is veiled, it nonetheless equates the sin of alcohol abuse with the sin of alcohol provision, detailing the devastating effects of alcohol on Native communities, where families are 'half-starved' and homeless, and children 'suffe[r] every day'.[17] Since the majority of Occom's white listeners would have been well aware of this less than Christian history, his 'call … to arms' that invites 'all orders ranks and degrees of people, to rise up against sin and satan',[18] and his insistence that all sinners of all races will be forgiven by a Christian God, is especially pertinent. Most importantly, Occom's endeavour can be interpreted as ultimately successful: his *Sermon* proved so popular that it was reprinted at least nineteen times and also translated.[19]

   This act of cultural negotiation is evident in the writings of another
Connecticut Christian Indian, William Apess (1798–1839). Apess was
of mixed ancestry: his father was part-Pequot and his mother a former
slave, possibly part-African. Apess's poverty, the physical abuse he
suffered at home, plus his experiences as an indentured servant, had a
direct impact on his interest in Christianity, and his subsequent role as
a Methodist minister and missionary. In spite of a very patchy formal
education, Apess published the first known Native American autobiography in 1829, plus four other influential texts that presented eloquent
arguments in support of Indian self-governance. Most significantly,
Apess's writings called for equal rights, as ordained by Christian teachings, for both Native peoples and African slaves. In this context, Apess is
highly significant not only as a forerunner of the abolitionist movement,
but also as the first advocate and activist for Indian civil rights, appro-
priating Christian discourse to directly challenge white racism: 'does the
proud white think that a dark skin is less honourable in the sight of God
...? All are alike ... To say they are not alike to him is an insult to his
justice. Who shall dare to call that into question?'.[20] The circumstances
of Apess's final years are unknown, and his death in 1839 of apoplexy was
possibly the result of alcoholism.

   Apess's cultural negotiations are far more forceful than those of
Occom, yet his writings were popular due to an ongoing fascination for
the details of Indian lives, especially of those who undertook missionary
activity among their own communities. Thus the appeal of Apess's texts
for a white audience is similar to the popular appeal of published slave
narratives, also beginning to appear more regularly from the 1820s
with the rise of the abolition movement. Significantly Apess's works,
including his life writings, all had a clear political focus. His discussion
of his near-fatal beating by his drunken grandmother argues that this
'cruel and unnatural conduct was the effect of some cause', namely the
role played by white settlers in introducing alcohol to the Indians who,
once intoxicated, were then 'wronged ... out of their lawful possessio[n]
... land' by settlers.[21] For Apess, 'the whites were justly chargeable with
at least some portion of my sufferings'.[22]

   Significantly, a topic to which Apess would repeatedly return was
the entrenched prejudice and racism he encountered as an Indian. To
Apess's mind, this prejudice was a 'flagrant ... breach' not only of
'good manners' but also – far more tellingly – of the '"civilization"'
that white American society claimed.[23] Apess extends this politically

aware approach to address multiple blunt questions to his white audience regarding their treatment of Native communities: 'I would ask you if you would like to be disenfranchised from all your rights, merely because your skin is white ... I'll venture to say, these very characters who hold skin to be such a barrier ... would be the first to cry out, "Injustice! awful injustice!"'.[24] The most powerful of Apess's works is the *Eulogy on King Philip* (1837), which reviews King Philip's War of 1675–6, one of the bloodiest encounters between the New England tribes and the English settlers. Comparing the values informing King Philip's 'revolution' with those of the fledgling Republic during the Revolutionary War, Apess 'go[es] on the offensive' by portraying King Philip as 'a freedom fighter ... acting in defence of his people'.[25]

Identified by Robert Warrior as 'a stunning revision of history' that 'condemns the historical and contemporary practices'[26] by which Native Americans were losing their lands, Apess's *Eulogy* clearly challenges the popular concept of Native Americans as a 'vanishing' race that was central both to the doctrine of Manifest Destiny and to the 1830 Indian Removal Act, which relocated all tribes west of the Mississippi. Thus Apess's comments not only confront white racism and hegemonic national history, but also the agendas of federal Indian policy; what Anne Marie Dannenberg identifies as a period of 'new ruthlessness' in federal–Indian relations.[27] It is as a Christian minister that Apess contests the racism inherent within Manifest Destiny to 'find no excuse in the Bible for Christians conducting toward us as they do'.[28] Significantly, Apess makes a clear comparison between the treatment of Native peoples and enslaved Africans within the Unites States, claiming that it was only through violent struggle that tribal peoples had evaded attempts to 'enslave a free people'.[29] In this sense, Apess is highly important not only as a forerunner of civil rights activism, but also for his conscious and highly visible attempts to ally Native interests with the concerns of the abolitionist movement.

Native Lives and Life Writings, 1883–1931

Popular American interest in Native lives increased throughout the nineteenth century, creating opportunities for a range of Indian authors to publish. Often a direct response to federal policies, or to events and atrocities of the Indian Wars, these 'life writings' publicised otherwise absent Indian histories. Like Occom and Apess, these writers proved of interest due to their negotiations between Indian and white worlds:

Dr Charles Eastman (Dakota, 1858–1939) was a graduate of Dartmouth College and a physician, while Sarah Winnemucca (Northern Paiute, c. 1844–91) was an interpreter and teacher. Significantly, both Eastman and Winnemucca were highly successful at 'translating' tribal cultures and concerns for wider American audiences, highlighting the need for reform within federal–Indian relations. Both devoted themselves to lecturing on Indian rights, yet both also attracted criticism for their active roles in promoting Indian cultural assimilation. However, as Andrew McClure comments, 'some degree of assimilation is essential to cultural and physical survival' within any colonial relationship.[30] Therefore recent reassessments of Eastman and Winnemucca's work can identify within their rhetorical strategies 'the language of survivance (survival + resistance)' by which they 'refigure "the Indian"' to successfully 'transfor[m] their object-status within colonial discourse into a subject-status'.[31]

Such rhetorical strategies are clearly evident within the writings of Charles Eastman (Ohiyesa). Born in 1858, Eastman was raised traditionally by his grandmother, before his Christian convert father[32] placed him within the Euro-American education system, from which he graduated with a medical degree in 1889. Given this unusual background and Eastman's successful negotiation of two often conflicting cultures, he proved of interest to those concerned with Indian assimilation and was subsequently employed by the Bureau of Indian Affairs (BIA). Eastman's work with the BIA was to prove a turning point in his writings when he was assigned to the Pine Ridge agency and, in 1890, amid fears of an Indian uprising, witnessed the aftermath of the massacre at Wounded Knee. Eastman later served as a physician to the Carlisle Indian School and the Crow Creek agency before devoting himself full time to writing and lecturing. Eastman died in 1939.

Eastman's own life had enormous bearing not only upon his writings but also upon his status as an object of fascination: he was a traditionally raised Indian who very successfully moved within Euro-American society. Yet Eastman's careful negotiations between two very different cultures are evident in his writings, which cater for an increasing Euro-American interest in ethnography and autobiography while simultaneously emphasising the value of key Indian cultural ideas. In this sense, Eastman clearly acts as a 'cultural broker',[33] and thus the totality of his assimilation into white society can be questioned. Eastman's autobiography, *Indian Boyhood* (1902), presents a snapshot of traditional Dakota life juxtaposed with examples of Indian stories. Eastman persistently emphasises the civilised habits of 'pagan' people, often in comparison to white American society: thus Euro-Americans are 'a heartless nation' who 'have made some of their people ... slaves!'.[34] The text carefully creates a dialogue between the young Eastman and a range of elder Dakota voices to present a series of important Indian values that he identifies as 'wonderful and lively conceptions'.[35] Significantly, Eastman describes his initial translation from tribal culture to white society in terms of absolute finality: 'I felt as if I were dead and travelling to the Spirit Land ... my life was to be entirely different'.[36]

Yet it is Eastman's later writings in response to the Wounded Knee massacre[37] that are the most vivid. Eastman was the only physician at hand to help the wounded and dying, and he pointedly comments on the 'many grievances' that the Dakota previously suffered at the hands of national bodies and local agents, before describing the sight of Indians 'frightfully torn to pieces of shells' or 'relentlessly hunted down and slaughtered while fleeing'.[38] Eastman's own reactions suggest a growing critique of his adoptive white culture: 'All this was a severe ordeal for me who had so lately put his faith in the Christian love and lofty ideals of the white man'.[39] Although a long-term advocate of acculturation and assimilation, Eastman's increasingly critical approach to Euro-American culture can be clearly detected: 'there was no "Indian outbreak" ... [only] dishonest politicians, who through unfit appointees first robbed the Indians, then bullied them, and finally in a panic called for troops to suppress them'.[40] Eastman's conclusion clearly indicates the difficulties he experienced in his negotiations between cultures: 'I am an Indian; and while I have learned much from civilization ... I have never lost my Indian sense of right and justice'.[41] As David Murray argues, there are thus many 'contradictions' of Eastman's cultural identity that 'are too pressing to be ignored'.[42]

Such contradictions are equally evident in Sarah Winnemucca's writings. Born about 1844 in Nevada, Winnemucca (Thocmentony) was raised primarily among white settlers and her family saw many benefits in white society and favoured acculturation. Winnemucca subsequently established strong links with the US military, both through marriage and her work as an interpreter. In 1880, she began a series of lecture tours that promoted Paiute rights and highlighted a range of mistreatments. Having founded an Indian school (1886) which was briefly successful, Winnemucca died in 1891. Like Eastman, Winnemucca made concerted and successful negotiations between Indian and white cultures, with the result that her work has been interpreted as problematic due to her constant accommodation of Euro-American cultural demands and her public support of the infamous Dawes General Allotment Act.[43] Nonetheless, Winnemucca also persistently argued in favour of Indian self-governance and her writings, which display these internal cultural tensions, are significant for the ways in which she 'imagine[s] new possibilities for Native resistance and survival'.[44]

The first Indian woman to publish an autobiography, Winnemucca's concerns are evident in her title: *Life Among the Piutes: Their Wrongs and Claims* (1883). Witnessing white settlement on Paiute land as a child, and settlers who 'kill[ed] everybody that came in their way', Winnemucca bluntly outlines her agenda in the first pages: 'I mean to fight for my downtrodden race while life lasts'.[45] Her strategy is significant: an embracing, and subsequent subversion, of popular and romantic Indian stereotypes such as the 'Indian Princess'. As McClure comments, Winnemucca's writing is significant for its ability to 'uphold Native identity and simultaneously adapt to the dominant culture'.[46] Like Eastman, Winnemucca depicts an idyllic childhood of freedom alongside images of traditional Paiute culture increasingly eroded by white settlement, which would appeal to a white audience interested both in ethnographic detail and in the notion of a 'vanishing race'. Yet Winnemucca's linguistic strategies are often subversive: persistently using the term 'our white brothers',[47] Winnemucca both invokes Christian discourse and critiques the less than brotherly or Christian behaviour of the white settlers. Facilitating a discussion on Paiute 'domestic and social moralities',[48] Winnemucca demonstrates implicit Native 'civilization' and contradicts persistent stereotypes of Indian 'savagery'. Her subsequent analysis of respect – for oneself, for others, and especially for other races and genders – is bluntly concluded by her comment on the partiality of Euro-American concepts of democracy and equality, and on Indian resistance: 'my own people are kind to everybody that does not do them harm; but they will not be imposed upon'.[49]

It is within this context of mutual miscommunication and cultural misinterpretation that Winnemucca draws upon her role as an interpreter to discuss white settlement, and acts of hostility between settlers and Natives. In her discussion of 'hostility', a term normally used solely in relation to war, Winnemucca outlines the repeated breaches of Indian trust by officials such as the Indian agents who persistently cheat the Paiute out of goods provided for them by the government which are sold on for profit. This extension of the notion of war to include hostile acts of settlement or colonisation is evident in Winnemucca's direct address to her audience, which contradicts Euro-American assumptions of blood-thirsty Indians: 'Dear reader, if our agent had done his duty ... there would be peace everywhere, on every agency'.[50] It is this emphasis on Indian morality and ethics, often in direct contrast to her experiences of Euro-American behaviour, which is evident in the most eloquent argument of the text:

> Oh, for shame! You who are educated by a Christian govern-ment in the art of war; the practice of whose profession makes you natural enemies of the savages, so called by you. ... you rise from your bended knees seizing the welcoming hands of those who are the owners of this land, which you are not ... [and] your so-called civilization sweeps inland ... but, oh, my God! Leaving its pathway marked by crimson lines of blood and strewed by the bones of the two races ... I am crying out to you for justice.[51]

Winnemucca's consciously rhetorical literary style emphasises her own education and civilisation while also clearly embodying the contradic-tions that she identifies within the Christian yet warlike, and civilised yet savage American nation. Most importantly, it also embodies those contradictions which she herself must negotiate in her complex media-tions between Indian and white cultures. In this context Winnemucca's writings, like those of Eastman, indicate that the 'greatest iron[y] of federal assimilation policy' was that it created a distinct 'space for the preservation of native cultural traditions'.[52]

One of the most damaging federal Indian policies was the enforced education of Indian children, beginning with the introduction of the boarding school system in 1879 at Carlisle. This type of enforced Indian education was to prove highly damaging to Native cultures: children were often forcibly removed from their families and relocated hundreds of miles from home, their hair was cut, their traditional clothing replaced, they were given Christian names, and their Native languages were banned.[53] Such cultural insensitivity played a crucial role in the assimila-tion process, where 'Indianness' (including traditional Native forms of education) was seen as a barrier to progress which had to be eradicated. Carlisle was a paradoxical blend of military discipline and misguided philanthropy: while Pratt clearly believed that Indian students could be 'educated' into civilisation, his emphasis upon the English language and vocational training caused cultural chaos. Many of his students lost their Native languages, causing them to become alienated both from their immediate family and from the wider tribal group. Additionally, Carlisle's focus upon vocational training (it was an 'industrial school') proved to be useless: students returned to reservation life where there were simply no opportunities for tinsmiths or domestic servants.

Yet Indian education did have one unexpected side effect: the creation of a range of Indian graduates well versed in white culture and discourse, many of whom became writers and/or educators, extending the type of mediation and negotiation undertaken by individuals such as Eastman and Winnemucca. One of the earliest students to arrive at Carlisle was Luther Standing Bear (Ota Kte, c. 1868–1939). Standing Bear is another interesting product of cross-cultural and inter-cultural negotiations: born into a traditional Lakota family, Standing Bear returned to the Pine Ridge reservation where he was elected as tribal chief in 1905. Although Standing Bear was in his sixties when he first published, his experience of inter-cultural negotiations was extensive, and his wide-ranging inter-actions with Euro-American culture ensured a clear understanding of prevalent white perceptions of Indians. As part of Buffalo Bill's Wild West Show, Standing Bear toured both America and Europe, and he later worked successfully in Hollywood as an actor and as a consultant for western films, both of which well situated him to assess the popularity of enduring Indian stereotypes for white society. Standing Bear died in Hollywood in 1939.

Standing Bear's analysis of Carlisle became far more critical in his later years. His reminiscences in *My People, the Sioux* (1928) view Pratt's experiment as beneficial, and express his disappointment that his father had sent him to Carlisle as if to battle, with the charge 'be brave and get killed', when he 'should have told me … to go and learn all I could of the white man's ways, and be like them'.[54] Here Standing Bear outlines his desire to assimilate: to learn how to 'be white'.[55] Indeed, Standing Bear initially believed so deeply in Pratt's mission that he returned home to successfully recruit 'more than fifty' Indian students despite strong resistance from parents.[56] However, Standing Bear's attitude toward the Indian education system was to change dramatically during the early 1930s possibly, as Frederick Hale argues, as a result of a growing 'disillusionment with … the unbridled greed … and other manifesta-tions of cultural decadence' that he witnessed in Hollywood.[57] As Hale comments, Standing Bear's increasing criticism may also have been encouraged by changing popular attitudes among Euro-Americans, who were themselves becoming more critical of assimilationist policies.[58]

In *Land of the Spotted Eagle* (1933), Standing Bear draws clear distinctions between traditional Lakota knowledge (the wisdom required for all individuals to lead morally and ethically sound lives) and the Christian education system (designed to make children 'conscious of ... [their] shortcomings'[59]). Standing Bear's analysis of Carlisle outlines his misgivings: although he 'truly liked' Pratt, he cannot forget 'those hours of silent misery I endured'.[60] As an alternative, Standing Bear presents a range of traditional Lakota wisdoms, covering the 'home and family', 'civil arrangements' and 'social customs'.[61] Like the works of Eastman and Winnemucca, the appeal for a white audience lay in the 'romance' of the ethnographic material, which had become popularised by Euro-American writers and artists in the 1920s.[62] The text is, significantly, a celebration of enduring Lakota values in the face of extreme cultural loss, emerging directly from Standing Bear's own sense of shock upon his return to Pine Ridge from Hollywood. In this context, he comments bluntly on 'the changed life of my people' who, as a direct consequence of federal assimilation policies, are 'degraded by oppression and poverty into but a semblance of their former being'.[63] Standing Bear's conclusion is that, due to 'nearly four centuries of ... misinterpretat[ion]', white attitudes to Indians are implicitly racist and have become embodied within federal Indian policy.[64] Like Apess before him, Standing Bear calls for a re-vision of accepted histories of federal–Indian relations to address 'the fact that a bonded and enslaved people lived in "the land of the free ..."' more than fifty years after the abolition of slavery.[65]

Standing Bear's emphasis upon the value of traditional Native cultural practices as a response to the failure of a range of assimilation programmes and the cultural devastation they caused, is also evident in the autobiography of Nicholas Black Elk (1863–1950). Another Lakota from Pine Ridge, Black Elk had also taken part in Buffalo Bill's Wild West Show. A participant at the Battle of the Little Bighorn (1876), and a survivor of the massacre at Wounded Knee, Black Elk was forced to convert to Christianity, under a federal ban making the practice of Native religious ceremonies illegal (1921).[66] Nonetheless, Black Elk remained committed to traditional spiritual practices and participated through a range of 'underground' activities, becoming a respected Lakota spiritual leader. Due to his expressed concern that crucial Lakota cultural and spiritual traditions were being lost, Black Elk decided in 1930 to preserve information through a collaboration with a white poet, John G. Neihardt. The resulting material, *Black Elk Speaks: Being the Life Story of a Holy Man of the Oglala Sioux* (1932), celebrated Oglala culture and warned of the dangers of assimilation. Black Elk died in 1950.

As with the works of Apess, Winnemucca and Standing Bear, the 'authenticity' of Black Elk's autobiography has been persistently questioned since its publication due to its collaborative nature.[67] As Murray comments, readers should 'be aware' that these are texts 'produced by, and in, white literate America'.[68] In this sense, the text can be identified as both autobiography *and* biography, a 'composite form' that embodies a combination of the ideas and cultural/religious biases of the subject, translator, transcriber and editor.[69] Black Elk's story appealed to a white fascination that, ironically, seemed to grow the more that Indian culture was perceived as 'endangered'.[70] This notion of the 'vanishing Indian' is evident in Black Elk's text, and remains one of the primary criticisms of Neihardt's role as an editor. Indeed, the text concludes with an image of inescapable cultural disintegration: the Oglala nation is described as 'broken and scattered. There is no center any longer, and the sacred tree is dead'.[71] This 'end of the dream'[72] is one of the most disputed statements of the text, and subject to repeated questions regarding Neihardt's culturally biased 'translations'. Yet to emphasise Neihardt's role is to negate Black Elk's own agency within the project. In this context, readers should read carefully, to avoid both 'the nostalgia of Neihardt' and 'any tendency to see Black Elk as ... an object of someone else's textual production'.[73] In this context, Black Elk and Neihardt's collaboration is an especially interesting example of inter-cultural negotiation.

Black Elk depicts a complex culture that directly challenges Euro-American assumptions of cultural inferiority which form the basis of the land losses associated with settlement and 'progress' during the nineteenth century. Chapter titles revise the history of the American West, emphasising 'the compelling fear' of the Lakota that culminates in 'the butchering at Wounded Knee'.[74] Black Elk's experience at Wounded Knee, which he recounts in great detail at the close of his narrative, is crucial for interpreting his concluding comments on the death of 'a people's dream'.[75] The piles of 'butchered' bodies remain very much burned into Black Elk's memory – 'I can still see [them] ... as when I saw them with eyes still young'[76] – and the tone at the close of the text reflects his inability in 1890 either to help or to save his people.

Accordingly, the postscript details his despair, the 'tears running' and his request to a greater power to 'make my people live!'[77] In this sense, it is likely that Neihardt's editing accurately portrays Black Elk's reaction both to the events of the Indian Wars, and to the range of social and economic measures by which the Indian Wars were continued, under the guise of federal Indian policy, in the early twentieth century. Thus Black Elk's text remains a pertinent intervention into the ongoing dialogue that Native writers were establishing with white American society.

Popular Fiction: The Native American Novel, 1854–1936

A further highly significant intervention into this ongoing dialogue was also the direct result of cultural assimiliation and the Indian education process: the emergence of the Native American novel. While the imposition of the coloniser's language is a crucial part of the process of colonisation, education does equate to power. A range of Native fiction writers were to usurp the imperial discourse and 'write back' to their oppressors, actively making an imposed and enforced language 'carry the weight' of the colonial experience.[78] Many Native writers thus undertook a form of 'translation', whereby elided Indian experiences found full expression in a form of discourse ordinarily associated, in the nineteenth century, with the white middle classes. Indian writers thus intervened within an almost exclusively white discourse to re-inscribe a Native presence, and critically engage with topics such as race and racism, the politics of land settlement, and American notions of 'freedom', 'justice' and 'democracy'.

One of the earliest Native fiction writers was John Rollin Ridge (Cherokee, 1827–67), who is significant for publishing a novel that is both the first Native American novel *and* the first Californian novel: *The Life and Adventures of Joaquín Murieta, the Celebrated California Bandit* (1854). As a mediatory cultural broker, Ridge (Yellow Bird) is especially interesting. Born in Georgia, he was a member of one of the 'five civilised tribes' who adopted a range of white cultural customs such as clothing, farming methods and housing; and, contentiously, introduced plantations and slave ownership. These tribes were also significant for having 'recognisable' (i.e. Euro-American modelled) legal systems, education systems, legislatures and written constitutions. The Cherokee also introduced a 'syllabary' (1819–21) by which the spoken language could be written,[79] and the first Native bilingual newspaper, *The Cherokee Phoenix* (1828), produced. While there was general public recognition that these tribes were 'civilised', they were nonetheless still subject to the 1830 Indian Removal Act which, in spite of well publicised attempts (including legal action[80]) to remain on their ancestral lands, forced the Cherokee to move west of the Mississippi. Internal divisions among the Cherokee led to one faction, including Ridge's father and grandfather, illegally signing away all Cherokee rights in the Treaty of New Echota (1833). In spite of widespread tribal protests, the treaty was ratified in 1836, leading directly to the infamous enforced removal of the Trail of Tears (1838) during which more than 4,000 Cherokee died from disease and adverse conditions.[81] Ridge's father and grandfather were subsequently assassinated by tribal members in 1839, with the young Ridge witnessing his father's brutal death. After killing a Cherokee believed to have been involved in his father's murder, Ridge was forced in 1850 to flee to California, where he died in 1866.

This tumultuous and unusual personal background, coupled with his 'mixed race' (his mother, Sarah Bird Northrup, was white), greatly influenced Ridge's subsequent interactions with Euro-American and Indian cultures. As a member of the 'civilised tribes', Ridge had experienced a 'white' education, had been a slave owner and remained opposed to abolition, and was a long-term advocate of assimilation. All of these views (some explicitly racist) are evident in his published work, and Ridge's position and personal convictions are even more contested than those of Eastman and Winnemucca. As a result, his writing exhibits a range of contradictions and cultural tensions. This is especially evident in his novel, *The Life and Adventures of Joaquín Murieta*. As the subtitle indicates, Murieta is a 'celebrated California bandit', which ironically pits Ridge's sympathies against established ideas of American law. The popular appeal of Ridge's character, a composite of several real figures, is immediately evident: Murieta (a prototype for Zorro) is a murderous yet strangely loveable rogue, robbing and killing racist white settlers both in revenge for his own ills, and for the wider benefit of dispossessed Californian Mexicans. The text displays complex internal tensions that reflect Ridge's own ideas and attitudes towards white America, Indian assimilation, his identity as a Cherokee and other Native American tribes. And Ridge illustrates his own biases towards 'progress' in his depictions of a range of unassimilated Californian Indians as 'poor, miserable [and] cowardly'.[82]

However, in spite of his commitment to full assimilation, what emerges in the text is a critique – at times damning – of Euro-American racism: in particular, the racist mistreatment of Mexicans in California by encroaching white settlers during the Gold Rush (1848–50). His land stolen, and forced to witness the rape of his mistress, Murieta is thus made a monster. Ridge comments upon prevalent popular Euro-American beliefs, after the US–Mexican war (1846–8), that Mexicans within the US were 'no better than conquered subjects' who 'ha[d] no rights that could stand before a … superior race'.[83] Significantly, Murieta becomes politically emblematic within the text as both 'a persecuted and exiled minority and a proto-guerrilla movement',[84] providing a range of dispossessed minority groups with the means to resist, even if only through fiction; and accounting for the enduring popularity of the character. Consequently, it is difficult to read Ridge's comments and not acknowledge his own experiences as a Cherokee at the hands of the American government: as John Lowe argues, 'the rape of Rosita … comments … obliquely, on the "rape" of the Cherokee … [which] is surely on Ridge's mind'.[85] In this context, Ridge's concluding remarks are highly pertinent: 'there is nothing so dangerous in its consequences as injustice … whether it arise from prejudice of color or from any other source'.[86]

This commentary on injustice is equally evident in the novel *Wynema: A Child of the Forest* (1891),[87] by S. Alice Callahan (Muscogee Creek, 1868–94), the first known novel to be published by a Native American woman. Callahan was of mixed ancestry – her father was part-Indian and her mother white – and, like Ridge, a member of one of the 'civilised' tribes, belonging to a wealthy slave- and plantation-owning group of Indians identified as the 'Creek Aristocracy'.[88] Her father was a prominent tribal figure, but little is known of Callahan herself except that she became a teacher and died in 1894. Yet Callahan's personal circumstances as an educated and wealthy mixed-blood Indian from a prominent tribal family are evident within her writing; her text is, as Ruoff notes, a complex negotiation between a range of ideas and positions, 'Indian and non-Indian … male and female'[89] which are, perhaps inevitably, suffused with her own ideas on cultural assimilation. Additionally, Callahan's negotiations are also extra-textual, commenting on many issues affecting Muscogee life in the early 1890s, such as land loss and the continuing Indian Wars.

Callahan's choice of genre – a domestic romance – is perhaps unusual for the politics of her subject matter: her story is of the Muscogee Wynema Harjo who finds first friendship with the Euro-American teacher Genevieve Weir, then love with Genevieve's brother Robin. Yet

Callahan's approach was to appeal to a white middle-class female reader-ship fascinated with the notion of a romanticised Indian (the 'child of the forest') who could then be educated into civilisation. Callahan therefore uses what Susan Bernardin identifies as the 'meeting grounds of senti-ment', already successfully employed by a range of 'reformist' novelists including Harriet Beecher Stowe.[90] Callahan's inclusion of arguments concerning the rights of women, which directly addressed the concerns of her readership while allying them with specifically Indian inter-ests, served to strengthen that appeal. Consequently, Callahan's novel addresses and mediates between deeply conflicting ideas and ideolo-gies. Callahan's primary focus is upon the white character Genevieve Weir, who provides appeal for her Euro-American audience but whose entrenched cultural ideas and prejudices are then persistently critiqued. Despite her initial 'mistaken belie[f]' in the inherent godlessness of Indians, Genevieve soon learns from her future husband that 'when you live among the Romans, you must abide by their laws and follow their customs', the majority of which are presented as both inoffensive and of equal cultural value.[91] While the novel focuses on Wynema's assimila-tion into Euro-American culture it therefore, unusually, also comments on Genevieve's education in Muscogee culture.

However, it is Callahan's focus on Indian politics and Indian women's rights that makes the novel especially significant. Recognising the damage caused by illegal sales of alcohol to the Indians, Wynema becomes a member of the Women's Christian Temperance Union to act against 'the unholy and unlawful practice'.[92] Genevieve makes a passionate case against allotment, arguing that Indians 'would be persuaded and threat-ened into selling their homes … until finally they would be homeless outcasts' rejected by white society.[93] And Wynema makes clear cross-cultural connections between the rights of Muscogee women and those being demanded by white women, which extend the racial boundaries and responsibilities of suffrage: '"we are waiting for our more civilized sisters to gain their liberty, and thus set us an example that we will not be slow to follow"'.[94] However, it is the focus upon the traumatic events at Wounded Knee that is most pertinent: Callahan's novel is the only known piece of contemporary Indian fiction to include a commentary on events. Callahan asks the blunt titular question: 'Is This Right?'[95] and, in answer, a range of characters provide commentary: the government and Indian agents have precipitated events by acting 'together to starve and slaughter this defenceless people'; and the massacre itself depicts the 'iron-clad hand of the white soldiers beating down ... helpless, defence-less women and children'.[96] Callahan purposefully presents an Indian account of Wounded Knee ('I am not relating the brave (?) deeds of the white soldier'[97]) and, although her negotiations between Indian and white worlds become more strained, her text ultimately is, as Ruoff argues, 'a moving and powerful call to action'.[98]

This 'call to action', and the increasing use of literature as a form of resistance, builds upon the tradition of activism established by writers such as William Apess in the early nineteenth century. A growing popular awareness of individual and civil rights enabled a new range of Native writers to call for recognition and action in the first half of the twentieth century. Consequently a continuing expression of Indian concerns, and an increasingly critical view of the devastating effects of federal Indian policies, can be traced in the novels of Mourning Dove (Okanogan, 1888–1936), John Joseph Mathews (Osage, 1894–1979) and D'Arcy McNickle (Chippewa-Cree, 1904–77). Additionally, an engagement with, and politicisation of, Modernist ideas of socio-cultural alienation can also be identified.

Born in 1888, Mourning Dove (Christine Quintasket) was from a relatively poor background (she was a migrant farmworker), from mixed ancestry (her father was part-white) and had less than four years of formal education.[99] Consequently her writings have, like the work of Black Elk, been subject to both close scrutiny and a certain amount of scepticism due to her close collaborations with a Euro-American editor and Indian rights activist, Lucullus McWhorter. In spite of McWhorter's sometimes heavy and overbearing editing of the text, the basis of what McWhorter helped 'develop' is Mourning Dove's own response to her role within tribal politics and campaigns for Indian rights, and to enduring negative perceptions of tribal peoples. In this respect, Mourning Dove was a highly active campaigner on legal issues and Native women's rights, and the first woman to be elected to her Tribal Council (1935). Mourning Dove's personal story as a writer is one of triumph over adversity: her poverty meant that her writing was undertaken after long hours of manual labour, and she published only with difficulty – her novel *Cogewea* took eleven years to emerge in print, while her autobiography was published posthumously. Mourning Dove died in 1936.

The extensive collaboration with McWhorter, undertaken due to Mourning Dove's sometimes hesitant translations of her ideas and dialogue into English, remains central to discussions of the novel

Cogewea, the Half-Blood (1927). Writing to McWhorter, Mourning Dove expresses her astonishment at the extent of some of the editorial polishing, which included glosses explaining Okanogan customs and language, and epigraphs for all chapters: 'I felt like it was someone elses [*sic*] book and not mine at all'.[100] As a result, the majority of the dialogue is one of two extremes: highly polished and full of rhetoric, or somewhat stilted and reliant upon slang. However, as Dexter Fisher notes, in spite of the difficulties we have in disentangling Mourning Dove's writing from McWhorter's editing, this collaboration is significant because it 'br[oke] new ground in bringing together two disparate traditions'.[101] In this sense, *Cogewea* presents an important picture of Okanogan culture as it struggled with the pressures of increasing assimilation and acculturation, and with the ramifications of ongoing Euro-American prejudice and racism. Most importantly, the linguistic tension within the text demonstrates the cultural tensions that both Cogewea and Mourning Dove attempt to negotiate.

Set on a ranch in Montana, *Cogewea* is a western romance yet Mourning Dove's analysis of the relationships between Cogewea, a Carlisle graduate, and her two potential love interests, Jim LeGrinder (another half-blood) and Alfred Densmore (a sophisticated white Easterner), also carefully considers the prevalence of racism, and the cultural and individual damage caused by assimilation. Thus the character of Densmore exposes the history of duplicity within white–Indian relations: although carefully courting Cogewea, Densmore is actually interested in her inheritance from her (white) father. Most significantly, *Cogewea* interrogates the cultural spaces available to the 'half-blood'. Situated between her grandmother Stemteema, who is emblematic both of traditional Okanogan culture and of a 'vanishing race', and the white world into which her sister has successfully integrated through marriage, Cogewea is 'regarded with suspicion by the Indian' and 'shunned by the Caucasian'.[102] This is especially evident when she enters – and wins – both the 'squaw' (Indian) and 'lady' (white) horse races, and is subsequently penalised for attempting to evade strictly enforced cultural and racial categories. In this context, *Cogewea* is an interesting intervention into established discussions on Indian assimilation, mixed blood and Euro-American fears of miscegenation. Rejecting standard Euro-American literary traditions that, as Alicia Kent comments, insist upon death for the mixed blood to resolve 'an unresolveable social anxiety',[103] the novel ends with the union of Cogewea and Jim, and thus a celebration

and proliferation of half-blood. While Mourning Dove has been criti-
cised for presenting stereotypical vanishing Indians and for advocating
assimilation, the novel belies these criticisms through its emphasis upon
adaptation – including textual and linguistic adaptation – as a useful form
of cultural negotiation and mediation during the transitional years of the
early twentieth century.

These types of cultural adaptation, negotiation and mediation are
all also evident in John Joseph Mathews' novel *Sundown* (1934) which
emerged just after *Cogewea*, during a new phase of federal Indian polices.
For example, Roosevelt's 'Indian New Deal' recognised the mistakes
of past federal Indian policies, such as allotment, and heralded the 1934
Indian Reorganization Act. Born in 1894 in Oklahoma, Mathews was an
unusual figure: a veteran of World War One and a graduate of Oxford
University, who travelled widely in Europe and Africa before returning
to his childhood home in the early 1930s. A founder of the Osage Tribal
Museum (1938), a member of the Osage Tribal Council and a participant
in the re-organisation of the BIA in the 1930s, Mathews was an active
campaigner for, and protector of, Indian rights. He died in 1979.

Of both Osage and white ancestry, Mathews' awareness of his liminal
cultural status can clearly be traced within *Sundown*, which discusses mixed
race, 'progress' and assimilation, and the possibilities and problematics
of cultural mediation.[104] Equally evident in the text is Mathews' awareness of the devastating effect of the Oklahoma oil boom of the 1920s and
30s on Osage culture, when tribal members were legally exploited by
self-interested white authorities and individuals. Mathews' mixed-blood
protagonist is Chal (Challenge) Windzer, pointedly named by his father
in the text as a 'challenge to the disinheritors of his people'.[105] Although
these disinheritors are identified primarily as self-interested and exploitative white groups, they also include the well-meaning yet culturally
insensitive, such as the white teacher who had fallen 'under the spell of
Fenimore Cooper'[106] and embraced the romantic stereotype of the 'noble
savage'. This type of cultural insensitivity is identified within the text as
equally damaging.

Introduced to Euro-American education and aspiring to become
white, Chal comes to despise and reject his Indian heritage as he moves
through university and military service, where he feels persistently 'out
of step' due to his inter-cultural position.[107] Once in the airforce, Chal
denies his heritage to claim Spanish ancestry with the result that, even as
he becomes 'a man among civilized men', he also becomes 'separated by

a great abyss' from both culture and home.[108] This is evident especially
when Chal returns home on his father's death and is subject to an ever-
increasing tension between the place he instinctively identifies as 'a
paradise on earth',[109] and the discomfort he feels when viewing traditional Osage culture alongside the values of the encroaching white
settlers. Chal's alienation is problematised by rapid changes in Osage
culture: the sudden vast wealth produced by oil discoveries on lands to
which the Osage retain mineral rights, which hastens acculturation and
assimilation; and the equally sudden influx of corrupt Euro-American
individuals and corporations interested in exploiting Indian wealth,
which polarises Osage culture between 'progressives' and 'traditionalists'. Mathews comments on the duplicitous role played by both local
Indian agents and the federal government: Congress 'made a new law'
identifying the Osage as legally incompetent to manage their financial
and business affairs and requiring white 'guardians', with the result that
'white mans that is lawyer and white mans that sells clothes and houses,
and white mans that is doctors, cheat Indian[s]'.[110] Significantly, by the
1920s the Osage were, as Carol Hunter indicates, in a 'unique' situation for Indians: 'the richest people per capita in the world'.[111] Osage oil
boom towns consequently become 'a lawless haven for ... [crime]',[112]
and it is in this context that Chal's father is murdered for the symbol of
his wealth, his new automobile. Reflecting actual events, *Sundown* ends
with the multiple murders of Osage individuals that force the intervention of FBI investigators.

It is against this backdrop of enforced Osage allotment, and the chaos
caused both by the oil boom and by the activities of the Euro-American
'Robber Barons', that Mathews interrogates Euro-American understandings of the concept of 'progress'. By the close of the novel, the promise
of Chal's youth has been undermined by a range of socio-cultural forces,
and he has become reliant upon alcohol to release his 'dammed up
emotion':[113] the pressure he feels to assimilate to an unreceptive Euro-
American culture, that is coupled with a concomitant sense of cultural
loss. It is through this emphasis upon an uncertain ending that Mathews
illustrates the cultural instability caused by the assimilation process and
by federal Indian policy, and demonstrates the difficulties of mediating
between disparate cultures. As Hunter comments, the 'human tragedy'
of the novel is the result of 'an abrupt assimilation' which 'alienated those
[like Chal] that were caught between the Indian and white values'.[114]

While the concept of alienation can be traced in Modernist concerns of the same period, for example in the writings of F. Scott Fitzgerald and Ernest Hemingway, there is no doubt that Native fiction of this era expands upon these ideas to express the ways in which a sense of alienation is exacerbated for those caught between cultures. Alienation is therefore also the topic of D'Arcy McNickle's 1936 novel *The Surrounded*. Born in Montana in 1904, McNickle was of mixed ancestry and consequently 'passed' as white during his university education. Like Mathews, McNickle also attended Oxford University and travelled in Europe, before returning to the US where he joined the Bureau of Indian Affairs (BIA). Euro-American interest in his Indian heritage was the basis for McNickle's role in the implementation of the 1934 Indian Reorganization Act, which aimed to rectify the culturally devastating mistakes of previous federal Indian policy by emphasising local tribal self-government. McNickle subsequently worked with the National Congress of American Indians (NCAI) to better co-ordinate campaigns for Indian Civil Rights, and was a lecturer at the University of Saskatchewan. In 1972, he was appointed as Director of the Center for the History of the American Indian in Chicago. McNickle died in 1977.

Continuing the themes of Mathews' *Sundown*, McNickle's novel *The Surrounded* analyses the problems facing Indian communities in the 1930s, where Euro-American demands for greater socio-cultural integration and assimilation are pitted against Indian attempts to maintain traditional cultural concepts and values. Significantly, as Birgit Hans argues, McNickle's novel failed to 'fit into [e]ither of the two accepted [Indian] catgories' of modern assimilation or romantic history.[115] In this sense, the novel is a 'realistic treatment' not only of contemporary Indian life, but also of the cultural alienation experienced by many Indian peoples as a direct result of the history of federal–Indian relations.[116] The pressures of external demands for cultural assimilation are evident in McNickle's choice of title: not only are the Indian textual characters 'surrounded' by hostile external forces, but their homeland is so-called because this is where 'they ha[ve] been set upon and destroyed'.[117] The protagonist, Archilde Leon, is a mixed-blood product of the Indian education system, and the novel traces his return to the Flathead reservation and his attempts to negotiate between the polarised cultural values represented by his Spanish rancher father and his increasingly traditionalist Indian mother. The complex difficulties of Archilde's negotiations are immediately apparent: within hours of arriving home, 'he was wishing to God that he had stayed away'.[118] Significantly, it is this emphasis upon religion, and upon the power of religion as a form of social control, that provides the basis for McNickle's discussion of Euro-American cultural imperialism.

McNickle traces the legacy of Christianity among the Salish through Archilde's mother, 'Faithful Catharine', who is so-called because she is one of the first tribal members converted by Jesuit missionaries.[119] The Jesuits subsequently bring 'progress' and 'civilisation' to the Salish in the form of religion and education, yet Catharine identifies the result as 'a chaotic world' where there are 'so many things dead' and so much 'confusion and dread and emptiness' that she is driven to ask '[w]hat had come about since that day of the planting of the cross?'[120] In terms of textual authority, it is significant that McNickle includes a text within his text – Father Grepilloux's journal – which provides a Euro-American, Christian and ethnographic commentary on Salish culture from the point of view of the colonising assimilative force. In this context what becomes apparent, as Laird Christensen comments, is the devastating impact of 'a new moral code' that 'will effect a culturally lethal separation' of the Salish people from their 'social and ecological' cultural traditions.[121] Most significantly, what McNickle demonstrates are the damaging results of cultural collision and the expectations of swift cultural assimilation, which demands 'a tremendous epistemological and psychological leap' of the newly converted Salish.[122] The results can be seen in the undermining of traditional Salish culture through an increase in alienation, alcoholism and crime brought on by the Jesuit education system that has taught the younger Salish generation to respect the Christian church and to reject (and thus to disrespect) Salish culture and their parents.

For the majority of the text, therefore, Archilde either seeks acceptance from a range of familial and cultural figures or becomes entangled in criminal activities, often as a passive witness. The text ends in multiple deaths that occur through both error and retribution: Archilde's horse thief brother Louis is shot by a hunting warden, who is then killed by Archilde's mother; when Archilde flees in order to shift the blame from his mother, the Sheriff tracking him is killed by his girlfriend Elise and Archilde is arrested for murder. In spite of distinct mutual cultural misinterpretations and misconceptions it is notable that, for the white Indian Agent who makes the final arrest, Archilde represents a failure for Indian assimilation and becomes a symbol of the Euro-American belief in the biological inability of Indians to 'progress': 'You had everything, every chance, and this is the best you could do with it! … It's too damn bad you people never learn that you can't run away'.[123] In spite of this emphasis upon facing facts, it is significant that the Indian Agent is equally representative of Euro-America's refusal to accept the damaging effects of its demands for Indian cultural assimilation. In this context, McNickle makes it emphatically clear that Archilde – and all of his problems – is, quite literally, 'our child'.

From the earliest works of the eighteenth century, Native American writing changed greatly in terms of form, eventually resulting, in the early twentieth century, in the emergence of the 'American Indian novel' which clearly engaged with more widespread literary developments and concerns. However, regardless of form, it is notable that all of these early texts expressed three clear objectives: a re-assertion (and cultural translation) of important Native cultural values; an exposure of ongoing Euro-American racism and its legacy in federal–Indian relations and policies; and an emphasis upon Indian rights. As a result, the emergence of highly focused and prominent Civil Rights movements in the 1950s and 60s heralded a further proliferation, and a new generation, of Native writers and writings.

Notes

1. While the majority of early American texts are available in literary anthologies such as *Norton* and *Heath*, they are now also easily available in online editions.
2. Thomas Harriot (2003), p. 82.
3. William Bradford (2003), pp. 186–7.
4. Ibid. p. 189.
5. Mary Rowlandson (2003), p. 337.
6. Ibid. pp. 311, 336.
7. Roger Williams (2003), p. 228
8. Gunther Barth (1998), p. 19.
9. Ibid. pp. 19–20.
10. For a detailed overview, see Eric Cheyfitz (2002).
11. David Murray (1991), p. 45.
12. Samson Occom (1997), p. 644, emphasis added.
13. Ibid. p. 650.
14. A. LaVonne Brown Ruoff (1992), p. 79
15. By the time of Occom's speech, it had become commonplace for self-interested white settlers to supply tribes, who often had no experience of alcohol, with spirits in order to influence trade and land deals in their own favour.
16. Occom (1997), p. 658.
17. Ibid. p. 657.
18. Ibid. p. 656.
19. See Ruoff (1992), p. 78.
20. William Apess (1992), p. ix.

21. Ibid. p. 7.
22. Ibid. p. 7.
23. Ibid. p. 36.
24. Ibid. p. 96.
25. Murray (1991), p. 63.
26. Robert Warrior (2004), p. 1.
27. Anne Marie Dannenberg (1996), p. 70.
28. Apess (1992), p. 136.
29. Ibid. p. 107.
30. Andrew McClure (1999), p. 29.
31. Malea Powell (2002), p. 400. Survivance is a term popularised by the Anishinaabe critic Gerald Vizenor (1994).
32. For the first fifteen years of his life, Eastman and his family believed that his father had been killed in battle.
33. See Margaret Szasz, *The Cultural Broker* (1994).
34. Charles Eastman (1971), p. 241.
35. Ibid. p. 18.
36. Ibid. p. 246.
37. At Wounded Knee, the seventh cavalry massacred 153 Dakota and wounded a further forty-four, primarily old men, women and children, who were camping under both American and white flags. The encounter was investigated and the army officers exonerated, but public opinion has always been damning, and in 1990 the US government finally offered a 'statement of regret' and redesignated the 'battle' as a massacre. For a full text of the statement, (House of Representatives, 25 October 1990), see the records for the 101st Congress at http://thomas.loc. gov/home/r101query.html.
38. Eastman (2001), pp. 272, 286, 290.
39. Ibid. p. 296.
40. Ibid. p. 301.
41. Ibid. p. 363.
42. Murray (1991), p. 76.
43. Responding to the need for more land for white settlement, the 1887 Dawes Act allowed the 'allotting' of reserved lands to individual Indians. The result was the rupture of tribal notions of communality in favour of Euro-American notions of private property, and – since there was more land available than individual Indians to take it – the opening up of Indian land to white settlement. Widespread misuse of the Act was condemned by the Meriam Report of 1928 and it was repealed in 1934. By this point, more than half of all tribal lands had been lost.
44. Powell (2002), p. 404.
45. Sarah Winnemucca (1994), p. 5, p. 11, p. 6.
46. McClure (1999), p. 31.
47. Winnemucca (1994), p. 12.
48. Ibid. p. 45.
49. Ibid. pp. 53–4.
50. Ibid. p. 136.
51. Ibid. p. 207.
52. Powell (2002), p. 427.
53. A substantial number of children died either as a result of separation from their

families (often accompanied by severe cultural shock) or from a range of epidemics. Standing Bear notes that parents were regularly given no warning that their children were ill, and no invitation to the burials (1975: 162).

54. Luther Standing Bear (1975), p. 141.
55. Standing Bear had to ask Pratt's permission to speak to his visiting father in his own language.
56. Standing Bear (1975), p. 166.
57. Frederick Hale (1993), p. 33.
58. Ibid. p. 33.
59. Standing Bear (1978), p. 16.
60. Ibid. p. 18.
61. Ibid. p. xx.
62. Living in self-proclaimed 'colonies' among a range of southwestern tribes were, among others, Georgia O'Keefe, D. H. Lawrence, Ansel Adams, Mabel Dodge Luhan and Willa Cather.
63. Standing Bear (1978), p. 226.
64. Ibid. p. 227.
65. Ibid. p. 245.
66. The criminalisation of Native American religions continued until 1978, with the introduction of the American Indian Religious Freedom Act.
67. As with nineteenth-century African-American slave narratives, questions tend to arise concerning the role of the white editor, and the extent to which that editor influences, shapes or even writes/rewrites texts and topics. This is especially pertinent when the subject matter is 'cultural' or ethnographic. Such questions, although important, do tend to negate the agency of the Indian authors, effectively erasing or discounting their voice/opinions.
68. Murray (1991), p. 65.
69. Ibid. p. 71.
70. The increasing popularity of Black Elk's text in the late twentieth century is indebted to the rise of a new kind of Euro-American fascination: the 'New Age' or 'Eco-Indian'.
71. Nicholas Black Elk (1979), p. 270.
72. Ibid. p. 263.
73. Murray (1991), p. 72.
74. Black Elk (1979), pp. vii–viii.
75. Ibid. p. 270.
76. Ibid. p. 270.
77. Ibid. pp. 273–4.
78. Chinua Achebe (1993), p. 434.
79. The exact origins of the syllabary are subject to some debate, but the general consensus is that the creator was Sequoya, or George Guess (c. 1760–1843), son of a Cherokee mother and English father.
80. In 1831, the Cherokee took their case to the US Supreme Court, who ruled in their favour and declared Georgia's action illegal. The case proved useless when President Jackson refused to uphold the ruling.
81. In total, more than 50,000 (numbers are still disputed) Native Americans lost their lands and were forced west.
82. John Rollin Ridge (2003), p. 27.

83. Ibid. p. 3.
84. John Lowe (1992), p. 115.
85. Ibid. p. 107.
86. Ridge (2003), p. 136.
87. *Wynema* was only recently 'rediscovered', and republished in the late 1990s.
88. Annette van Dyke (1992), p. 124.
89. Ruoff (1997), p. xix.
90. Susan Bernardin (2001), p. 209.
91. S. Alice Callahan (1997), pp. 6, 18.
92. Ibid. p. 44.
93. Ibid. p. 52.
94. Ibid. p. 45.
95. Ibid. p. 94.
96. Ibid. pp. 74, 90.
97. Ibid. p. 92.
98. Ruoff (1997), p. xliii.
99. Mourning Dove did return to education at a later date in an attempt to improve her writing skills.
100. Cited in Dexter Fisher (1981), p. xv.
101. Ibid. p. xxvi.
102. Mourning Dove (1981), p. 17.
103. Alicia Kent (1999), p. 48.
104. *Sundown* is often loosely autobiographical.
105. John Joseph Mathews (1988), p. 4.
106. Ibid. p. 26.
107. Ibid. p. 98.
108. Ibid. pp. 230, 208.
109. Ibid. p. 233.
110. Ibid. pp. 235–6.
111. Carol Hunter (1982), p. 67.
112. Ibid. p. 68.
113. Mathews (1988), p. 297.
114. Hunter (1982), p. 71.
115. Birgit Hans (1996), p. 236.
116. Ibid. p. 236.
117. D'Arcy McNickle (1994), frontispiece.
118. Ibid. p. 14.
119. Ibid. p. 22.
120. Ibid. p. 22.
121. Laird Christensen (1999), p. 3.
122. Ibid. p. 7.
123. McNickle (1994), pp. 296–7.

CHAPTER 3

Seminal Writers: N. Scott Momaday, James Welch and Leslie Marmon Silko

The 'Renaissance' of Native American Literature: 1968–77

The development of a highly politicised African American Civil Rights movement from the 1950s heralded the emergence of equally active demands for Native American civil rights and posed the first real challenge to entrenched Euro-American racism. Movements such as 'Red Power' and political groups such as the American Indian Movement (AIM) raised the profile of Native Americans within the United States and acted to promote wider Indian activism. Both Red Power and AIM were given impetus by developments within federal Indian policy which, from the relatively philanthropic Indian Reorganization Act (1934), had seen a return to disastrous policies that caused further socio-cultural chaos and suffering. For instance, Indian calls for tribal self-government or sovereignty were interpreted as a means by which the federal government's responsibility to its colonised peoples could be 'terminated' and through which Indians could, as with the removals of the nineteenth century, be 'relocated'. In what was effectively a cost-cutting exercise, between 1953 and 1968 many relationships between tribal peoples and the government were severed, with devastating economic results: tribal communities had been made dependent upon welfare, and had no independent economic resources or means to develop them. Significantly, this legislation directly attempted to undermine historical federal–Indian relationships that were protected by treaty and American law. The situation was compounded in 1956 with the Indian Relocation Act, when individuals were paid to relocate to urban areas. Little if any support was given to these new 'urban Indians', and no monies were available to allow a return home if desired. The result was a widespread depopulation of traditional tribal communities, which directly affected Indian culture and cultural activities.

In direct response to these events, and to almost five hundred years of dispossession and oppression, a new era of Indian political activism developed, accompanied by a more public discussion of Native American culture and identity.[1] Public political protests by AIM included the occupation of Alcatraz Island (1969–71), which demanded the return of tribal lands no longer used as guaranteed by treaty; the occupation of the BIA office in Washington (1972) as part of the 'Trail of Broken Treaties' march; and a siege at the Wounded Knee site on the Pine Ridge reservation in 1973 when, following the suspicious deaths of more than sixty traditional tribal members and a reclamation of the site by the Oglala, AIM activists were involved in a gun battle with the FBI that resulted in three deaths.[2]

Media coverage of such events raised popular American awareness of contemporary Native American communities, and many of the Indian writers finding publication – whose sudden increase was identified by Kenneth Lincoln as a Native American literary 'Renaissance' – expressed a common 'sense of dispossession', a 'mutual sense of historical displacement' and a 'shared struggle for cultural survival and rebirth'[3] in the face of enduring Euro-American racism and active attempts to eradicate Native cultures through a wide range of federal Indian policies. The works of these new Indian writers provided pertinent political commentary on the realities of contemporary Native life in the US: a crucially important non-fiction Indian text of 1969 was Vine Deloria Jnr's *Custer Died For Your Sins: An Indian Manifesto* which, as its title suggests, presented a Native view of the federal–Indian relationship. Significantly, fictional texts also celebrated and promoted Native values and world-views, developing innovative literary styles and structures designed to portray and incorporate traditional oral storytelling devices, by which the colonial language could demonstrate the colonised experience. Thus, as Louis Owens comments, Native literature enabled an 'oppressed and marginalized minority [to] continually subver[t] the authority of the dominant discourse'.[4] Indian writers of this period, such as N. Scott Momaday (Kiowa), James Welch (Blackfoot/Gros Ventre) and Leslie Marmon Silko (Laguna Pueblo), therefore build upon the more politicised work of authors such as Mathews and McNickle to engage in conscious and deliberate acts of cultural mediation and translation.

The Indian Pioneer: N. Scott Momaday (b. 1934)

In 1969 the Pulitzer Prize for fiction was, unexpectedly, awarded to an unknown Kiowa writer, N. (Navarro) Scott Momaday, for his first novel, *House Made of Dawn* (1968). Momaday had previously been awarded a series of accolades in recognition of his talent: a Wallace Stegner Creative Writing Fellowship (1959), the Academy of American Poets Prize (1962) and a Guggenheim Fellowship (1966). Nonetheless, it was Momaday's Pulitzer success that heralded a burgeoning of Native artistic expression, especially in the field of literature. Crucially, Momaday's success, his pioneering literary representation of the Kiowa oral story-telling tradition and his ability to integrate rather than polarise Native and non-Native worlds, transformed contemporary Native American literature, providing both publishing opportunities and artistic inspiration for subsequent generations of Native writers.

Born in 1934 in Oklahoma to the teacher/writer Natachee Scott (part-Cherokee) and the painter Al Momaday (Kiowa), Momaday was raised primarily in the Southwest among highly diverse communities: Euro-American, Mexican-American, Navajo, Apache and Pueblo. Alongside the cultural diversity of his own family background, which included Euro-American ancestry, the influence of this early experience can clearly be identified in the multicultural concerns and perspectives of Momaday's writing and his love of language. Momaday commented in his collection of stories and poetry, *In the Presence of the Sun*, that he very early 'fell in love with' a range of languages.[5] Educated at the mission school at Jemez Pueblo, Arizona, and further schools in Sante Fe and Albuquerque, Momaday attended a Virginia military academy before completing a BA in Political Science at the University of New Mexico, and an MA (1960) and PhD (1963) in English at Stanford. While Momaday is a poet, playwright and novelist, he has also long been an established literary critic and academic, teaching at both Stanford and Berkeley. Until recently, Momaday was Regents Professor Emeritus at the University of Arizona.

At Stanford, Momaday's thesis (on the poetry of Frederick Goddard Tuckerman) was supervised by the often controversial theorist and poet Ivor Winters, who was enormously influential upon Momaday's own creative work. His highly structured Euro-American post-symbolist stylistics had a significant influence on Momaday's writing,[6] as did Euro-American modernist writing: Louis Owens suggests that one significant result of Momaday's Pulitzer Prize was a recognition of Native literature as 'recognizably modernist', and thus Native cultures as recognisably modern.[7] One importance of Momaday's work for subsequent Native writers is its emphasis upon Indian cultures and worldviews, and its ability to fuse cultural and stylistic approaches, to present multiple and multicultural perspectives and voices, without polarisation or hierarchy.

Following the success of *House Made of Dawn* (the subject of the case study below), Momaday published numerous texts focusing on his mixed-blood ancestry and Kiowa culture, including three autobiographical volumes, *The Way to Rainy Mountain* (1969), *The Names: A Memoir* (1976) and the earlier private publication *The Journey of Tai-me* (1967). All three provide a detailed analysis of what it means to be an Indian – especially one of mixed ancestry – in modern America, developing themes evident in the writings of earlier writers such as Mourning Dove, Mathews and McNickle. *The Names* devotes much consideration to the ways in which Momaday's primarily Euro-American mother 'began to see herself as an Indian ... as it enabled her to assume an attitude of defiance'.[8] Thus, for Momaday, his identity as an Indian derives as much from the imagination as from ancestry and resistance: 'we are what we imagine. Our very existence consists in our imagination of ourselves'.[9] All three volumes of life writings are, therefore, an attempt to imagine and recover a more traditional form of Kiowa culture, for example the cultural and linguistic translation of traditional Kiowa stories and myths in *The Journey of Tai-me*. This form of recovery is especially evident *The Way to Rainy Mountain*, which retells what Owens identifies as 'a crucial mythic moment in the history of the Kiowa':[10] the emergence and migration of the Kiowa, then their eventual defeat in the nineteenth century by invading white settlers. Significantly the text also emphasises the importance of Rainy Mountain as the spiritual home of the Kiowa, thus highlighting Indian cultural understandings of ongoing federal Indian land claims cases. This more politicised reading of federal–Indian relations is subsequently evident in the essay collection *The Man Made of Words* (1997), where Momaday discusses his perception of Indian–white relations in 'The Morality of Indian Hating', alongside considerations of Kiowa perceptions of land and sacred space. In 1992, Momaday was awarded a Lifetime Achievement Award for Literature by the Native Writers Circle.

In his early writings, Momaday clearly negotiates between Indian and white worlds to produce language that reflects the influence both of his Euro-American literary studies and of traditional Kiowa oral forms.

This is best demonstrated in Momaday's poetry, such as *Angle of Geese* (1974), *The Gourd Dancer* (1976) and *In the Bear's House* (1999). As Matthias Schubnell comments, Momaday combines Native 'oral poetry' with 'the strict formal tradition of English verse' and also post-symbolist concepts.[11] All three volumes are highly eclectic and provide some fascinating cross-cultural insights: while *Angle of Geese* employs a stark post-symbolist approach to death, it also provides an analysis suffused with Kiowa cultural understandings. Similarly, *The Gourd Dancer* juxtaposes traditional Kiowa worldviews and ceremonies with American cultural figures such as Georgia O'Keefe and Billy the Kid (also a key figure in Momaday's second novel *The Ancient Child* (1989) and his volume *In the Presence of the Sun* (1992)), yet with an emphasis upon integration rather than opposition.

This integrated cross-cultural approach is perhaps best illustrated in the volume *In the Bear's House*, where Momaday attempts to 'understand something about the spirit of the wilderness, of which the Bear is a very particular expression'.[12] Here, distinctly cross-cultural 'Bear–God Dialogues' are created between 'Urset', 'Yahweh' and Momaday himself to explore the relationship of a variety of cultures, religions and spiritualities to the American land. Drawing upon his own intimate connections with the bear – 'Bear and I are one'[13] – Momaday's text attempts to recover more profound understandings of the connections between culture and nature. These connections are also evident at the close the novel *The Ancient Child* (1989) whose mixed-blood protagonist is 'Set', the Kiowa word for 'bear'. Analysing the mixed-blood's complex search for cultural identity and the need to imagine and recover that identity, *The Ancient Child*'s emphasis upon mythic Kiowa bear stories effects a cultural translation. Thus, as Craig Frischkorn argues, the concept of '[t]ransformation ... is crucial to [our] understanding' of Momaday's cultural considerations.[14]

House Made of Dawn (1968)

Momaday's 1968 novel *House Made of Dawn* tells the story of a Walatowa (Jemez Pueblo) Indian, Abel, whose sense of alienation and search for identity forms the basis of the plot. Focusing on events between July 1945 and February 1952, the text explores Abel's uncertain parentage (he is of unidentified 'mixed blood'), his military service in World War Two and related alcoholism, his murder of an albino tribal member and subsequent imprisonment, his urban relocation to Los Angeles, and his return home to re-engage with his Indian cultural heritage. Within this context, Momaday analyses the profound impact of federal Indian policy and enduring Euro-American racism on Indian communities and individuals, evident in his emphatically Biblical choice of the name 'Abel' which embodies Christian understandings of the nature of brotherhood and the damage caused by violence. Moreover, through this emphasis upon religion and the sacred, Momaday also considers the effect of the Christian church on Indian lives and traditional ceremonial practices. All of the primary Indian influences on Abel's journey towards self-understanding are key cultural mediators of religion and the sacred: Abel's uncle Francisco is both a tribal traditionalist and a leading member of the local Catholic church; and the Navajo Ben Benally and the Kiowa 'Priest of the Sun' John Tosamah both negotiate the complex cultural translations inherent within living as 'urban Indians' while practising traditional Native religious ceremonies and maintaining traditional worldviews and values. This emphasis upon Native religious practices is especially significant given that public practice of traditional Indian ceremonies and rituals was illegal until the passing of the American Indian Religious Freedom Act in 1978.

Formally, the text is clearly influenced by modernist writings and ideas. As Owens comments, a crucial part of *House Made of Dawn*'s Pulitzer success was a 'recognizably modernist' style, which is evident in the fragmented and 'formally experimental, discontinuous narrative replete with multiple perspectivism'.[15] The opening descriptions set the scene of the Walatowa landscape through a series of concise statements that display the influence of writers such as Ernest Hemingway:

> The seasons lie hard upon the land. In summer the valley is hot, and the birds come to the tamarack on the river … The fields are small and irregular, and from the west mesa they seem an intricate patchwork of arbors and gardens …[16]

This environment is unexpectedly disrupted by the sudden introduction of flashbacks to Abel's childhood, to the 'bright red [canyon] walls' that 'seemed to close over him' to produce a sense of suffocation that makes the young Abel 'afraid and cr[y]'.[17] The sense of threat evoked by this change of atmosphere and its direct relation to Walatowa or 'home', suggests that Abel's problems as an adult – evident in his increasing alcoholism – are rooted in and engulfed by something much deeper: cultural identity and its relationship to geographical/spatial location.

In this context, the text's prologue opens with the Walatowa word
'*Dypaloh*' (the word with which traditional Walatowa oral stories are
introduced, i.e. 'once upon a time') and with Abel participating in a
Walatowa running ceremony. Both act to clearly situate both the action
and the reader within the world of the sacred:

> *Dypaloh*. There was a house made of dawn. It was made of pollen and
> of rain, and the land was very old and everlasting.[18]

While the text is therefore ostensibly easily accessible for the European
or Euro-American reader (and also likely to appeal to and attract such
an audience), Momaday makes specific and strategic breaks with the
modernist tradition to 'translate' an indigenous oral storytelling tradition into a western textual form. As Owens comments, this 'transformative act' is significant for 'privileging' American Indian discourse while
simultaneously challenging and devaluing 'modernism's emphasis upon
a placeless iconography' that promotes a worldview that is problematically depoliticised if not apolitical.[19] While Momaday's focus upon the
Walatowa landscape is undeniably 'mythic', his presentation of a specifically Pueblo worldview privileges Indian cultural values in a discussion
of contemporary Indian lives that is emphatically political.

As a result, the relocation of the reader is highly pertinent to promoting
successful inter-cultural understanding: as Momaday states in *The Names*,
'The events of one's life take place, *take place* ... [they] have meaning in
relation to the things around them'.[20] Consequently Momaday's suggestion that 'who we are' equates to 'where we are' provides a much more
complex and political reading of Native communities, reflecting not
only a range of indigenous values informing many long-standing federal
Indian land claims cases,[21] but also the problems associated with the
Indian Relocation Act, and with ongoing Indian alcoholism, especially
among military veterans. Tapping into the long history of alcohol provision and abuse among Native communities and emphasising the social
effects, Momaday clearly demonstrates that Abel's reliance upon alcohol
is a key factor in his increasing alienation: 'He [Abel] was drunk, and he
fell against his grandfather and *did not know him*'.[22] Additionally, Abel's
alcoholism is itself a symptom of his ongoing alienation from the tribal
community, evident in his ejection from the Eagle Watchers Society,
one of the traditional clans, for killing the live eagle entrusted to him
whose imprisonment 'filled him with shame and disgust'.[23] It is within
this complex context of 'home' that Abel's dis-ease and healing can be

understood, ultimately effected by his return home and relearning of familial and cultural relationships. Building on the foci of writers such as Mathews and McNickle, Momaday's conceptualisation of the 'return home' not only foregrounds the significance of Native understandings of land and its relationship to ideas of 'home', but also critiques the Euro-American conceptual separations of culture and nature that are evident within the notion of land ownership and federal Indian policies such as the Dawes Allotment Act. As William Bevis comments, while modernist Euro-American literary individualists, in accordance with the established traditions of the *bildungsroman*, 'keep leaving home' in order to find themselves, Native American literary protagonists tend to 'hom[e] in' as 'a primary mode of [self] knowledge'.[24] As Bevis suggests this is, significantly, for more than merely individualist goals, it is for a wider and more communal 'primary good'.[25]

This notion of 'homing' is central to Momaday's presentation of indigenous concerns and worldviews. *House Made of Dawn* therefore traces the attempts of Abel to locate himself culturally. Having lost his Walatowa mother at an early age, Abel never knows the identity of his father (speculated to be 'a Navajo ... or a Sia, or an Isleta, an outsider anyway') with the result that he is persistently identified by the Walatowa community as 'somehow foreign and strange'.[26] Indeed, Momaday's awareness of the dis-ease caused by cultural dis-location is evident in his choice of title: the 'house made of dawn' derives from the Navajo Nightway, a chant specifically devoted to healing. Abel's cultural dis-ease and dis-location, his inability to locate himself either culturally or geographically, is evident both in his alcoholism and in his constant attempts to situate himself throughout the text. One significant reason for Abel's inability to locate himself upon his return from war is his experience of Post-Traumatic Stress Disorder (PTSD), evident in the graphic and forceful nature of the flashbacks that Abel suffers which have a physical impact that makes him 'shake violently'.[27] Significantly, this physical symptom relates to Abel's very real need as a returning warrior to undergo the purification or healing ceremonies specified by Indian traditions. The 'ceremony of recovery'[28] that Abel requires is, therefore, both physical and cultural; and one that has a wider application for contemporary Indian individuals, communities and cultures.

Abel's initial attempts to locate himself are clearly detrimental to his Indian identity. His drunkenness erodes his ability to communicate, which represents a serious problem within a primarily oral culture. Further, his

relationship with the wealthy Euro-American Angela St John perpetu-
ates the established Indian stereotypes with which she identifies him: he is
both highly physical (Angela's descriptions of Abel are deeply sensuous)
and also a 'wooden Indian', which Angela interprets as simultaneously
noble ('grave, distant, intent on something she could not see') and primitive ('dumb and immutable'[29]). Abel's reactions to the Pueblo albino Juan
Reyes Fragua attempt to embrace southwestern indigenous understandings of 'witchcraft' (i.e. the manifestation of evil or bad feeling), and to
enact a traditional response to its threat: '[a] man kills such an enemy if
he can'.[30] It is significant, especially in the context of the ongoing colonisation of contemporary Native peoples in the United States, that this
concept of witchcraft has been discussed in detail by subsequent writers
such as Leslie Marmon Silko as a concept that encompasses all forms of
destruction, oppression, exploitation and manipulation. Interpreting the
albino as a 'witch' (as actively intending to harm him both physically
and spiritually, i.e. *culturally*), Abel responds to the albino's 'terrible
strength' and his own 'terror' by stabbing him to death.[31]

Abel's killing of the albino is perhaps the most significant event of the
text, and the simplest interpretation of the albino is as Momaday describes
him: 'the white man' who is 'an enemy'.[32] In this context, Abel's destruction of 'whiteness' can be interpreted as an act of self-defence, to thwart
the persistent threat of cultural erosion – in effect, cultural death – represented by Euro-America. However, in the context of Indian concepts of
witchcraft, the figure is a far more complex embodiment of evil. Indeed,
while Abel attempts to act traditionally in his ritual killing of the albino,
it becomes evident that he has, due to his own cultural alienation, misin-
terpreted Walatowa traditions: as Owens comments, Abel 'has seriously
erred' because, by being physically embraced by the albino in the moment
of his death, Abel therefore 'has become one with' him, and with the
evil he represents.[33] Therefore, Abel's physical relationship to the albino
(and therefore to his death) additionally acknowledges not only his own
mixed-blood status, and its potential to further erode traditional Native
cultural ideas, but also his own cultural dis-location. In this context, Abel's
action can also be interpreted both as an act of self-negation (emerging
from his own problematic and liminal tribal position), and as an attempt
to locate himself culturally. Given Abel's cultural dis-location, his action
can be identified as culturally transgressive: 'evil cannot be destroyed'
but must be dealt with correctly, i.e. 'acknowledged and avoided, never
killed'.[34] While the act of murder and the figure of the albino are clearly a

crucial focus of the text, it is significant that Momaday leaves the episode open for interpretation and thus forces his reader not only to be highly active but to re-locate him/herself within a Pueblo worldview.

Abel's impressions of his subsequent trial for murder emerge as hallucinations that result from his near-fatal beating by a corrupt LA policeman, Martinez, whose nickname 'culebra' (snake) exposes his own close relationship to evil, and perhaps also the intrinsic and historic biases of the US legal system.[35] The figure of Martinez additionally emphasises Pueblo understandings that evil continues, internalised by Abel through his injuries and suffering. In spite of his inability to communicate, Abel recognises the power of language and its role in the imperial process as '[w]ord by word by word these [Euro-American] men were disposing of him in language, *their* language'.[36] Abel's interpretation of Euro-American language use as an instrument of power is equally evident in the sermon of the Kiowa 'Priest of the Sun' Tosamah:

> And he [Saint John] said, 'In the beginning was the Word ...' ... old John was a white man, and the white man has his ways ... He talks about the Word. He talks through it and around it. He builds upon it with syllables, and prefixes and suffixes and hyphens and accents. He adds and divides and multiplies the Word. And in all of this he subtracts the truth ... the white man deals in words, and he deals easily, with grace and sleight of hand.[37]

Providing both a critique of the Bible (and its role in the colonising process) and white abuses of linguistic power, Tosamah's sermon is a pertinent comment on federal Indian history. Indeed, Momaday's focus on the role of language within the colonial relationship can be traced in the diaries and letters of the Catholic priest Father Nicolas, whose written presence within the text marks their authority. In this context, Tosamah's subsequent comments that the white man 'may ... perish by the Word'[38] underlines the very real distinctions that Momaday draws between the perception of language within Euro-American and Native American cultures. For Tosamah, the Kiowa relationship to language is an understanding of its ability to give a culture 'whole and consummate being', that storytelling is both 'to utter and to hear', and that 'the simple act of listening is crucial'.[39]

Abel's ability to listen and communicate is tested by his relocation to Los Angeles, which is crucial for his re-integration within Walatowa culture. An ability to communicate effectively is an important aspect of inter-cultural negotiations, and is evident in the attempts made by a variety of characters to heal Abel. For example, effective communication is demonstrated not only in the cultural negotiations of Tosamah's sermons, but also in the narrative of the Navajo Ben Benally which incorporates both Indian oral traditions and a modernist stream-of-consciousness style to compare Native and Euro-American literary traditions. Benally's partially successful negotiations between Indian and white worlds is evident in Momaday's incorporation of a range of Navajo ceremonial stories and ritual chants, including the healing Nightway Chant, through which Benally attempts to heal Abel: 'House made of dawn,/ ... Restore my body for me,/ Restore my mind for me'.[40] While these healings are only partial, they are necessary for Abel's return home and cultural re-integration, the initial stages of which are evident at the close of the text in Abel's participation as a dawn runner.

Abel's attempts to locate himself are mirrored by the ways in which the text's structure relocates the Euro-American reader within an emphatically Pueblo worldview. The text is therefore divided into four sections plus a prologue, which resonate with the ceremonial understandings of a range of southwestern tribal groups who acknowledge the significance of four as a representation of the natural world (i.e. the seasons and human age cycles), and of the directions that orient Native ceremonies. Most importantly, in the context of Abel's need for healing, four is representative of Native perceptions of wholeness. The novel thus also echoes and privileges Native ceremonies and ceremonial perceptions through its cyclic structure, with the text framed by images of Abel as a Pueblo dawn runner. Momaday emphasises concepts of the sacred throughout the text, outlining a range of religious and spiritual worldviews, including Christian, Navajo, Kiowa and Pueblo. Perhaps the most significant figure is Abel's uncle Francisco, who is condemned by Father Nicolas as 'evil' for his ability to successfully negotiate between Euro-American and Pueblo cultures in his role as 'sacristan' for the Catholic church coupled with his participation in traditional kiva ceremonies.[41] Returning home as Francisco is dying, Abel listens to Francisco's important tales of Pueblo history and traditions, but remains confused by what he hears, by the words that 'ran together and were no longer words'.[42] It is only Francisco's death that ultimately ensures that Abel is 'wide awake and listening'[43] and enables the beginnings of his cultural re-integration into Pueblo ceremony as a dawn runner. The final image of the text, of Abel 'running on the rise of the [sacred] song',[44] reveals the start of his integration (although partial) back into Walatowa culture through a correction of his 'faulty vision':[45] at the close of the text, Abel finally 'could see'.[46] In this context, *House Made of Dawn* can be interpreted as a vision quest that demonstrates the importance of Indian ceremonial worldviews as vehicles for cultural recovery, and the text closes with '*Qtsedaba*', the Jemez term by which a story is concluded.[47] Significantly in the ongoing context of the federal–Indian relationship, this conclusion of the text, while it is still 'in action', carefully ensures that the success or extent of Abel's cultural re-integration remains ambivalent.

Resistance Writings: James Welch (1940–2003)

The influence of Momaday's work can be detected in a range of subsequent Native writers, including the work of James Welch. Welch was born in 1940, in Browning, Montana, to a Blackfoot father and Gros Ventre mother, both of whom were also of Euro-American ancestry. Schooled on both the Blackfoot and Gros Ventre reservations, Welch went on to study creative writing at the University of Montana, and subsequently taught at Cornell and at the University of Washington. While his wider social awareness can be detected in his service for the Parole Board of the Montana Prisons System, his commitment to his Indian heritage is evident in his work as a Director at the Newberry Library D'Arcy McNickle Center. The cultural and literary value of Welch's writing was recognised in 1997 with a Lifetime Achievement Award for Literature from the Native Writers Circle. In 2003, Welch died at the age of 62 while battling against cancer.

Welch's engagement with traditional Native lives and his analysis of the impact of Euro-American culture is evident throughout his writings. In particular, the political realities of contemporary Native life can be traced in works that ground the federal–Indian relationship within specific historical eras and events. Above all, Welch's writings are powerful because they do not shirk from demonstrating the truth of Euro-American colonisation that often devastated traditional Indian cultures and senses of community and which, through assimilative policies, alienated a whole generation of Indian children. In this sense, Welch's writings can be interpreted as resistance or protest literature, giving expression to this cultural alienation. Acting on the advice of his tutor, the poet Richard Hugo, to write about what he knew, Welch published his first volume of poetry, *Riding the Earthboy 40*, in 1971. Although Welch's style, much like Momaday's, indicates the influence of Euro-American literature, his choice of topics mediate Blackfoot culture for a Euro-American audience and give a voice to Native peoples often rendered both absent and silent. *Riding the Earthboy 40* presents detailed comparisons of urban and rural scenes and lives, and beautifully drawn images of Welch's own world, 'a world full of bones and wind – the world of my ancestors'.[48] Welch's images challenge popular assumptions of the reservation as 'a depressed "bleak" place' and contemporary Indian culture as 'dying' and 'hopeless', and present alternative scenes that reflect his own childhood experience of friends, parents, and a culture that 'you loved'.[49] Yet Welch's work is inherently political: an intrinsic part of this world is the lasting effects of a series of poorly designed and badly executed federal Indian policies, coupled with ongoing Native resistance.

However, it is Welch's fiction for which he is best known. In 1974, Welch published *Winter in the Blood*, whose title demonstrates the effects of colonisation on the colonised. Significant for its emphatically first person Indian voice, *Winter in the Blood* remains one of Welch's most important texts, and is the subject of the case study below. The problem of cultural alienation is evident not only in Welch's first novel but also his second, *The Death of Jim Loney* (1979), where the realities of contemporary Native lives are made manifest through a bleak imagery and sparse style reminiscent of naturalist writers such as John Steinbeck. As his name suggests, Loney is alienated from his Native culture, due in part to his mixed blood. Thus Welch joins an ongoing discussion to which the majority of prominent twentieth-century Native writers have contributed. The novel traces the events leading to the textual climax: Loney's death. Throughout, Welch traces the impact of colonisation to present the bleak truth that the only control Loney maintains over his life is the ability to choose the form of his own death. In this context of unremitting tragedy, critical opinion on the novel remains divided between readings of Welch's vision as an eradication of any concept of hope, and analyses that attempt to draw out a more positive reading. However, as Arnold Krupat and Michael Elliott comment, it is difficult to interpret Loney's alienation as anything other than an 'inability to heal the culturally split personality that is his colonial legacy'.[50]

Welch's subsequent two novels engage further with the problems that beset Jim Loney, presenting two separate readings of very different potential outcomes – one Euro-American, *The Indian Lawyer* (1990), and one Native, *Fools Crow* (1986) – as a tentative solution to the problems of mixed blood.[51] *The Indian Lawyer* is a highly contemporary analysis of a successful Indian attorney, Sylvester Yellow Calf. Although raised in poverty after being abandoned by his parents, Yellow Calf has 'made good' in Euro-American terms as a lawyer and parole board member; and the novel considers his inter-cultural negotiations as he embarks on a political career. Welch focuses on the ways in which Yellow Calf mediates his own Indian identity – elided by his expensive suits, yet clearly marked by his name – within a white world. Significantly, the mediation is ultimately unsuccessful: Yellow Calf is blackmailed and eventually professionally destroyed by an ex-convict who is refused parole. While Welch's tale emphasises the problems of building an Indian identity in a Euro-American world, it also, as Krupat and Elliott argue, demonstrates the 'cost entailed by the loss of tribal connection'.[52]

By contrast, in *Fools Crow* Welch re-imagines a crucial period of Blackfoot history: the battles against the US military and devastating epidemics of smallpox in the 1860s. Welch quite specifically engages with the revisionist aims of 'New Historians' of the 1980s, who had begun to review the accepted histories of American settlement and the American West, often from the perspective of Native peoples and other minority social groups. This new focus is evident in the title of Patricia Nelson Limerick's seminal text *The Legacy of Conquest*, which argues that the legacy of conquest on 'the conquered' – Native peoples – is a trauma directly comparable to '[t]he legacy of slavery'.[53] This approach, therefore, exposed the violence and racism that formed the basis of American colonisation. *Fools Crow* engages with this new emphasis to present a history of Euro-American western settlement from a Pikuni (a band of the Blackfoot) viewpoint. *Fools Crow* emphasises the protagonist's submersion within traditional Pikuni culture, presenting an effective ceremonial and ritual way of life that Ron McFarland describes as an 'epic design'.[54] Welch's novel therefore is a depiction of a fully functioning culture that offers a powerful alternative to an encroaching and assimilative Euro-America. In this sense, Welch's vision is one of both protest and resistance: as Owens comments, *Fools Crow* represents a 'profound act of [cultural] recovery'.[55]

While the text ends hopefully, with the return of spring and its ceremonial recognition by the Pikuni, a key moment of *Fools Crow* is nonetheless the Massacre on the Marias River (1870), where more than two hundred Pikuni (mostly women, children and the elderly) were gunned down by the US military. Welch's unflinching depiction acknowledges a forgotten and elided moment of American history, and one that is crucial for anyone wishing to understand the causes of the subsequent Battle of the Little Bighorn (1876). Indeed, Welch continued his revision of this historical period with a film script, a PBS documentary series, and an accompanying non-fiction text, *Killing Custer: The Battle of the Little Bighorn and the Fate of the Plains Indians* (1994). Engaging with what has become a momentous and defining moment of Euro-American history – the unimaginable defeat of the US military by Indians – *Killing Custer* outlines a powerful historical background of Euro-American duplicity and military violence as the catalyst for Native retaliation. Most interestingly, Welch's discussion provides a clear analysis of contemporary Native political activism as part of the same historical continuum.

Welch's final novel, *The Heartsong of Charging Elk* (2000), widens this historical focus to address the impact of the events of the Indian Wars on the Lakota. With his tribal cultural identity dis-located by the introduction of the reservation system and the loss of traditional activities such as hunting, the text traces Charging Elk's new career as a member of Buffalo Bill's Wild West Show on its European tour, and his subsequent injury and prosecution for vagrancy while in France. Welch's discussion of Charging Elk's often thwarted attempts at cultural negotiation in France, whose authorities refuse to return him to a United States that declines to acknowledge any Native peoples as US citizens,[56] pertinently mirrors the simultaneous cultural struggles occurring in America. This final novel is significant for its depiction of the highly complex problems of intercultural negotiation, ranging from the relative simplicities of linguistic translation (Charging Elk speaks little or no English or French) to the almost insurmountable dilemma of conceptual and ideological translation (Charging Elk's traditional Oglala worldview).

Winter in the Blood (1974)

Momaday's emphasis upon cultural loss and recovery can be traced in Welch's 1974 novel *Winter in the Blood*, whose very title suggests the adverse physical effects of the long history of federal Indian relations. Indeed, as Sidner Larson argues, Welch's novel has, quite explicitly, 'colonization as subtext', where '[a]lienated Indian men and their estranged relationships ... reflect the colonial assault on the identities of Indian people[s]'.[57] In this context, Welch's mixed-blood protagonist remains un-named, trapped in a bleak and devastated landscape where, at the deepest emotional and psychological level, it is always winter. This 'dormancy', as Owens suggests, represents the ways in which

'Blackfoot culture and identity have been appropriated by the dominant white culture, leaving a kind of nothingness in their place'.[58] Having no name, the narrator has no cultural identity or place, and also no power. This sense of powerlessness becomes increasingly significant throughout the text, as do the narrator's attempts to locate himself within both family and the wider Blackfoot community. In this sense, Welch's textual structure echoes Momaday's, with a four-part division that reflects traditional concepts of ritual to suggest that, in spite of the bleak outlook, recovery of some kind is perhaps possible. Like Momaday's Abel, a clear problem for the narrator seems to be internal, related to his own mixed blood: 'the distance I felt came not from country or people; it came from within me. I was as distant from myself as a hawk from the moon'.[59]

As with Momaday's writing, an engagement with the Euro-American literary tradition is clearly evident in Welch's novel, and Welch himself often expressed his desire for success within American literature more widely. In this sense, Ron McFarland identifies *Winter in the Blood* as an 'American picaresque classic',[60] a description that reflects Welch's juxtaposition of the despair of the narrator and his attempts to locate his cultural identity with moments of bleak and very dark humour which contrast starkly with, and so add weight to, the concerns of the text. For example, the grandmother's grave which is dug 'too short' so that the coffin has to be 'jumped up and down on' to make it fit; and the fact that the catalyst for the narrator's one moment of clear vision, in a text composed of blindness, is an old horse's fart.[61] These moments of black humour act, as Larson notes, to emphasise 'the absurdity of negative and self-feeding cycles such as colonization'.[62] Structurally, the text therefore embodies the kind of alienation experienced by Welch's narrator, with highly discrete sections that prevent any sense of synthesis through a series of abrupt transitions that offer a sense of the narrator's mental, emotional and cultural fragmentation. This fragmentation is evident both in Welch's use of flashbacks, which demonstrate the narrator's increasing attempts to locate himself, and in the descriptions and sentiments of the opening chapter which engages with notions of 'homing':

> Coming home was not easy anymore. It was never a cinch, but it had become a torture … Coming home to a mother and an old lady who was my grandmother. And the girl who was thought to be my wife. But she didn't really count. For that matter none of them counted; not one meant anything to me. And for no reason, I felt no hatred, no

love, no guilt, no conscience, nothing but a distance that had grown through the years.[63]

Here, the narrator's cultural alienation is evident in the tortuous experience of 'coming home'; his familial alienation demonstrated by the linguistic distancing apparent in his choice of terminology: 'a mother', 'an old lady'. Moreover, the presence of the girl who is 'thought' to be his wife emphasises the dysfunctional nature of the family unit, where meaningful communication has ceased to exist. The effects of this inability to communicate, and tendency to miscommunicate, clearly influence every aspect of the narrator's life: as Catherine Rainwater suggests, it is evident that his 'depressive condition results partially from gaps in memory and from his inability to put all the stories of his life together'.[64]

Welch's characters demonstrate both this dysfunction and persistent miscommunications and misunderstandings. The narrator's mother Teresa eschews traditional Blackfoot culture as a 'Catholic', and conducts an ambiguous relationship with the local priest; Teresa's new husband Lame Bull's motives are questionable as he is described as having 'married 360 acres of ... some of the best land in the valley'; and the elderly grandmother attempts to recreate violent inter-tribal feuds as she watches the narrator's Cree girlfriend with 'a paring knife ... heavy in [her] ... eyes'.[65] The Cree girlfriend, Agnes, is perhaps the most pertinent character in this context of dysfunction, running away in the narrator's absence and, in a move that is potentially emasculating, stealing the emblems of his masculine identity, his 'gun and ... electric razor'.[66] In contrast to both Momaday's *House Made of Dawn* and Silko's *Ceremony*, what compounds this narrator's sense of isolation and alienation is the fact that the text is very noticeably culturally unmarked: there is little that can be specifically identified as 'Indian' on which the narrator can 'home in'. As Larson comments, this not only distinguishes Welch's 'high plains' writing from southwestern writers such as Momaday and Silko, but also reflects the extent to which southwestern Indian cultures 'were left comparatively [culturally] intact' in direct contrast to the resource-rich plains regions which were 'dispossessed ... with extreme prejudice'.[67] Drawing upon a long and established history of assimilationist goals to eradicate Indian cultures by 'killing the Indian to save the man', Welch thus creates a very real sense of Indian absence.

In this context, it is pertinent that the textual action is framed at both start and close with images of death and closure: with graves and burials. Specifically, they are the graves 'of all the Earthboys', a traditional Blackfoot family who are all now 'gone'; and of the narrator's grandmother, presented as a remnant of Blackfoot history. As Owens notes, the significance of these individuals is that they represent the last of those 'who knew what it meant to be Blackfoot in the old [i.e. traditional] sense'.[68] Welch's narrator has additionally lost his father, First Raise, to an alcohol-related death from exposure, and a brother (Mose) to a violent accidental death during childhood. In this sense, the text is largely marked by tribal absence,[69] and this is echoed by the environment of Welch's text whose desolation exposes the history of Euro-American settlement of these once 'rich' Native lands. Reflecting T. S. Eliot, the land is effectively a wasteland where attempts to create local employment 'die' and even the fish 'simply vanis[h]'.[70] Indeed, the textual action is framed by a persistent erosion of the family's livestock: by the death of the ducks won by the narrator at a fair as a child, and by the death of the narrator's elderly horse Bird as he attempts, unsuccessfully, to save a stricken cow at the close of the text.[71]

The sense of death-like stasis that Welch evokes becomes inextricably linked to the narrator and is emulated by the structure of the text with the result that, as Welch himself commented, 'nothing much happens'.[72] Indeed, the narrator deliberately names himself as 'servant to a memory of death'.[73] Moreover, the narrator's quest to find himself is marked by stalled or thwarted attempts, by misunderstandings and miscommunications, ultimately by a lack of direction. Part of the problem seems to be that the narrator interprets his search for self as a search for Agnes, indicating the extent to which his self-definition and identity depend on others in the absence of a tribal matrix to provide 'meaning and order'.[74] It is especially significant that male identity seems defined through the female: as Owens comments, one of the 'radical displacement[s]' of the text is colonisation's dramatic and adverse effect on traditional gender relationships. This erodes traditional understandings of gender roles and interaction to ensure a growing 'marginalisation' of the men and an 'embitter[ing]' of the women.[75] The legacy of this socio-cultural transformation can be detected in the opening images of the narrator, which depict him as physically marked from an encounter with a 'white man' with his 'right eye swollen up' from an alcoholic altercation that he cannot entirely remember.[76] He is subsequently compared by Teresa to his father, the 'wanderer' through whom Teresa in 'outrage' condemns

'all these damned Indians' and so highlights the narrator's own failure
to 'become something' and potential to die an equally 'foolish' death.[77]
This initial impression provides that basis for the recurring theme of
brief and violent or unsatisfactory encounters, as the narrator searches
for a place that he 'fits' and so exposes the ongoing legacy of federal–
Indian relations. As the elderly Yellow Calf surmises, the world – socio-
cultural, emotional and, more disturbingly, environmental – has become
'cockeyed'.[78] Marked at the start of the text by the narrator's blindness
(his eye is swollen shut[79]), this twisted vision is evident in the narrator's
ongoing inability to locate himself culturally within the textual 'vision
quest'.

   The search for Agnes becomes transformed into a series of extra-
familial encounters that emphasise the narrator's alienation. These
encounters are marked in terms of gender, highlighting not only the
sterility of the narrator's sexual relationships (evident in a series of disap-
pointing one-night stands), but also the ways in which male relationships have degenerated into violent and alcohol-fuelled encounters and
potentially criminal activities. All of these encounters are, significantly,
negotiated within the seedy night life of the desolate reservation towns.
The sexual encounters with Malvina and Marlene both prove highly
unsatisfactory. While Malvina refuses to tell the narrator her last name,
the narrator's attempts at further intimacy are met with blunt rejection:

   'Beat it.'
   My hand froze.
   'Beat it.'
   My groin froze.
   'Beat it.'[80]

Malvina's repeated rejection reiterates Welch's 'wintering' theme as the
narrator 'felt the quick desire dying in my crotch'.[81] This sexual death is
compounded by the narrator's encounter with the Indian Marlene, who
helps him after he is beaten in the street. Like the last, this encounter
merely serves to emphasise the narrator's alienation: he realises that 'it
was not enough'. As the encounter descends into violence (he 'slap[s] her
hard across the cheek'), the narrator becomes ever more detached and
the theme of death resurfaces, as he 'star[es]' with a 'lack of emotion' and
'curiosity' as if Marlene were 'a bug floating motionless down an irriga-
tion ditch, not yet dead but having decided on death'.[82] In this context,
death becomes directly equated to cultural alienation and stasis.

This deathly detachment can also be detected in the narrator's sense of powerlessness, accentuated by his interactions with other male characters, most of which take place in bars. Agnes's brother Dougie turns out to be a sneak thief, tricking the narrator into helping him rob a man, before refusing to pass on information about Agnes and later beating the narrator unconscious. The narrator's subsequent friendship with the 'airplane man' is exposed as racial exploitation when the airplane man – 'a fugitive from justice' (later to be arrested) – reveals that his desire to include the narrator in his plans is because Indians can cross the Canadian border more easily.[83] Significantly, the narrator is attracted to the scheme by its apparent glamour, which produces one of the narrator's only discernible emotional reactions in the text, a 'funny feeling of excitement and sadness'.[84] Perhaps most significant is the narrator's recognition of the dangers posed to him by both Indian and white worlds due to his own liminal status, evident in the repeated assaults that he endures: 'I was a stranger to both and both had beaten me'.[85]

At the heart of the narrator's lack of emotion is the absence of any kind of love. Indeed, the only love he has ever encountered derived from his father. Unlike Teresa, from whom the narrator 'never expected much … and I never got it',[86] First Raise's relationship with his sons is marked by more than absence and dissociation. This is especially evident when First Raise usurps Teresa's traditional domestic role, preparing food for his sons: 'First Raise smiled' as he 'watch[ed] us eat' because '[h]e loved us'.[87] First Raise's love is crucial for the narrator's 'return home', as Owens argues it is First Raise's 'ability to demonstrate his love for his sons [that] is vital to whatever chances the narrator has for renewal'.[88] Significantly, valuable and nurturing male relationships are therefore central to the narrator's healing within the text, which is marked by the true moment of epiphany: his recognition of a 'lost' family member, and his realisation that he is not mixed blood. Visiting the elderly Yellow Calf to pass on news of his grandmother's death, the narrator finally realises the reason for First Raise taking him to visit the old man as a child: Yellow Calf is Teresa's father who, significantly, she has always identified as part-white. Yellow Calf therefore functions as a mediator for traditional Blackfoot culture, and his powerful stories of the winter starvation which killed many tribal members act to create a cultural link for the narrator. Given vision by a blind man, and thus tracing his ancestry historically for the first time, the narrator achieves a first real sense of cultural connection and reconstruction: 'we shared this secret in the presence of ghosts, in wind that called forth the muttering teepees, the blowing snow, and the white air of horses' nostrils'.[89] Moreover, this moment also marks the narrator's first real experience of emotion as 'the wave behind my eyes broke' and he is finally able to weep.[90]

At the close of the text, the narrator buries his grandmother in a scene that embodies the enduring ambiguity of the text. Alternating between the actual burial and the narrator's unrelated interior monologue, the text emphasises the passing of the old while indicating a slightly more positive note for the future, the narrator's desire to find Agnes and 'maybe offer to marry her on the spot'.[91] Through such tentative terminology, Welch reflects the partial nature of the narrator's recovery. However, the final image of the text suggests that the first steps are positive: throwing a traditional pouch into his grandmother's grave, the narrator indicates his awareness of the ongoing need for ritual. In this context, Welch's narrator has, however partially, come home.

Un-settling Hi/Stories: Leslie Marmon Silko (b. 1948)

This sudden burgeoning of Native writing also influenced the Laguna writer Leslie Marmon Silko. Born in 1948 in Albuquerque, New Mexico, of mixed Mexican, Native American and Euro-American ancestry, Silko was educated primarily at off-reservation Euro-American schools before graduating from the University of New Mexico in 1969, the year she published her first short story, 'The Man to Send Rain Clouds'. Silko subsequently enrolled in Law School, influenced by the lawsuit undertaken by the Pueblo of Laguna against the State of New Mexico. However, when the Laguna case was disappointingly resolved, with compensation for land losses awarded at nineteenth-century land values, Silko rejected a career in law due to her realisation that 'injustice is built into the Anglo-American legal system'.[92] In 1971 Silko turned to writing in order to portray Pueblo storytelling traditions, and understandings that stories which are told well can actively change the world. Silko has subsequently taught at the Navajo Community College, and at the universities of Arizona and New Mexico, and been awarded numerous prestigious awards, including the Native Writers Circle of the Americas lifetime achievement award (1994), a MacArthur Foundation 'genius' Award (1981) and the Pushcart Prize for poetry (1977). Named as a 'Living Cultural Treasure' by the New Mexico Humanities Council, Silko has in recent years relocated to Mexico as part of her ongoing resistance against the politics and policies of the US government.

The influence of Silko's own background, both familial and tribal, can clearly be detected in her work, and she repeatedly emphasises the significance of her heritage: 'what I know is Laguna. This place I am from is everything I am as a writer and a human being'.[93] However, Silko's own family have been a cause of some internal conflict at Laguna: her Euro-American ancestors were railroad surveyors (and so deemed responsible for Laguna land losses), and their subsequent involvement in Laguna tribal politics caused rifts both with tribal members and with local Euro-Americans. From an early date, Silko's family thus occupied an ambiguous social position within Laguna, forced into complex inter-cultural negotiations. This social marginality was reflected physically in the location of the Marmon household at the edge of the Laguna reser-vation, visibly situated between Indian and white worlds. Nonetheless, an essentially Laguna worldview is evident as the foundation of Silko's writings, which develops two primary inter-related foci: an exploration of Laguna culture and functions of the oral storytelling tradition, and a powerful and often controversial critique of Euro-America.

Silko's writing career has been built upon her understanding of story as an alternative form of 'justice'. Therefore, Silko's writings engage with and subvert conventional Euro-American literary forms and ideologies, to privilege alternative worldviews evident within Native storytelling. Silko is best known for her widely anthologised 1977 novel *Ceremony*, which is the subject of the following case study, yet her cultural emphases are evident in her earlier volume of poetry, *Laguna Woman* (1974). Poems such as 'Indian Song: Survival' emphasise what Louise Barnett and James Thorson identify as her 'formative influence':[94] the concept of story as a vehicle for cultural identity and continuity, and as an embodi-ment of the Laguna landscape. This interest in literary representations of landscape formed the basis of Silko's subsequent correspondence with the poet James Wright, published after his early death as *The Delicacy and Strength of Lace* (1986). Silko's commitment to poetry can be detected not only in her use of verse as a structural and ideological device within *Ceremony*, but also in her development of multi-genre works such as *Storyteller* (1981). A combination of autobiography, biography, revisionist history, photography, poetry and prose, *Storyteller* attempts to translate the oral storytelling tradition through the creation of an internal dialogue that gives voice to a range of contrasting viewpoints and stories to depict the dynamics of Laguna culture. Central to this conceptualisa-tion of Laguna culture is Silko's discussion of the mythic figure 'Yellow

Woman', the subject of multiple stories and poems, who re-appears as the focus of Silko's 1996 essay collection, *Yellow Woman and a Beauty of the Spirit*, which analyses multiple aspects of contemporary Native life in the American southwest within an explicitly political context. This interest in the multi-genre is explored in two further volumes, *Sacred Water: Narratives and Pictures* (1993), and *Rain* (1996), a collaboration with Silko's photographer father, Lee Marmon. Both volumes combine written word and visual images to present highly political readings of the southwestern landscape and its multiple cultures.

In the titular 'Storyteller', Silko's protagonist insists that, regardless of personal cost, the story 'must be told as it is'.[95] This ideology is most evident in Silko's second novel, *Almanac of the Dead* (1991). Taking ten years to write, *Almanac* is physically vast (more than 760 pages and seventy-two significant characters), with a plot that spans 500 years and the entire Americas. Highly political, the novel presents a disturbing vision of America's future based on the legacy of 500 years of colonialism: widespread destruction, oppression, exploitation and manipulation. In this sense, *Almanac* is an extension of *Ceremony*'s consideration of 'witchery'. As its title suggests, the text is peopled by the thousands of 'furious, bitter spirits' who represent the true cost of American settlement and who demand justice.[96] The textual action ends with the emergence of a People's Army who rise up to peacefully retake stolen indigenous lands, and to play upon a range of contemporary Euro-American fears. Deeply un-settling to Euro-American readers and vastly different to the widely celebrated *Ceremony*, *Almanac* provoked a notably hostile critical reaction and received no concentrated critical attention for almost a decade.

Silko's most recent novel, *Gardens in the Dunes* (1999), is also political but with a less overt historical focus. Focusing on the fictional Sand Lizard tribe of the southwest, *Gardens* analyses the relationships between imperialism, collecting and horticulture, yet also evokes the dead through a discussion of the Ghost Dance phenomenon of the late nineteenth century that resulted in the Wounded Knee massacre. Through an exploration of a range of attitudes to the land, the text explores concepts of hybridity and cross-pollination within a cultural context to provide a focus upon the problems and potentials of mixed blood and the possibilities of inter- or trans-cultural relationships.

Ceremony (1977)

The relationship between Silko's 1977 novel *Ceremony* and Momaday's *House Made of Dawn* can be clearly seen: like Abel, Silko's protagonist Tayo is mixed blood, a fact that is constantly commented on by his Auntie, who makes 'sacrifices' for 'her dead sister's half-breed child'.[97] Both Auntie and her son Rocky are products of assimilation: Auntie is a converted Christian even though she exhibits very little 'Christian' spirit, and Rocky 'deliberately avoid[s] the old-time ways' because he 'understood what he had to do to win in the white outside world'.[98] Tayo is therefore alienated from his family, including his uncle Josiah and Grandma, by Auntie's persistent acts of exclusion. However, this is exacerbated by Tayo's wider rejection by both white and Indian worlds, evident in the racism and hostility he suffers due to his mixed race. In this context, Tayo's description of his experiences provides a pertinent comment on the paradoxical nature of assimilation: '[e]verything ... was white. Except for me. I was invisible'.[99] In spite of his mixed blood and best efforts, Tayo remains, to paraphrase Homi Bhabha, 'almost the same but not quite/white'.[100] Tayo's confusion is made manifest by the textual stream of consciousness, and the constant transitions between times and places that emulate traditional Laguna beliefs in a temporality that is not, as with Euro-American concepts, strictly linear.

Tayo's suffering is compounded by his status as a returning World War Two veteran. Accepted to serve for America because '[i]n a time of need, *anyone* can fight for her',[101] Tayo is taken prisoner of war in the Philippines and endures the notorious Bataan Death March,[102] during which Rocky dies. Crucially, at this point Tayo curses the relentless rain, a culturally prohibited action that, to his mind, causes the subsequent drought at Laguna. In this context Tayo, like Momaday's Abel, has committed a range of transgressions and finds himself in very real need of healing and purification as a returning warrior. Yet his experience of Euro-American medicine reduces him to invisibility, to 'white smoke', as it 'drained memory out of hi[m]' and sentences him to silence.[103] However, traditional cures from Laguna elders such as Ku'oosh also fail because they cannot recognise the kinds of mass destruction unleashed during World War Two with the creation of the atomic bomb: 'the old man would not have believed anything so monstrous ... [n]ot even oldtime witches killed like that'.[104] Significantly, Tayo's cure eventually lies with the mixed-blood Navajo medicine man Betonie, whose successful cultural negotiations are evident in his discussion of the necessity for change as a prerequisite for cultural health. As Welch's nameless narrator realises in *Winter in the Blood*, Betonie knows that 'things which don't shift and grow are dead things'.[105] The central lesson of the text therefore is, as Owens comments, that 'through the dynamism, adaptability, and syncretism inherent in Native cultures, both individuals and ... cultures ... are able to survive, grow, and evade the deadly traps of stasis and sterility'.[106] Tayo's recovery lies equally with the female character Ts'eh Montano, with whom he has a sexual relationship and who is an embodiment both of the mythic figure Changing Woman and of the land itself, the sacred southwestern mountain Mount Taylor. It is therefore the storied Laguna land that Tayo must embrace in order to achieve healing.

Silko's emphasis upon myth and ritual is central to the structure of the novel, which presents Tayo's return home and re-integration into traditional Laguna culture that Krupat and Elliott define as 'still functionally available and vital' in spite of the best efforts of assimilation.[107] The text begins and ends with the single word 'sunrise' to emulate Laguna religious practices and convey a sense of completion and renewal.[108] The text presents two intertwined narratives: the story of Tayo, which is delivered largely in prose; plus a series of poems retelling Laguna myths that mirror Tayo's own journey. In this context, Silko celebrates Tayo's mixed blood as emblematic of a range of Laguna mixed-blood mythic heroes, who act to save the people in times of trouble. The text therefore provides a powerful argument in favour of the continuing applicability of mythic stories and knowledges. Moreover, in the face of Tayo's cultural forgetfulness, the novel emphasises the importance of remembrance, of recognising the nature of events in order to understand how to deal with them. At the close of the text, Tayo has himself become a figure re-enacting, and re-integrated within, Laguna culture; a transformation that is recognised by Grandma's response: '[i]t seems like I already heard these stories before ... only thing is, the names sound different'.[109]

Significantly, Silko's structure has no chapter divisions, but relies upon a series of 'natural' breaks that emulate the pauses of oral storytelling (whose speech patterns are evident within the poetic narrative of the text) in order to create a dialogue. Structurally, the novel opens with three poems that emphasise the mythic basis of the story: the novel has been created by Thought Woman and Silko herself is only 'telling you the story/she is thinking'.[110] These poems provide insight into Laguna ideas of the role of story as a carrier of culture: stories are 'all we have to fight off/ illness and death'.[111] In this sense, Silko's comment that 'you don't have anything/if you don't have the stories' carries real weight.[112] Crucially, Laguna understandings of the power of story are evident in the events that are 'set in motion' as stories are told.[113] In this way Silko insists not just upon Native presence but, more importantly, upon Native agency. Most importantly, in terms of the drought, of Tayo's illness, and of a more general cultural malaise, Silko makes it clear that '[t]he only cure … is a good ceremony'.[114] The text itself therefore functions as a ceremony, not just for Tayo and the land but also for Silko's readers.

   This concept of communal healing and recovery is particularly significant in the context of 'witchery', the term Silko uses to denote the full range of human oppression and exploitation, including the violent legacy of colonialism. Oppression and exploitation therefore saturate the text, from the racism that Tayo experiences to the hatred evident in the actions of Tayo's fellow Laguna servicemen Emo, Pinkie, Leroy and Harley. However, witchery is most evident in Silko's analysis of atomic and nuclear power, whose development on Pueblo lands and original use against Japan becomes symbolic of the racism endemic within Euro-American culture. By naming this attitude 'witchery', Silko equates this destructive form of thinking to traditional Laguna notions of evil. As Owens comments, witchery equates to 'the evil that strives to separate and thereby destroy'.[115] As a result, the notion of ceremony within the text becomes expanded as a means by which to ward off these kinds of separatist and hierarchical thinking. Silko's moral is outlined by Josiah's reminder: '[t]he old people used to say that droughts happen when people forget, when people misbehave'.[116] This type of separatist thinking is embodied by the 'witches' of the text, the Destroyers who fail to recognise Native concepts of relatedness and so:

> … see no life
> When they look
> they see only objects.
> The world is a dead thing for them
> the trees and rivers are not alive
> the mountains and stones are not alive.
> The deer and bear are objects
> They see no life.[117]

Failing to see the connections, the Destroyers not only 'fear the world' but 'destroy what they fear'.[118] This is evident in the behaviour of the

Laguna veterans who return home 'full of stories' of self-hatred.[119] The veterans embrace the ideals of witchery by celebrating and ritualising their war experiences, 'repeat[ing] them like long medicine chants, the beer bottles pounding on the counter tops like drums'.[120] Thus Euro-American separatist concepts are internalised and Emo, in particular, loses any concept of the connections between nature and culture, insisting that 'the Indians' mother earth' is an irredeemable '[o]ld dried up thing!'[121] Emo's terminology clearly indicates his deliberate disasso-ciation of himself from his culture. Indeed, his wholehearted embracing of witchery is perhaps most evident in the tortures that he inflicted during war on the 'Jap bastard[s]' whose teeth he keeps as 'war souve-nirs' in a 'little bag'.[122] An essential part of Emo's destructive drinking ritual, this bag of souvenirs inverts traditional Laguna understandings of the healing medicine pouch. Tayo's reaction is evident in his constant vomiting which attempts to purge his system of this type of poison.

For Silko, this self-destruction ultimately finds expression in the concept of atomic and nuclear power: as Helen Jaskoski comments, *Ceremony* is an 'extended critique of the nuclear age' which recognises that 'nuclear weapons and nuclear power ... [are] the logical and inevitable culmination of western empirical thought'.[123] The text therefore unites apparently disparate forms of oppression to trace connections wrought by imperial Euro-American worldviews. For example, the discovery and conquest of the New World – the '[s]tolen rivers and mountains' and the introduction of 'terrible diseases' that cause '[e]ntire tribes to die out'[124] – is connected with the discovery of uranium on Native lands, and with the subsequent economic reconquest of southwestern Native peoples by the uranium industry. This uranium discovery will, to Silko's mind, produce 'the final pattern' that will enable wholesale destruction.[125] Silko's concerns, therefore, extend to incorporate all peoples, as the Destroyers are intent upon laying their nuclear pattern 'across the world' to 'explode everything'.[126] It is at the abandoned Jackpile uranium mine at Laguna, where the earth is 'piled ... like fresh graves', that Tayo finally recognises the source of his illness.[127] As Jaskoski indicates, the site is carefully chosen for the final clash between Tayo (humanity) and the other Laguna war veterans (the Destroyers) that exposes the uranium as a 'deadly counter-symbol to the Pueblo understanding of the earth as literally the mother of all life'.[128]

Remembering Grandma's story of the first atomic test when, despite her failing eyesight, she thought she was 'seeing the sun rise again',

Tayo can finally see the pattern he has been searching for: '[h]e had been so close to it, caught up in it for so long that its simplicity struck him deep inside his chest'.[129] At the Jackpile site, Tayo traces the connections between the siting of Trinity atomic test site on colonised Native lands and the vast human costs of the bombs exploded at Hiroshima and Nagasaki. Tayo's exposure of these connections provides a solution for his constant confusion of the 'enemy' Japanese soldiers with his own family members: namely that all human beings are, through the forces of racial hatred, 'united by the fate the destroyers had planned for them'.[130] It is through connections such as these that Silko clearly indicates the ongoing power of racial hatred.

In this context, Jane Caputi argues that Silko's context of global 'nuclear annihilation' allows the reader to trace Tayo's illness 'to the same evil that now threatens the planet with nuclear destruction' and also to recognise that his healing is representative 'of a much larger [more communal] ritual'.[131] Significantly, it is the role of the reader that Silko emphasises within *Ceremony*, drawing on traditional Laguna stories of the power of the witness against witchery: it 'won't work/if someone is watching'.[132] In this context, the reader is invited to understand how, from a Laguna perspective, one result of the nuclear industry is that 'the balance of the world had been disturbed'.[133] The reader is therefore invited to see that Tayo's illness is 'part of something larger' and that 'his cure would be found only in something great and inclusive of everything'.[134] The cure, as Silko indicates in the poems that open the text, is 'a good ceremony',[135] an embracing of Laguna notions of reciprocity and relatedness. An integral part of Tayo's cure is a growing understanding of his own relationship to both land and traditional Laguna culture and how he is 'connected ... to the earth'.[136] This connection is perhaps most evident in Tayo's relationship with the mythic Ts'eh. While Tayo initially fails to understand that Ts'eh is representative of the land itself, it is through their physical relationship/connection that he realises that 'he couldn't feel where her body ended and the sand began'.[137] However, notions of inter-relatedness are most clearly emphasised by Ku'oosh, the elderly Laguna holy man:

> 'But you know, grandson, this world is fragile'.
> ... It took a long time to explain the fragility and intricacy because no word exists alone, and the reason for choosing each word had to be explained with a story about why it must be said this certain way. That was the responsibility of being human, old Ku'oosh said.[138]

Relating to the types of linguistic power discussed by Momaday, Ku'oosh's emphasis is upon the constant care that is needed to maintain correct and mutually beneficial relations. Above all, Ku'oosh underlines the inter-relatedness of the world and of all of its inhabitants, none of which 'exists alone'. In the context of responsiblity, Ku'oosh warns that '[i]t took only one person to tear away the delicate strands of the web, spilling the rays of the sun into the sand, and the fragile world would be injured'.[139] While Silko depicts Tayo overcoming the dangers of witchery at the close of the text, she maintains the need for watchfulness on the part of the reader to emphasise the need for us all to remain constantly vigilant against the destructive forces of witchery. At the close of Silko's text, witchery 'is dead' but only 'for now'.[140]

The burgeoning of a Native American literary 'renaissance' in the late 1960s and early 1970s demonstrated clear interactions with Civil Rights concerns of the era, as diverse Native writers offered increasingly complex articulations both of valuable and surviving Native cultural traditions, and of Native political demands within modern America, to communicate the social and cultural results of the history of federal–Indian relations and policies. Demonstrating an emphatic Indian presence in spite of a lengthy history of racism and oppression, often enshrined within federal Indian policy, these writers and their texts also expressed and illustrated continued Indian agency. Perhaps most significantly, the complexity of these articulations made even further demands upon readers of Native literature, who were required to engage not only with intricate political histories and trace their relationships with modern America, but also with the cultural translations evident within innovative literary techniques. The successful usurpation of Euro-American language and literary form as an expression of the colonial experience enabled further, more far-reaching developments in Native writing and publishing.

Notes

1. In the late 1960s, there was a greater acceptance of Indian culture due in part to an emerging ecological awareness and interest in alternative lifestyles. In this context, the 'Keep America Beautiful' Campaign of 1971 very successfully used a 'crying Indian' image to indicate the damage being done by pollution. This appropriation of Indian culture is increasingly evident within the 'New Age' spiritual movement.
2. Two FBI agents and one Indian, Joseph Stuntz, died at Wounded Knee. Of the three Indians tried for the murder of the agents, one – Leonard Peltier – was

convicted. Identified by the United Nations Commission on Human Rights and Amnesty International as one of the most outrageous abuses of justice in American history, Peltier remains incarcerated for a crime he almost certainly did not commit, with every appeal for parole or re-investigation turned down. The killer of Joseph Stuntz has never been identified.

3. Kenneth Lincoln (1983), p. 13.
4. Louis Owens (1992), p. 34.
5. N. Scott Momaday (1992), p. xviii.
6. Matthias Schubnell (1985), p. 200.
7. Owens (1992), p. 91.
8. Momaday (1976), p. 25.
9. Cited in Schubnell (1985), p. 10.
10. Owens (1992), p. 126.
11. Schubnell (1985), p. 189.
12. Momaday (1999), p. 9.
13. Ibid. p. 9.
14. Craig Frischkorn (1999), p. 24.
15. Owens (1992), p. 91.
16. Momaday (1989), p. 5.
17. Ibid. pp. 10–11.
18. Ibid. p. 1.
19. Owens (1992), p. 92.
20. Momaday (1976), p. 142.
21. For example, the Lakota battle for the return of the Black Hills (South Dakota) to Native ownership is based on the spiritual value of the land and not its value as a mineral site: the Black Hills were one site of the late-nineteenth-century Gold Rush. As a result, an eighty-year legal battle by the Lakota for the return of the land which resulted in a legal ruling (1980) in favour of $106 million compensation was unacceptable to the Lakota because the sacred nature of the land could not be valued in monetary terms.
22. Momaday (1989), p. 13, my emphasis.
23. Ibid. p. 22.
24. William Bevis (1987), pp. 581–2.
25. Ibid. p. 582.
26. Momaday (1989), p. 11.
27. Ibid. p. 24.
28. Robert M. Nelson (1993), p. 43.
29. Momaday (1989), pp. 34–6.
30. Ibid. p. 103.
31. Ibid. p. 83.
32. Ibid. p. 83
33. Owens (1992), p. 103.
34. Ibid. pp. 104–5.
35. Momaday (1989), p. 141.
36. Ibid. p. 102.
37. Ibid. pp. 93–4.
38. Ibid. p. 95.
39. Ibid. p. 94.

40. Ibid. p. 147.
41. Ibid. p. 51.
42. Ibid. p. 196.
43. Ibid. p. 209.
44. Ibid. p. 212.
45. Nelson (1993), p. 47.
46. Momaday (1989), p. 212.
47. Ibid. p. 212.
48. James Welch (1997), online essay.
49. Ibid.
50. Arnold Krupat and Michael Elliott (2006), p. 134.
51. Ibid. p. 134.
52. Ibid. p. 134.
53. Patricia Nelson Limerick (1988), p. 18.
54. Ron McFarland (2000), p. 109.
55. Owens (1992), p. 166.
56. Although many Native peoples gained American citizenship through the 1887 Dawes Allotment Act, many were only legally recognised in 1924 with the passing of the Indian Citizenship Act.
57. Sidner Larson (2005), p. 276.
58. Owens (1992), p. 129.
59. Welch (1986), p. 2.
60. McFarland (2000), p. 52.
61. Welch (1986), pp. 174, 158.
62. Larson (2005), p. 276.
63. Welch (1986), p. 2.
64. Catherine Rainwater (1999), p. 148.
65. Welch (1986), pp. 4, 13, 15.
66. Ibid. p. 3.
67. Larson (2005), p. 277.
68. Owens (1992), p. 129.
69. Larson (2005), p. 277.
70. Welch (1986), pp. 5–6.
71. Ibid. pp. 15–18, 144–7.
72. Cited in McFarland (2000), p. 57.
73. Welch (1986), p. 38.
74. Owens (1992), p. 134.
75. Ibid. pp. 135–6.
76. Welch (1986), p. 2.
77. Ibid. pp. 19–20.
78. Ibid. p. 68.
79. Ibid. p. 2.
80. Ibid. p. 84.
81. Ibid. p. 84.
82. Ibid. p. 123.
83. Ibid. p. 97.
84. Ibid. p. 102.
85. Ibid. p. 120.

86. Ibid. p. 21.
87. Ibid. pp. 105–6.
88. Owens (1992), p. 135.
89. Welch (1986), p. 159.
90. Ibid. p. 159.
91. Ibid. p. 175.
92. Leslie Marmon Silko (1996), pp. 19–20.
93. Cited in Dexter Fisher (1981), p. 18.
94. Louise Barnett and James Thorson (1999), p. 2.
95. Silko (1981), p. 39.
96. Silko (1991), p. 424.
97. Silko (1986), p. 30.
98. Ibid. p. 51.
99. Ibid. p. 123.
100. Homi Bhabha (1994), p. 89.
101. Silko (1986), p. 64 emphasis added.
102. After the Battle of Bataan in 1942, approximately 75,000 prisoners of war were forcibly relocated by Japanese troops. More than 10,000 died.
103. Silko (1986), pp. 14–15.
104. Ibid. p. 37.
105. Ibid. p. 126.
106. Owens (1992), p. 167.
107. Krupat and Elliott (2006), p. 139.
108. Silko (1986), p. 4.
109. Ibid. p. 260.
110. Ibid. p. 1.
111. Ibid. p. 2.
112. Ibid. p. 2.
113. Ibid. p. 135.
114. Ibid. p. 3.
115. Owens (1992), p. 177.
116. Silko (1986), p. 46.
117. Ibid. p. 135.
118. Ibid. p. 135.
119. Ibid. p. 163.
120. Ibid. p. 43.
121. Ibid. p. 25.
122. Ibid. pp. 60–1.
123. Helen Jaskoski (1990), p. 2.
124. Silko (1986), p. 136.
125. Ibid. p. 137.
126. Ibid. p. 137.
127. Ibid. p. 245.
128. Jaskoski (1990), p. 10.
129. Silko (1986), p. 245.
130. Ibid. p. 246.
131. Jane Caputi (1992), p. 14.
132. Silko (1986), p. 247.

133. Ibid. p. 186.
134. Ibid. p. 126.
135. Ibid. p. 3.
136. Ibid. p. 104.
137. Ibid. p. 222.
138. Ibid. p. 35.
139. Ibid. p. 38.
140. Ibid. p. 261.

CHAPTER 4

Writing Women: Louise Erdrich, Anna Lee Walters and Luci Tapahonso, 1980–2000

The successes of the first wave of writers of the Native American Renaissance are evident in their achievements: Momaday, Welch and Silko all clearly 'wrote back' to Euro-American literary traditions through their engagement with specific literary styles and concerns, even while they subverted these through their privileging of traditional Native cultural practices and worldviews. Moreover, the fact that all three were also recognised by literary awards and prizes, not least of which was Momaday's Pulitzer, ensured that their writings became even more influential through a rapid incorporation into the American canon. The influence of Silko, in particular, is crucial to a whole range of subsequent Native women writers: Silko not only set a positive example as a highly successful female author but, while she discussed the alienation of the individual, she also carefully foregrounded the role of community in cultural re-integration. This emphasis upon the communal, often as an expansion of the family, is central to the development of Native women's writing from the 1980s, which began to focus much more fully on the complex realities of Native women's lives. This new generation of Native women writers were therefore, in every way, writing women.

These new Native women writers thus presented a focus on often elided aspects of Native culture, engaging with some of the emerging concerns of feminism to respond to the ways in which the traditional roles of Native women had been eroded by colonialism, and by contact with the institutionalised sexism of Euro-American culture. These analyses also responded to developments within feminism, such as the emergence of 'Third World' feminism to address the implicit (sometimes explicit) racist assumptions of a seemingly 'colour blind' feminist movement. Such colour blindness allowed claims, for example, that all women were linked by shared experiences of oppression. Identified as the assumptions of the white middle classes, such claims were subsequently denounced as highly offensive by women's groups who had experienced extreme socio-cultural conditions such as slavery, poverty or colonisation. As Julia V. Emberley aptly comments, 'the unequal relations between women cannot be reduced to a universal sisterhood composed of an essential plurality of differences'.[1] This denunciation refused to define women as 'socially constituted as a homogeneous group' or as a 'category of analysis',[2] and instead highlighted key cultural and political specificities which were crucial to the development of Native women's literature in this era. In her feminist analysis of the recovery of 'the feminine' in Native cultures, Paula Gunn Allen engages directly with this socio-politico-cultural specificity to trace the ways in which firmly patriarchal Euro-American culture had imposed, to varying degrees of success, the same rigid forms of patriarchy on Native cultures through the imposition of Christianity and European forms of government. In this manner, traditional social, political and religious roles undertaken by Native women were either eroded or eradicated, leading to a more general 'devaluation of women'.[3]

A key benefit of feminist theory, especially in terms of historiography, has been the recovery and privileging of previously silenced female voices. In the context of Native American history, and within published Native literature, most Native voices have been silenced to some degree, yet none so successfully elided as the female voice. As part of the legacy of colonialism and federal–Indian relations, this silencing has often also been compounded at a local level by communal or individual circumstances: poverty, alcohol abuse, domestic violence. Yet such silences belie the traditionally powerful roles that women occupied within many Native cultures. For example, the Seneca historian Barbara Mann has carefully traced the traditional gender relationships of Iroquois culture to recover and foreground the powerful political roles occupied by Native women during America's revolutionary war, where the 'all-important Clan Mothers' Councils' and 'Women's Grand Council' of the Iroquois League decided all matters relating to war and any assault on or reduction of female power was interpreted as an assault on Iroquois culture.[4] The history of Native American politics since colonisation has been dominated by the voices of Indian men, largely because European and Euro-American politicians and negotiators refused to recognise Indian women politically, instead conceptualising them physically and sexually, resulting in an erasure of traditional ideas of equality. Significantly, Native women are increasingly beginning to occupy powerful political roles again, with the emergence of activist groups such as WARN (Women of All Red Nations), and the election of high-profile tribal politicians such as Wilma Mankiller, Chief of the Cherokee Nation (1991–5), and Joyce Dugan, Principal Chief of the Eastern Band of Cherokee Indians (since 1995).

The works of major women writers of this period clearly engage with this need to express Native women's experiences more fully, and all build upon the firm foundations laid by Silko's earlier (and ongoing) success at presenting Native women's voices and views, and gaining a wider Euro-American audience. In this context, this chapter will consider the range of public successes and political interventions evident in the three very different voices and worldviews of Louise Erdrich (Turtle Mountain Chippewa), Anna Lee Walters (Pawnee/Otoe-Missouria), and Luci Tapahonso (Navajo).

International Successes: Louise Erdrich (b. 1954)

A member of the Turtle Mountain Chippewa, Louise Erdrich is one of the most popular, prolific and internationally successful contemporary Native American writers. Born in Little Falls, Minnesota in 1954 to a German-American father and Ojibwe-French mother, the significance of this mixed-blood status can be traced in the majority of Erdrich's writing. Primarily analysing her Indian heritage (her grandfather was a Tribal Chairman), Erdrich's works have in recent years explored her German ancestry in more detail, notably with the publication of *The Master Butcher's Singing Club* (2003). Raised in North Dakota, both Erdrich's parents taught at the BIA Indian school at Wahpeton and encouraged her to pursue a university education. Erdrich joined Dartmouth College in 1972, the year that Dartmouth first admitted women, to study on the new Native American Studies programme.[5] Encouraged by her parents and influenced by the Ojibwe storytelling tradition embraced by her wider family, Erdrich wrote throughout her university career, during which she won several literary prizes for both poetry and fiction. At Dartmouth, Erdrich also met her future husband and literary collaborator Michael Dorris (then Director of the Native Studies programme), with whom Erdrich would later publish the collaborative novel *Crown of Columbus* (1991) tracing the legacy of 500 years of New World colonialism upon contemporary Native American societies. Having gained a master's degree in creative writing from Johns Hopkins University, Erdrich returned to Dartmouth in 1979 as a writer-in-residence. After a lengthy correspondence, Erdrich and Dorris married in 1981 and went on to collaborate on several works of fiction before Dorris's suicide in 1997.

Like Welch, the success of Erdrich's writing lies in her focus upon what she knows: the world of the mixed-blood Ojibwe. As with Silko, Erdrich's first focus was on poetry, resulting in the publication of three volumes, *Imagination* (1981), *Jacklight* (1984) and *Baptism of Desire* (1989), all of which emphasised her Ojibwe heritage through a focus on Native culture, myths and stories, and on the lengthy and troubled history of federal–Indian relations and the assimilative intentions of Euro-American culture. In spite of this early focus, Erdrich was not to publish a further volume of poetry until 2004, when *Original Fire* appeared. Nonetheless, Erdrich's essentially poetic style is equally evident in her works of fiction which produce strikingly visual imagery. Significantly, the majority of Erdrich's fiction, until her separation from Dorris just before his death in 1997, was the product of an intensive collaborative process, and as a result most of her early novels are dedicated to her husband. The publication of the 1984 novel *Love Medicine*, which won the National Book Critics Circle Award, ensured Erdrich's popular appeal and her critical acclaim. Her success is notable for being not only national but increasingly international: unusually for a Native writer, Erdrich's works are easily available in the UK through a British imprint.[6] The subject of the case study below, *Love Medicine* introduces the reader to a distinctly Ojibwe world that is firmly geographically and textually located, and to four complex and inter-related Indian families: the Lamartines, the Kashpaws, the Morriseys and the Pillagers. *Love Medicine* also introduces Erdrich's distinct style which juxtaposes disparate and often ostensibly chronologically unrelated temporal episodes to present a rich and multi-vocal textual dialogue that many critics have compared to William Faulkner. By these means, Erdrich demonstrates the significance, often elided within hegemonic Euro-American history, of past events that continue to have a profound effect on contemporary Indian lives.

This powerfully drawn Indian cultural landscape subsequently became the focus of the majority of Erdrich's works, including the three texts that, with *Love Medicine*, are identified as her 'tetralogy': *The Beet Queen* (1986), *Tracks* (1988) and *The Bingo Palace* (1994). All volumes of the tetralogy trace the experiences of the same four families across the twentieth century, to emphasise the complex problems that derive from 500 years of assimilative pressure on Native communities. These communities are, problematically, experiencing increasing internal divisions deriving not only from growing numbers of culturally alienated mixed-blood Indians, but also from diverse and conflicting allegiances to Indian or Euro-American cultures and values between those who can be identified as 'traditionalists' and 'progressives'. Following *Love Medicine*'s Indian focus, *The Beet Queen* presented a more peripheral focus on Indian stories, emphasising a largely white community as a means through which cultural alienation and its ramifications can be assessed, while *Tracks* provided an historical analysis of the effects of allotment on the Ojibwe at the turn of the twentieth century, and its effects upon the traditional Ojibwe beliefs that were inseparable from both the land and geographically specific cultural relationships. Erdrich's novel *The Bingo Palace* has a much more emphatically political focus in its explorations of the potentials and pitfalls of Indian gaming,[7] and its relationship to traditional Indian culture in the late twentieth century.

Erdrich's subsequent novels provide an increasingly detailed and complex consideration of the same Ojibwe families and cultural world-views. *Tales of Burning Love* (1996) provides a tangential development of *Love Medicine* through its focus on the husband of one of the principal characters, and explores the nature of gender relationships. While *The Antelope Wife* (1998) also retains Erdrich's favoured familial focus, it relocates the textual action to Minneapolis to provide a consideration of the specific cultural difficulties of urban Indians, and the ways in which traditional Ojibwe stories and myths retain contemporary relevance. The textual action of the 2001 novel *The Last Report on the Miracles at Little No Horse* spans almost a century, and this timespan allows Erdrich to fully trace and examine the ongoing effects of enforced Christianity on the Ojibwe. In 2004, Erdrich published *Four Souls*, which continues the storyline begun in *Tracks*, and her most recent novel is *The Painted Drum* (2005) which, while it departs from Erdrich's usual focus on very specific Ojibwe family groups, nonetheless retains several of her major characters from earlier texts, most notably Fleur Pillager.

In recent years, Erdrich's work has begun to diversify, and she has expanded beyond her purely Ojibwe focus to analyse the other ethnic components of her own mixed blood: for example, *The Master Butcher's Singing Club* (2003) considers German immigrants in America. This diversification is evident in the publication of an autobiographical volume, *The Blue Jay's Dance* (1995), and a non-fiction consideration of the Chippewa landscape and culture, *Books and Islands in Ojibwe*

Country (2003). Erdrich has also branched out into children's literature, producing three well-received volumes: *Grandmother's Pigeon* (1996), *The Birchbark House* (1999) and *The Game of Silence* (2005). Arguably, it is Erdrich's continuing popularity with mainstream audiences in America and Europe that has enabled this diversification and ensured her publisher's willingness to experiment in new directions. While her Chippewa-focused material, including the children's books, has been well received, the material focusing on her German heritage has, however, received mixed reviews, reiterating the enduring fascination of Native America for a Euro-American audience.

Love Medicine (1984)

While Erdrich's writing clearly owes a debt to the approaches and themes of earlier Native writers such as Momaday, Welch and Silko, her works also engage directly with both Euro-American literary traditions and with the conventions of Native oral storytelling. Erdrich's *Love Medicine* (1984) is significant not only as her first novel (which was very well received by public and critics alike), but also as the first book of a tetralogy focusing on the Chippewa landscape and its diverse inhabitants: Indian, Euro-American and mixed blood. The concept of four inter-linked volumes was clearly highly important to Erdrich, as she published a further revised edition of *Love Medicine* in 1993 with four extra chapters to ensure that the original text was better integrated with the subsequent volumes. One reason for these revisions can be interpreted as a desire on Erdrich's part to more clearly convey the ongoing legacy of colonialism and ongoing tribal negotiations with, and resistances to, external forces such as cultural assimilation, education policy and imposed Christianity. In this context, the entire series addresses a wide historical period covering the majority of significant federal Indian policies and their effects across the twentieth century. Continuing the themes introduced by Mourning Dove and developed by subsequent Native writers, Erdrich's series also addresses complex tribal identity politics which have been further problematised by the liminal socio-cultural status of the mixed-blood. In *Love Medicine*, the impact and legacy of Euro-American colonisation is clearly presented from the perspective of Lyman Lamartine, a would-be Indian entrepreneur:

> They gave you worthless land to start with and then they chopped it out from under your feet. They took your kids away and stuffed the

English language in their mouth. They sent your brother to hell, they shipped him back fried. They sold you booze for furs then and told you not to drink. It was time, high past time the Indians smartened up and started using the only leverage they had – federal law.[8]

The action of *Love Medicine* ranges from 1934 to 1984, presenting multiple perspectives and cultural viewpoints that are often contrasting or conflicting, to represent not only the complex interactions of families and communities but also, on a larger scale, the complex and long-standing internal divisions that are the result of colonisation and subsequent interactions with Euro-America. Erdrich's multiperspectival and multivocal narrative has been compared to William Faulkner's writing, in particular to the multiple narrators of texts such as *As I Lay Dying*, where distinct voices and opinions make themselves heard and compete for dominance. While *Love Medicine* does indeed owe a debt to the Euro-American literary tradition, it nonetheless owes an equal debt to Erdrich's own tribal and familial background which emerges through textual emulations and recreations of Native oral storytelling traditions. This is especially pertinent since all voices are therefore presented equally with no one voice or perspective privileged because, as E. Shelley Reid comments, 'any story that is told is always a *version* of the story, altered as the ... [narrator] sees fit'.[9] While this means that the narrative of the text often appears fragmented as it switches between narrators, viewpoints and time periods, crucially it is this very multiplicity that allows a representation of *wholeness*: the complex totality of Erdrich's Chippewa community. Thus individual characters create dialogues with each other and, more importantly, create an extra-textual dialogue with the reader: the reader is required to engage with the text by actively piecing together the numerous narrative fragments into a coherent whole. In this context, the reader also becomes a negotiator of cultures and, as Rainwater argues, the alienating experience of marginality becomes 'the foremost component of the reader's response', allowing an effective 'reading between worlds'.[10]

Erdrich's title emphasises the concerns of the text: the 'love medicine' refers both to traditional Ojibwe love spells and, in a wider sense, to the healing processes by which cultures can be 'cured' of dis-ease. Significantly, Erdrich's consideration of those healing processes explores the role of gender, and the text therefore writes women and their lives to examine the ways in which a dominant and firmly patriarchal Euro-

American worldview (including the strident patriarchy of the Catholic church) has disrupted traditional Ojibwe culture and continues to dislocate Ojibwe women. Erdrich's analysis of medicine thus considers the manner in which healing can occur through an emphasis upon the home and its relationship to the female/feminine. The focus upon the legacy of the imposed religions of colonisation is evident in the opening action of the text, which begins 'the morning before Easter Sunday'.[11] This Easter setting juxtaposes Christian and Ojibwe traditions, to provide a focus upon the concept of salvation and the resurrection, that is culturally focused.

Focusing on the Chippewa June Kashpaw's attempt to return home to the reservation, Erdrich emphasises the alienation of urban Indians, many of whom, like June, simply cannot afford to return home. This poverty is visually represented by June's clothing, the 'pink top' that is 'ripped across the stomach' and, much like the Indian Marlene in Welch's *Winter in the Blood*, by her obvious reliance upon men for money: the bus ticket home has been paid for by 'the man before this one'.[12] Indeed, June is only tempted to stay with 'this one' because 'she couldn't help but notice ... that he had a good-sized wad of money'.[13] Given this marginalised and marginal existence, it is unsurprising that June 'felt so fragile' that she could 'fall apart at the slightest touch'.[14] After another unsatisfactory sexual encounter, June's decision to walk home over the plains into a snowstorm and her resulting death is not only out of character – '[e]ven drunk she'd have known a storm was coming'[15] – but also provides a focus in the subsequent analysis of June's death by her extended Ojibwe family. In this sense, the descriptions of June's death clearly negotiate and mediate between Christian and Ojibwe worldviews: '[t]he snow fell deeper that Easter than it had in forty years, but June walked over it like water and came home'.[16]

While this opening emphasis on death can be interpreted as negative, it is significant that Erdrich's text remains firmly fixed upon 'those who hang on in spite of it all' to 'confront with humor the pain and confusion of identity'.[17] The Ojibwe engagement with June's death is therefore highly positive, allowing June to effectively and metaphorically be 'brought home', as existing communal and community ties become renewed and strengthened, specifically through story. Indeed, story is the means by which June is resurrected through cultural re-integration. As with Silko's *Ceremony*, Erdrich's emphasis is, crucially, upon the power of memory and June is literally re-membered into wholeness. This re-membering is undertaken by all of the seven narrators of *Love Medicine*: Albertine Johnson, who has escaped the reservation to study as a nurse in the city; the 'love triangle' of Marie Lazarre, Nector Kashpaw and Lulu Nanapush (later Lulu Lamartine); Lyman Lamartine, a progressive Indian capitalist; Lipsha Morrisey, who wants to be a traditional 'medicine man'; and Howard Kashpaw, whose father and white mother are locked in a persistent cycle of abuse. The narratives and perspectives presented, therefore, represent a wide range of experiences, ideas, concepts, worldviews, religious and political beliefs, generations and genders.

Gender relationships are especially important to the text. Like Momaday and Silko, Erdrich's analysis of cultural dis-ease takes place within the context of the 'return home'. However, the textual settings are emphatically domestic, not only exposing gendered conceptualisations and interpretations of home but also foregrounding a feminised domestic space and the women of the text. In this sense, the text emphasises and explores traditional gender roles within Ojibwe society. Albertine first hears the news of June's death via letter while 'sitting at my linoleum table', and the recollections that are instantly evoked are of June 'sitting ... in Grandma's kitchen'; when Albertine returns home two months later, it is to a kitchen occupied by her mother and aunt, baking for a family gathering with a room full of 'beautiful pies'; the men's traditional hunting stories are told 'across the kitchen table'.[18] Significantly, when Marie Lazarre takes advantage of the light skin associated with her mixed blood to join the Sacred Heart Convent (in 1934), her greatest battle is with the fanatical and dangerous Sister Leopolda and not only takes place in the kitchen but focuses on domestic weapons such as the 'monstrous iron stove', the kettle of 'scalding' water with which Leopolda burns Marie's back, and the fork with which she 'stabbed' Marie's hand.[19]

In this context, the kitchen soon emerges as a site for conflict and for gendered power struggles. When the men tell their stories of hunting, they are drinking and so starkly contrast the elderly Eli's traditional skills at the expense of King's experiences as a Vietnam veteran: Eli is a 'real old-timer'[20] while King lacks traditional hunting skills or knowledge of the Ojibwe language. The subsequent degeneration of the storytelling into abuse and violent argument thus occurs because there is a lack of respect between the generations, and also a lack of understanding of King's contemporary experiences and his attempts to negotiate between Indian and white worlds. In particular, there is a refusal to equate his war experiences with the traditional role of the warrior that, as is evident in both Momaday and Silko's novels, is potentially dangerous. King's resulting violence primarily focuses on his white wife Lynette, who seems to represent both Euro-American culture and the processes of assimilation that are responsible for King's own sense of cultural loss. The episode exposes King's inability (and, more widely, the inability of the other male characters) to deal effectively with cultural change, and, given the impact of colonialism upon male employment and status, it also exposes an inability to deal with changes in gender relations. Crucially, the climax of the power struggle between King and Lynette takes place at the kitchen sink, where King invades the gendered space of female power and attempts to 'drown Lynette ... in the sink of cold dishwater'.[21] The moment is important because it also destroys all the carefully and communally made pies which 'blee[d]' their contents across the kitchen, offering a significant comment on King, on his marriage and on gender relations more widely: as Albertine states, 'once they smash there is no way to put them right'.[22]

The epic battle between Marie and Sister Leopolda also takes place in the domestic kitchen space. Marie sees the convent partly as a means by which she can assimilate into Euro-American culture as the nuns 'were not any lighter than me' and she is convinced she can 'pray as good as they could';[23] and partly as a means of escaping the grinding poverty of the reservation. However, Marie also views her decision to join the convent as a means by which she can subvert traditional federal–Indian relationships, to assimilate so fully that 'they'd have a girl from this reservation as a saint they'd have to kneel to'.[24] The dangerously fanatical Sister Leopolda's ability to recognise the presence of 'Satan' in the Indian children evokes the legacy of Christian attitudes to Indians and the specific terminology used by Puritan writers to describe Native cultures. Moreover, her ability to recognise the presence of Satan in Marie – '[s]he always said the Dark One wanted me most of all'[25] – suggests a recognition of Marie's attempts at subversion which becomes evident when Marie challenges Sister Leopolda's authority: 'I'll inherit your keys from you'.[26] Staking her claim to the convent hoarded food, and also commenting on the history by which Euro-America has controlled Native America by economics and food distribution, Marie is subsequently burnt with scalding water by Sister Leopolda who, tellingly, identifies any resistance to her authority as a manifestation of evil. Significantly, Marie's subsequent vision is deeply un-Christian and, like many

Puritan texts, focuses on her own naked body, with bare breasts that 'flashed' and 'winked' with 'diamonds'.[27] The battle that then ensues, during which Marie attempts to push Sister Leopolda into the hellfire represented by the oven, results in the injuries inflicted on Marie by Sister Leopolda. Ironically, to save herself from accusations of cruelty, Sister Leopolda accomplishes the first step in Marie's desire for recognition by (and power within) the Catholic church by identifying her wounds as stigmata, and her (highly unsuitable) vision as 'holy'.[28] Marie's experiences provide a pertinent commentary not only on the complex cultural negotiations that she has to make as a mixed-blood Indian, but also on the legacy of Christian power within Indian country, and the highly unequal relationship between Euro-American and Native American women.

These complex inter-cultural negotiations are most obvious within the struggles of June's son Lipsha. Lipsha's own cultural crisis derives from his lack of knowledge of his mother and father, and the text charts his painful progress towards the truth of his birth and eventual cultural re-integration. This cultural and communal liminality is due, in part, to Lipsha's inability to 'fit' – his half-brother King had beat him up 'so badly so many times' as children that Marie 'wouldn't let them play on the same side of the yard'[29] – and Lipsha is emotionally scarred by the knowledge of his mother's attempt to drown him as a baby. Lipsha's problem is partly his lack of overtly male aggression and his seemingly feminine interaction with others; and partly his own intuitive response to Ojibwe culture which is inherited from his father's Pillager family of tribal traditionalists and medicine people. These problems are, paradoxically, also the solutions to Lipsha's crisis, evident in his innate ability to physically heal. For his contemporaries who are struggling with the forces of assimilation, Lipsha's identification with Ojibwe tradition represents a step backwards, yet his successful adoption of traditional Ojibwe beliefs is crucial to his own cultural integration, comparable to Tayo's need for a ritual in *Ceremony*. Questioning the continued applicability of Christianity to Ojibwe life, Lipsha comments that 'God's been going deaf ... God used to raineth bread from the clouds ... He even used to appear in person every once in a while. God used to pay attention, is what I'm saying', before recognising that while the Chippewa gods 'aren't perfect' they nonetheless 'at least ... come around'.[30] Lipsha's own healing emerges from his desire to heal the pain of his grandmother Marie, after her husband Nector leaves her for Lulu. Resorting to 'love medicine', in spite of his own instinctive awareness of the 'danger',[31]

Lipsha attempts to create a love potion to bring Nector home. Yet the attempt backfires when Lipsha cuts corners, killing Nector and almost resulting in the deaths of both Lipsha and Marie. However, what Lipsha learns is that the power of love transcends time and place, even death: as Marie comments, the love medicine is 'stronger than we thought. Nector came back even after death to claim me to his side'.[32]

In this context, Lipsha can finally respond to his discovery of his true parentage and reconnect with June. This discovery heals Lipsha's own inability to forgive his unknown mother for abandoning and attempting to kill him. At the close of the text, Lipsha creates his love medicine by performing the final act required to re-member June. Having helped his new-found fugitive father (Gerry Nanapush) escape across the border to Canada, Lipsha realises that, in order to complete himself, 'there was nothing to do but cross the water and bring her home'.[33] As Owens comments, in this final act of recovery for June, the real love medicine is therefore exposed: an Ojibwe 'ability to care deeply for others, individuals and Indians as a whole'[34] and, perhaps most importantly, oneself.

Political Interventions: Anna Lee Walters (b. 1946)

Born in 1946 in Pawnee, Oklahoma, Anna Lee Walters is of mixed Pawnee and Otoe-Missouria heritage. Raised initially by her traditional grandparents, Walters comments that as a result, as a child, she 'believed the whole world was Indian'.[35] This perception was to change dramatically when she simultaneously returned to live with her parents and entered the Euro-American education system. Walters' experience of the Pawnee boarding school, expressed in her autobiographical volume *Talking Indian* (1992), is especially pertinent as it reflects not only the experiences of earlier writers such as Luther Standing Bear, but also of deeply alienated fictional characters such as Abel and Tayo. The boarding school achieves the desired assimilative effect as absence from her family 'sever[s] a tie between all of us', to the extent that '[t]he picture I held of myself forever enmeshed within the Otoe world was now really gone'.[36] Suffering a crisis of identity as a direct result of the Indian education system, Walters relocated to Santa Fe at the age of sixteen and began attending the Institute of American Indian Arts, where she discovered an interest in creative writing. Walters later received a BA and MA, before working in a range of roles, including administration, publishing and education. Settling in Arizona with her Navajo husband and family, Walters has long been involved in teaching and curriculum development with the Navajo Community College. Currently devoted to producing literature in both of her tribal languages, Walters' writing has received a range of awards, including the American Book Award from the Before Columbus Foundation.

Walters personally experienced such a loss of identity that she 'stopped believing in *everything*' due to an education system that demanded she stop listening to the 'answers' available in 'the tribal voice'.[37] However, what she did retain of her Pawnee and Otoe traditions was an understanding of the oral storytelling tradition, of the words 'that gave shape and substance to my being and form to the world around me'.[38] Like the majority of the Native writers discussed so far, Walters therefore emphasises the power of language to 'create or destroy'.[39] This linguistic power is evident within Walters' writing, which foregrounds Native concerns, and presents female Indian characters 'who are unusually strong because they are modelled after Otoe and Pawnee women'.[40] In this context, it is significant that the subtitle of Walters' autobiographical volume is *Reflections on Survival and Writing*, and traces the connections between writing (and thus self-expression) and not only cultural identity but also the ability for cultural survival. Much of Walters' writing has, therefore, been non-fictional and devoted to celebrating Native American cultures, while also presenting non-stereotypical images for a Euro-American audience and detailing Native American political concerns.

Walters' first text, published in 1977 and co-authored with Peggy Beck and Nia Francisco, was *The Sacred: Ways of Knowledge, Sources of Life*, an exploration of diverse Native worldviews and epistemologies. Presenting challenging concepts for a Euro-American audience, *The Sacred* incorporates photography, oral testimonies of Native elders, and a chapter discussing the impact and legacy of 'the colonizers and genocide' which, pertinently, traces 'the historical events that have led up to the present-day situation'.[41] In this context, Walters et al.'s politics and political objectives refuse to be hidden or silenced:

'Government policy' here means the main currents of thought regarding the ways in which federal government has (1) defined its attitude towards Native Americans, (2) the plans it devised for the containment, extermination, or assimilation of Native Americans, and (3) the methods used by the Federal Government (through the war department, territorial agents, Department of Interior, missionaries, and Bureau of Indian Affairs Commissioners) to carry out its plans.[42]

Walters' sentiments here engage directly with those of William Apess in the 1820s, bypassing the more covert commentary of many Native writers of the early twentieth century (whose voice was subdued by the violence of American racism in the years leading up to the emergence of the Civil Rights movement) to make overt political interventions. Moreover, what makes this an especially significant volume is its timely focus upon historical and contemporary Native religious and spiritual practices in the year before the official passing of the American Indian Religious Freedom Act (1978) that effectively 'legalised' the Native spiritual practices that had been outlawed since the late nineteenth century.

This political engagement and emphasis upon key contemporary political debates and issues is evident throughout Walters' writing, both fiction and non-fiction, and signifies the importance of her work. For example, Walters' 1989 text *The Spirit of Native America: Beauty and Mysticism in American Indian Art* demonstrates the connections between art and religion/spirituality for many Native peoples, and therefore calls into question the collecting and displaying – by museums and private individuals – of Native religious artefacts and art pieces. This emphasis upon religious freedom and respect for Native spiritual traditions and artefacts is perhaps most evident in Walters' 1988 novel *Ghost Singer*. Although ostensibly a simple ghost story, the text engages directly with the inherent problems of the Euro-American museum mentality, and traces the ways in which collecting has an inbuilt disrespect that can be directly and historically related to colonialism, to racism and, ultimately, to resulting acts of genocide. The topic is especially pertinent to the histories and legacies of American settlement and, in this context, *Ghost Singer* is an important text and the subject of the following case study.

Walters' direct political interventions are also evident in her auto biography, *Talking Indian*, which covers topics such as history and identity, and expresses frank views on the damaging legacies of federal-Indian interactions. Importantly, the text illustrates the ways in which Walters' writing, as an expression of her Indian identity, is a direct resistance to ongoing and pervasive forces of assimilation which, through an imposed Indian education system, taught her and other Native American children that 'all the real Indians are gone: conquered, subdued, extinct, assimilated'.[43] Walters' own writing presents a direct challenge to this popular belief. For example, her short story collection *The Sun is Not Merciful* (1985) presents snapshots of contemporary Indian lives influenced by land loss, federal law, imposed Christianity, yet also traditional notions of identity and home. Walters' commitment to promoting a more positive view of contemporary Indian peoples is evident both in her working life in the educational roles she has occupied, and also in her recent published works which include two educational children's volumes, *The Two Legged Creature: an Otoe Story Retold* (1993) and *The Pawnee Nation* (2000). Walters has also edited an anthology of south-western Native literature, *Neon Pow-Wow: New Native American Voices of the Southwest* (1993).

Ghost Singer (1988)

Walters' 1988 novel *Ghost Singer* is, ostensibly, a very simple tale of museums, ghosts and hauntings: the principal action is set in the Smithsonian Museum of Natural History in the 1960s, with additional episodes that span back into the 1830s and forward into the mid-1970s to indicate the ways in which the events of the past continue to influence the present. The text is significant for a number of reasons: for the ways in which Native worldviews are presented and discussed; for the ways in which the text demonstrates an innate Euro-American sense of cultural superiority; and the intrinsic disrespect for other cultures that is evident within imperial concepts of museums and collecting. Most importantly, Walters' text makes a clear political intervention into the increasing debate, emerging in the late 1980s, surrounding the collection and display of Native American artefacts and human remains. A key criticism of the 1978 American Indian Religious Freedom Act had been its failure to adequately protect Native sacred sites, and growing concerns over the sheer numbers of Native remains and body parts either displayed within or held by American museums: for instance, in 1986 the number of remains held by the Smithsonian alone was estimated to be 18,500.[44] This factor, coupled with growing and increasingly well-publicised Native protests and wider Euro-American awareness of the highly emotive issue, resulted in the 1990 Native American Graves Protection and Repatriation Act (NAGPRA).[45] NAGPRA attempted to address the concerns being expressed by Native peoples: that Native remains (and by implication contemporary Native peoples) continued be scientifically identified as 'natural history'; that scientific freedom was being valued over the rights and dignity of human beings; that Native cultural beliefs continued to be disrespected by Euro-American institutions; and, most problematically, that there are inherently imperial notions of 'ownership' linked to both collecting and collections.

Walters' novel is significant not only because it anticipates and prefigures the NAGPRA legislation, but also because it sets the scene for subsequent non-fictional Native debate such as *The Repatriation Reader*, which presents a powerful argument that basic human rights are being denied if Native American bodies cannot 'rest in peace (not in pieces)'.[46] As the writer and critic Gerald Vizenor bluntly asserts, 'death is not the absolute termination of human rights',[47] and it is inconceivable that Euro-American bodies from a comparable period (in most cases, from the nineteenth and twentieth centuries) would be disinterred, studied and displayed in museum collections. Most problematically, for many Native peoples there is a distinct connection between the military campaigns of the nineteenth century and the museum mentality, providing clear links between the kinds of battle 'trophies' assembled from Native body parts and publicly displayed, and the collecting of Native bodies during the latter half of the nineteenth century, often from battlefields or robbed graves. For example, there are few distinctions that can be made between the public parading of scalps and severed genitalia by the US military in theatres throughout Colorado after the Sand Creek massacre of 1864,[48] and the kinds of body parts kept in American museums. In Walters' text, these dubious collections include a 'necklace of twenty human fingers', a 'full scalp with the ears attached', a 'mummified child', and 'strings of human ears … at least two hundred pairs'.[49] Common Native reactions to the issue are displayed textually through the Creek-Cherokee character George Daylight and his response to the collection of human ears:

> George walked around Donald's desk, his eyes on the coiled strings of human ears hanging on the nail above it … 'Are those ears? … Indian ears …? … Where's the rest of those people? … Those people are still probably mad as hell.'[50]

It is within the context of human rights abuse and Native outrage that, interestingly, Walters chooses to locate her story within the horror tradition. By doing so, Walters negotiates and subverts the gothic literary tradition to evoke popular and long-established Euro-American perceptions of monstrosity and evil. What makes Walters' text both haunted and haunting, however, is her engagement with Native realities, and this is evident in the carefully placed textual 'disclaimer' at the start of the text which comments that:

[a]lthough the Smithsonian Institution is a real place with collections of Native American artifacts, references to it in this book, including its collections and employees, are fictional. Any resemblance of characters to actual persons, living or dead, is purely coincidental.[51]

This disclaimer comments on Walters' own experience working in the National Anthropological Archives at the Smithsonian, yet it comments also on the range of disrespectful Euro-American attitudes and perceptions that the text addresses. These disrespectful Euro-American attitudes are telling as the majority are linked in some way to institutions that have and/or maintain authority over contemporary Native peoples. For example, anthropologists whose perceptions of Native cultures have directly informed some of the most devastating federal Indian policies; museums and their curators, whose collections are a form of cultural appropriation and thus, as James Clifford argues, a 'powerful discrimination';[52] and historians whose constructions of American history are exclusionary, presenting partial and often prejudiced views of Native peoples. This Euro-American authority is addressed by Thomas Biolsi and Larry Zimmerman, who argue that Indian 'disempowerment' through their conceptualisation as 'primitive Others' has ensured the 'privilege' of 'elite white intellectuals ... authorised to study the primitive as professional anthropologists'.[53]

In this context, disciplines such as anthropology are identified by Native writers such as Vizenor as a 'statement of academic power'[54] as anthropologists are often the primary 'authenticators' of Indianness, and thus also of the wide-ranging political, social and economic 'benefits' that federal tribal recognition entails.[55] The situation raises problematic and complex questions regarding authority and representation, and the widespread reactions of Native communities unsurprisingly combine bitterness, resentment and subversive irony. It is both this complex Native perception and disrespectful Euro-American attitude that Walters evokes through her representations of the Euro-American characters Donald Evans (a museum curator) and David Drake (an historian). Significantly, Evans defines contemporary Native peoples as 'curiosities', whose view of life is founded on 'superstition'.[56] Moreover, to Evans' mind, it is inconceivable that contemporary Native peoples still exist at all when they should 'have become extinct'.[57] Walters makes Evans' views explicit:

George's kind was already over-extended – they were on borrowed time anyway. It was simply an accident that such simple heathen types had made it this far – all the way to the twentieth century ... By all odds, sooner or later, all the [ethnic] groups would be sucked up into one big vacuum. Consequently, Donald couldn't, and wouldn't, encourage ethnic plurality and diversity.[58]

In Evans' view, the museum is doing Native peoples a favour by keeping its Indian collection hidden away in drawers and cabinets, as it is an 'embarrassment' to contemporary Native people.[59] Indeed, Evans cannot see anything wrong in his treatment of the strings of ears in his office, which he plays with while he takes a coffee break: '[w]ith his left hand, he fingered the strings of ears ... [while] [w]ith his right hand, he poured himself a cup of coffee'.[60] Evans sees nothing disrespectful in hanging human body parts 'in coils on the key-ring nail'.[61]

David Drake's views are equally problematic. With an interest in Indians that dates from his childhood, Drake perceives himself as a '"do-gooder" for the Indian cause'.[62] In this context, Drake admirably plans to write a Navajo history from a Navajo viewpoint but his convictions fail in the face of hostile academic reactions and his own inability to perceive history from a Navajo perspective. Drake's inability to see the connections and interactions between story and history that are evident within the Navajo worldview derive from his clear distinction between 'fact' and 'fiction', and lead him to comment of his Native 'informant' Jonnie Navajo: 'I don't get it ... Why is he telling us all this?'[63] Drake cannot conceive how Jonnie Navajo can be considered to be a tribal historian without any formal academic qualifications, and Drake's failure to recognise the validity of oral traditions emphasises Euro-America's privileging of the written or printed word and the concomitant de-privileging of Indian forms of knowledge. Indeed, Drake is so sceptical of unproven historical instances of Navajos being taken by the Spanish as slaves during the early nineteenth century that he asks '[c]ould he [Jonnie] have made it all up?'[64]

Drake's question exposes Euro-American academic prejudice against oral histories that are perceived as inherently unreliable and illegitimate. Significantly, this viewpoint ultimately affects the progress of his academic work, and he finds that his 'Navajo' history progresses far 'more efficiently' without 'the old man's input'.[65] Rejecting actual Navajo history (i.e. that told by Navajo historians) as 'uneducated' in its inability to separate Euro-American ideas of 'History' from a mythic 'time of dragons', and as problematic since it forces him to 'rethink his own history of the Navajos', Drake decides not to put his 'profes-sional reputation ... at stake'.[66] Despite his text 'add[ing] nothing new' to Euro-American understandings of Navajo history, his exclusion of 'sentimental hogwash' ensures that he remains 'a historian, and a damn good one, too'.[67] For Walters, a clear problem is the basis of both history and anthropology in the entrenched racism of nineteenth-century Euro-America: for example, the histories of American 'conquest' that celebrated acts of genocide as legitimate 'battles'; the federal policies that were informed by former military 'educationalists' such as Captain Pratt of Carlisle; and the racial theories of early anthropologists such as Samuel Morton, whose 'polygenesis' theory justified slavery through its promotion of ideas of biological inferiority. As George Daylight comments, 'It's a hell of a thing, the ideas they had 'bout "red Indians". It's enough to scare the crap out of you. What's even more spooky is that people acted on these ideas, made decisions based on them, decisions that still affect us guys ... you and me's lucky even to be sitting around here at all'.[68]

This, for Walters, exposes the true nature of the federal–Indian relationship. Conceptually, the relationship is evident within the text in the kinds of imperial 'souvenirs' collected by nineteenth-century settlers, and Walters' presents a letter with a trunk of Indian items stating:

> ... Get what you can for this Indian stuff. It should be worth something in $. *Try a museum first* ... Daddy ran across the ears in New Mexico and won them in a poker game about 1890. They're Indian ears all right. They won't be of much use to anyone, except to someone who may want to hang them on a *trophy mantle* – a *conversation piece* for sure.[69]

Through this exposure of an imperially informed, highly partial and deeply flawed Euro-American understanding of Native cultures and worldviews, Walters attempts what Rainwater defines as an 'ambitious, historically instructive project' that provides 'metatextual instruction' for her Euro-American readers.[70]

This is made manifest through the Indian characters of the text, who make a concerted effort to present explicitly Native worldviews. Moreover, they also attempt to overcome the 'Drakeian' interpretation of history as a series of linear progressions, to show that events continue to have deep significance because the present cannot be divorced from the past, however convenient that might be to the national narrative. One example is George Daylight's ability to trace the connections between the events of the past and those of the present through his comparison of the atrocities of the Vietnam War with nineteenth-century atrocities against Native peoples: 'There's a savagery here alright, no doubt 'bout it ... right now, it's probably over in Saigon. They're probably taking ears and scalps over there'.[71] George's subsequent comment, that this behaviour is '[f]irst class savagery',[72] challenges perceptions of Euro-American 'civilisation' and the reader's conceptions of good and evil, and of morality and ethics.

It is in this context that the figure of the Ghost Singer should be read, not only as a representation of ongoing Native outrage at the treatment of Native peoples, alive and dead, but also as a warning against the very real spiritual dangers of continued Euro-American disrespect. Claiming kinship to the dismembered collections that he acts to protect, the Ghost Singer begins a campaign against the museum curators, causing alienation, disease, physical harm and, in several cases, death. In this context, the text traces the continued influence and presence of a range of dead Indian characters, including the long-dead Navajos White Sheep and Red Lady, and the more recently departed Ioway medicine man LeClair Williams, whose influence continues because for Anna and Wilbur Snake he is 'still around'.[73] In this manner, Walters emphasises the humanity of *all* of the dead, and of *all* of the collected human remains, which demands the respect of the living. Thus Geoffrey Newsome realises that the odour of the remains he curates is one 'of living, breathing people', and Donald Evans is physically attacked by a 'living, breathing' Ghost Singer who 'raise[s] him to eye level' in an attempt to make Evans *see* his humanity.[74]

An inability to see this humanity is the result of dissociating collected body parts with actual human beings and, from the Native viewpoint of the text, represents a dangerous lack of understanding of the lasting effects of violent death. Walters emphasises the spiritual and physical dangers of this lack of comprehension through the illnesses and deaths that subsequently occur: quite apart from the Euro-American illnesses and deaths, the Navajo Willie Begay becomes ill after inadvertently touching a Navajo scalp and his subsequent suffering suggests he remains haunted by the unacknowledged demands of the Smithsonian spirits. Significantly, as Rainwater suggests, *Ghost Singer* quite specifically 'equates the illnesses of those involved in the appropriation and misuse of sacred Indian artifacts with the greed of an acquisitive western mentality'.[75]

Presenting a detailed argument in favour of growing Native calls for
the repatriation of human remains, *Ghost Singer* acts also to call attention to the need to eradicate dangerous prejudices within the Euro-
American worldview. In the final pages of the text, Walters provides
a clear warning of what will happen should these prejudices continue,
when the elderly Jonnie Navajo is buried by his family, complete with
traditional grave goods:

> 'Let's hope not too many people come out here, Willie,' Nasbah said.
> 'They're sure to haul everything away, bones and all! It wouldn't
> matter whose bones they are.'
> ... By the time Willie left there, Nasbah's comments about stolen
> bones had made him very uneasy. If only he could be sure his grand-
> father's grave would be safe there ...[76]

By emphasising Jonnie's humanity throughout the text, Walters therefore
emphasises the ways in which the issues that Euro-Americans relegate to
the past impact directly upon contemporary Native cultures. For Jonnie
himself there are thus clear connections between slavery in America and
the trade in Native remains which are 'still being bought and sold'.[77] The
greatest achievement of *Ghost Singer*, therefore, is its direct intervention
into a heated political debate, and Walters' text powerfully challenges
our perceptions of what is and what is not morally and ethically acceptable.

Oral Traditions: Luci Tapahonso (b. 1953)

One of the most influential contemporary Navajo (Diné) poets and story-
tellers, Luci Tapahonso was born in Shiprock, New Mexico in 1953 to
Lucille Deschenne Tapahonso (Salt Water clan) and Eugene Tapahonso
Sr (Bitter Water clan). Tapahonso was raised in traditional Navajo
surroundings on the largest reservation in the United States, the Navajo
homeland of Dinétah, which has greatly influenced her writing. While
Navajo is Tapahonso's first spoken language, due to her Euro-American
education English is her first written language, and this complex linguistic
blend is evident within her work. Having attended the Navajo Methodist
Mission Boarding School in Farmington, New Mexico, Tapahonso went
on to receive a BA and MA from the University of New Mexico, where
she was taught and influenced by Silko. Tapahonso has herself taught
at the universities of New Mexico and Kansas, and is currently a faculty
member at the University of Arizona. A member of the Board of Trustees

for the new National Museum of the American Indian (Washington), Tapahonso tours extensively at a national level for poetry readings and performances. Having published extensively, Tapahonso has received a range of awards, including an Eminent Scholar Award from the New Mexico Commission of Higher Education, the Wordcraft Storyteller of the Year Award (1999) and the 2006 Lifetime Achievement Award from the Native Writers Circle.

A key influence on Tapahonso's writing is her love of language, and she has written extensively of the power of language and the role of the storyteller within Navajo culture:

> There is such a love of stories among Navajo people that it seems that each time a group of more than two gather, the dialogue eventually evolves into sharing stories and memories, laughing, and teasing. To be included in this way is a distinct way of showing affection and appreciation for each other.[78]

For Tapahonso, this idea and use of story is highly significant since it demonstrates that, culturally, 'daily conversations strengthen us'.[79] Moreover, she also emphasises the complex cultural negotiations of her work, which mediates 'two, sometimes three languages' and which 'originat[es] in Navajo' before being presented in their 'English translation' for publication.[80] A key part of Tapahonso's composition is a 'combination of song, prayer, and poetry', which she indicates is 'a natural form of expression for many Navajo people'.[81] Most importantly, however, Tapahonso is in agreement with Momaday over the significance and power of all language and the importance of using language correctly. Corresponding with the conceptualisation of oral (hi)storytelling within *Ghost Singer*, Tapahonso's view is that:

> A person who is able to 'talk beautifully' is well thought of and considered wealthy. To know stories, to remember stories, and to retell them well is to have been 'raised right'; the family of such an individual is also held in high esteem ... People are known then by their use of language.[82]

Significantly, Tapahonso's view of linguistic interaction and mediation is one of cultural gain and not of cultural loss, and she emphasises that in spite of 'the influences of [Euro-American] television, radio, and video' the 'value of the spoken word is not diminished' for the Navajo, rather the Navajo language has been 'enriched' by cultural interaction.[83]

In this context, Tapahonso's writing actively and consciously combines English prose and poetry with Navajo phrases to highlight the relevance of Navajo worldviews and values, and to reproduce the rhythms and styles of the oral storytelling tradition: 'the imaginative and clever wordplay and the subtle uses of humor and silence at crucial moments'.[84] Tapahonso's writing therefore actively attempts to engage with 'the basis of Navajo philosophy', the concept of '"hozho" or beauty' (i.e. a perfectly balanced or harmonious physical and spiritual environment) by which the Navajo have traditionally conducted their lives.[85]

Tapahonso published her first two volumes of poetry, *One More Shiprock Night* and *Seasonal Woman*, in 1981. Both emphasise the strength of the ties that Tapahonso feels to her family, to her cultural heritage and to the Navajo homeland. Many of Tapahonso's poems therefore directly address her own children and grandchildren, and those which she composed during her tenure at the University of Kansas express her absence from and yearning for her immediate and extended family back home. Two significant and recurring themes within Tapahonso's work are the important role and power of Navajo women, and the centrality of the storytelling tradition to Navajo culture. Tapahonso published her third volume of poetry, *A Breeze Swept Through*, in 1987. All three volumes attracted instant critical attention, and Tapahonso's style, which evokes the oral tradition, proved especially interesting. While her poems and stories appear simple in their style, language and content, they nonetheless make powerful and effective social and political comments upon contemporary Native American life.

Tapahonso's subsequent publications have received critical acclaim and ensured her recognition as a highly significant Native writer. In 1993, Tapahonso published *Sáanii Dahataal: The Women Are Singing*, which began a detailed experiment with form as well as language that was continued in the 1997 volume *Blue Horses Rush In* (the subject of the case study below). In both volumes, Tapahonso continued to blend Navajo with English, but also seamlessly blended poetry with prose. Like Silko's *Storyteller*, these two volumes are multi-genre and, through Tapahonso's emphasis upon 'the first person narrative because it is the stronger voice',[86] both volumes are also multi-perspectival and polyvocal. Both texts emphasise the continuing significance of Navajo spiritual traditions, to present powerful images that successfully mediate between cultures. Most significantly, Tapahonso foregrounds the legacy of federal–Indian relations, and traces the continued impact of events that dramatically reconfigured Navajo lives upon contemporary Navajo communities. An important short story from *Sáanii Dahataal*, 'In 1864', discusses the effect of the Navajo Long Walk of 1864 on Navajo culture, when more than 8,000 Navajo were forced to relocate to a military fort in an attempt at enforced cultural assimilation. After being held in captivity for four years, during which 'more than 2,500 died of smallpox and other illnesses, depression, severe weather conditions, and starvation',[87] the federal government finally allowed the Navajo to return to Dinétah in 1868. Tapahonso's story employs the present tense to emphasise the ongoing legacy of the era, as she describes the communal memories of pregnant women murdered because they could not match the pace of the march; and the drowning of those who were forced to cross the Rio Grande. The continued pain of this era for contemporary Navajos is evident: the historical narrator's 'heart [that] hurts so to remember'; and the tears of the contemporary narrator's daughter 'stream down her face'.[88]

This translation not only of Navajo cultural values and perceptions, but also of the still painful legacy of historical events and of the federal–Indian relationship, is perhaps the most significant feature of Tapahonso's work. This emphasis upon the continued importance of past events to the present and, crucially, also to the future, underlines Navajo understandings of storytelling primarily as a form of 'teaching' that remains crucial to predominantly oral cultures.[89] Most importantly, Tapahonso's stated aim is to facilitate the '"active" participation' of her reader to produce an 'exploration of possibilities'.[90]

Blue Horses Rush In (1997)

Tapahonso's 1997 collection of stories and poetry, *Blue Horses Rush In*, takes its title from a poem in her previous volume, *Sáanii Dahataal*, which celebrates the birth of her granddaughter Chamisa Bah. A degree of inter-textuality is a feature of Tapahonso's work which, importantly, also acts to emphasise feminine roles within Navajo life such as child-birth. Perhaps most significant to Tapahonso's discussion of Navajo women's lives is her consideration of maternal responsibilities that, within an emphatically oral culture, include storytelling both as a form of instruction and as a means of cultural transmission. This emphasis upon the ongoing survival and transmission of Navajo culture makes Tapahonso's writing essentially political, as her comments engage directly with the extreme racial prejudice evident in the wide range of

Euro-American assimilation policies. It is a combination of the highly personal with the deeply political that makes Tapahonso a fascinating and extremely significant contemporary Native writer.

While the majority of Tapahonso's writing is implicitly (and often explicitly) political, this engagement is, somewhat subversively, often softened and even belied by the gentle tone and simplicity of her style. In the poem 'Blue Horses Rush In', Tapahonso adopts what de Ramirez identifies as 'a conversive style' to effectively convey and mediate Navajo culture.[91] The baby's arrival occurs 'amid a herd of horses/ ... of different colors'[92] that represent traditional Navajo cultural perceptions and values but which also illustrate the 'power and strength of [Navajo] women' through the repeated connections that are made between the women and horses.[93] The birth is therefore set against a landscape peopled with Navajo history, which locates the new child and her family firmly within a Navajo universe of ceremonial directions represented by the '[w]hite horses from the east' who 'ride in on the breath of the wind'; the '[b]lue horses ... from the south' who 'brin[g] the scent of the prairie grasses'; the '[y]ellow horses ... from the desert' where 'your grand-mothers went to war long ago'; and '[b]lack horses ... from the north' who evoke 'lush summers' and 'still white winters'.[94] By the end of the poem, the new child, Chamisa, has been firmly culturally located within her immediate family, the wider Navajo community, and the mythic world of the sacred: 'Chamisa, Chamisa Bah. It is all this that you are'.[95] Most importantly, the ongoing significance of Navajo history is reiterated: '[y]ou will grow strong like the horses of your past'.[96]

The continued power and relevance of Navajo culture is evident in the story 'Notes for the Children' which, as its title suggests, is presented as a means by which important cultural ideas are transmitted or taught via the oral tradition. Here, four stories present a range of important female-related topics, including the home, the role of women, the significance of names, and food. While these are discussed and explained, they are – most importantly – related to Navajo ceremony and the teachings of the sacred stories. Emulating the simple style and approach of the 'just so' story, 'Notes for the Children' presents its statements as self-evident, beginning with a sacred story that presents the reasons behind Navajo ceremonies relating to the traditional home, the 'hooghan'.[97] Opening with a traditional and, for both Native and non-Native reader, a comfortable and instantly recognisable phrase, '[l]ong ago',[98] Tapahonso immediately signals that the story is located within the mythic framework of 'once upon a time'. It is therefore no surprise when the first line of the story details the labours of 'the Holy Ones' as they 'build the first hooghan for First Man and First Woman'.[99] The remainder of the story suggests that continuing with such traditions as 'offer[ing] prayers and songs in each [ceremonial] direction' will ensure that all homes 'would embrace us' and families 'will be nourished and protected' as a result.[100] Moving swiftly into the temporal present, Tapahonso concludes with the assertion that although 'you can ask a medicine or clergy person to do this', the Holy Ones nonetheless 'appreciate it if you ... perform this yourself' as, most importantly, '[t]hey understand English, too'.[101]

The second and third stories have language in common, beginning with an analysis of the role of women through a discussion of the Navajo term for woman, 'Asdzání'.[102] Tapahonso's father's question, 'Have you ever seen your mother wear slacks?', opens a meditation on the ramifications of the fact that 'Asdzání' also means 'skirt'.[103] Connecting together childhood memories of the multiple uses that a Navajo mother finds for her skirt, including 'tablecloth', play mat, 'blanket, towel, and ... washcloth', the subsequent sentences compare 'the round roof of a female hooghan' to a woman's flared skirt' since, crucially, 'the woman is the center of the Diné home'.[104] Emphatically, therefore, '[b]eauty extends from the woman' in the Navajo universe.[105] This meditation upon language is evident in the subsequent interconnected story, which considers the role and uses of names and naming as a means by which relationships and family/community ties can be reiterated and thus strengthened. In this context, Tapahonso stresses that, before 'English names' became commonplace among the Navajo, such forms of naming taught the importance of 'acknowledging ... relationship[s] ... each time we speak' to convey 'love and respect'.[106] Emphasising that this is an especially important lesson for young people to learn, so as to 'show respect' for their elders and 'for Diné culture', Tapahonso's closing remark on cultural endurance is at once pertinent and deeply tongue-in-cheek: 'One must remember that good manners last for centuries and centuries'.[107]

The final story of 'Notes for the Children' explores the importance of food as a carrier of culture, thus emphasising the ways in which assimilation has profoundly affected traditional practices such as hunting or the production of culturally specific foods and livestock. Discussing the food cravings experienced by Diné away from home for specific foodstuffs such as mutton, Tapahonso thus highlights the relationship of sheep and sheepherding to Navajo culture which, as she states in the short story 'In 1864', are 'like our family'.[108] In this context, '[m]utton has long been a staple of Diné life' and therefore 'is a literal reminder of the many meals at home, celebrations and events of all types, fairs, and ceremonies'.[109] Tapahonso emphasises the power of foodstuffs to hold and evoke highly specific and powerful individual and communal memories: '[w]hen we taste mutton, we are reminded of the mountains, the air, the laughter and humor surrounding a meal, but mostly we are reminded of loved ones'.[110] This concept of food as a cultural carrier is especially significant in the face of Euro-American attempts to assimilate and even eradicate Navajo culture: 'mutton has healing powers and brings happiness because sheep have been a part of our history since the beginning of time'.[111] Moving between such historical memories and an emphatic present (where gifts of mutton have to be explained to bewildered 'airline agent[s]': '"it's meat"'), Tapahonso's story ends on a gently mocking yet insistent tone: '[t]his mutton business is a distinctly Diné trait'.[112]

Another distinctly Diné trait is weaving, for which Navajo women have become renowned, and which has become the centre of a powerful economy and means of negotiation with Euro-America. The short story 'Above the Canyon Floor' presents Tapahonso's version of the sacred story that explains the introduction of weaving to the Navajo by the mythic figure Spider Woman, a key figure in the stories of many of the diverse Southwestern Indian peoples. Here, the story is clearly physically located, '[i]n Canyon de Chelly',[113] both to provide a physical anchor for the lessons of the tale, and to expose the ways in which many Native cultures traditionally relate to the natural world through story. Contradicting popular Euro-American conceptualisations of an empty and undeveloped continent ripe for settlement, America is therefore presented as a complex storied and peopled land, and tribal relationships to the landscape are traced through physical sacred ceremonies and more domestic concerns such as the raising of livestock and development of commercial skills such as weaving. In this context, the story opens with a shepherd, Áshiih Neez, whose bewilderment at seeing an unknown young woman derives from his wide-ranging familial and tribal relationships: 'he knew all the families in the area'.[114]

Clearly situating the story in a timeless mythic arena, Tapahonso emphasises the longevity and endurance of Navajo culture by emphasising both Navajo language and traditional beliefs: both Áshiih and the young woman are obliged to trace their clan relationships for each other to ensure that they 'weren't related', a taboo for Navajo marriage.[115] And, while Tapahonso makes it clear that Áshiih 'hadn't asked her about her clans', his subsequent question remains untranslated: 'Ha'át'íísh dóone'é nílí?'[116] The effect, for the Euro-American reader, is one both of dis-location and re-location within a specifically Navajo worldview. Having spent the night singing songs from 'a healing ceremony', the young woman disappears leaving Áshiih to find himself stranded as the rock he has slept on 'had risen almost seven hundred feet' overnight.[117] His only chance of escape arrives in the form of 'an elderly woman' who 'weav[es] a rope' for him, causing some surprise as she is clearly Navajo and 'at that time only the Pueblo people wove'.[118] Recognising on his descent that the old woman is the love he has lost overnight, Áshiih realises that he has been in the presence of the 'wise and powerful being' known as Spider Woman. Tapahonso's story explains key elements of Navajo skills and economics: the meeting has been engineered to ensure 'the Navajos will never be destitute', as Spider Woman passes on the secrets of weaving.[119] Most importantly, Spider Woman emphasises the economic importance of Navajo women: '[o]nly the women will weave'.[120] This, in the final lines of the story, is just as well since, in a note that is both practical and slyly humorous, Spider Woman comments that '"[j]ust because a man wants to marry you doesn't mean he's going to take care of you forever"'.[121]

This note of wry yet pithy humour is equally evident in Tapahonso's more overtly political considerations of contemporary issues, creating an interesting counterpoint of irony to highlight the serious nature of the issues being discussed. For example, Tapahonso presents four interlinked poems that discuss the 1990 Phoenix Arts Commission collaboration not only as a means by which to 'interpret the history and development of an ancient Hohokamki settlement', but also as a way of 'documen[ting] the effects of the construction of the Hohokam Expressway' which poses a threat to the ancient ruins.[122] Tapahonso's engagement with the issue is framed by two poems discussing the significance of rain to desert regions. The poem 'Rain in the Desert' is a meditation on the 'overwhelming beaut[y]' of rain that makes the world 'shine with a newness'.[123] Significantly, this extended musing is interrupted by two sharply juxtaposed images: an archaeological dig at the Pueblo Grande Museum where complex drainage pipes have been dug to 'protect the ... site'; and the many 'homeless people' who huddle 'a few hundred yards away' and attempt to 'catch a bit of rainwater'.[124] The stark contrast of the two images indicates clearly where Euro-American interests lie and funds are directed. In this context, Tapahonso's subsequent question has enormous relevance: '[h]ow must the remaining spirits of the Hohokamki feel?'[125] The remainder of the poem comments on the humanity of the dead through references to the uses to which they would have put rainwater for 'drinking,/cooking, mixing pottery clay, and for mixing paints'.[126] Yet for Tapahonso, the most significant problem is the lack of recognition given to the Hohokamki for their engineering innovations, the 'earthen covered canals' that 'were witnesses' to Native 'ingenuity and success', yet are now 'lined with cement'.[127] As Tapahonso bluntly comments, '[t]hat the trees and the land survived is a wonder in itself'.[128]

This commentary on the misuse and abuse of the land, the socially dis-located and the dead is a theme that continues through the remaining three pieces. The short story 'Conversations at the Gila River Arts Center' begins, significantly, with a story about the ways in which the land and '[t]he Holy People take care of themselves'.[129] This emphasis upon Native culture is evident in the discussion of cultural crafts such as 'traditional basket weaving', which have been re-introduced due to an increased contemporary demand 'to learn the old ways'.[130] Tapahonso's consideration of 'the excavated area' shows an 'imperceptible'[131] Hohokamki presence that contrasts harshly with the vibrant presence of the contemporary Native peoples she had met earlier. This erasure seems to emulate Euro-America's desire to eradicate Native cultures through assimilation, and Tapahonso is careful to speak aloud to the Hohokamki: '"We're still here … And we're still the same"'.[132] Significantly, the short-sightedness of the construction of the Expressway is clearly contrasted with more holistic Native worldviews, to the concept that the 'prayers and hopes' that future generations experience derive directly from the present as 'we cast our prayers seven generations ahead'.[133] While this concept is clearly compromised by the construction of the Expressway, Tapahonso is nonetheless adamant about the longevity of Native culture: 'memories and stories … are too powerful for things as new as cement and asphalt to destroy'.[134]

The meditation is completed with two further pieces that make specific links between the past and the present evident for her reader. In 'Daané'e Diné', the discovery of 'a cache of clay animals' at the excavation site causes 'a ripple of excitement' among the archaeologists, who instantly determine that they are 'ritual ceremonial images'.[135] The following prose section of the piece subtly subverts the 'authority' of such experts as Tapahonso 'dream[s] of my childhood' to equate the figures found with the 'toy people' made by her mother,[136] and expose the tendency of such cultural theorists to complicate something that is, essentially, uncomplicated. Tapahonso's subsequent questions return to the concerns of the first poem, to question Euro-American values that prioritise archaeology over basic human rights: 'I wondered if ... the wandering spirits of the Hohokamki gathered with the homeless, some of whom were recent war veterans and feel similarly displaced in modern America?'[137] The final poem of the sequence, 'Dust Preceded the Rain', reiterates the importance of water while linking together the fragmented topics of the previous pieces to provide a comprehensive analysis of the significance of cultural endurance: the 'quiet gratitude', 'still concentration' and 'exuberant spirits' that all 'still remain'.[138] Most significantly, in the final lines Tapahonso reiterates the ongoing importance of history through powerful presence of the past in the present, and the continuing inter-connection of southwestern cultures:

> They recognize the old history that is theirs
> They recognize the old history that is ours.[139]

Through such creative juxtapositions of personal story and communal politics, Tapahonso emphasises the continued cultural survival of Native peoples and their resistance to the damaging forces of assimilation. Language is, for Tapahonso, therefore a powerful force for both 'represent[ing] and affect[ing] the world'.[140] In this context, de Ramirez comments that the significance of Tapahonso's work is its invitation to reader and critic alike to understand that her writing is 'speaking' and that her words are 'creative and living stories'.[141]

The increased publication of texts by Native American women clearly demonstrates a growing audience for writings that explore female cultural experiences, voices and views. Native women's writing continues to experiment with literary forms, and to incorporate and translate cultural ideas and values in order to express and celebrate an Indian worldview that is specifically feminine. Furthermore, Native women's writing also continues to investigate the connections between women's roles in tribal and wider American political contexts, making textual interventions that echo the recent political successes of Native women. In this context, many Native women writers interrogate external claims of 'universal sisterhood' through an emphasis upon cultural specificity, and this interconnection with wider feminist issues, especially with the concerns of Third World feminism, has ensured a broad and diverse readership and given Native women a powerful audible literary voice. Significantly, the absence of any comparable politico-cultural Native men's movement, coupled with the federal challenges to the Red Power civil rights movement, has ensured that writings by Native American men have followed an alternative trajectory.

Notes

1. Julia V. Emberley (1993), p. 92.
2. Chandra Talpade Mohante (2003), p. 22.
3. Paula Gunn Allen (1992), p. 196.
4. Barbara Mann (2005), p. 12.
5. The introduction of the programme is both ironic and pertinent: Dartmouth had been founded on the funds raised by Samson Occom in 1762, and had subsequently excluded Indian students.
6. The only other Native writer to be singled out in this manner is Sherman Alexie, the subject of Chapter 7.
7. Because of a legal loophole, casinos and bingo palaces are allowed on reserved Indian lands even if they are prohibited elsewhere in the state. As a result, so many tribes have become reliant upon the income from gaming that the 1988 Indian Gaming Regulatory Act was introduced. The 1991 Indian Gaming Commission noted that the bingo industry alone involved over 130 tribes, with an estimated annual revenue between $225 million and $1 billion.
8. Louise Erdrich (1994), p. 326.
9. E. Shelley Reid (2000), p. 69.
10. Catherine Rainwater (1990), pp. 405–6.
11. Erdrich (1994), p. 1.
12. Ibid. pp. 4, 2.
13. Ibid. pp. 2–3.
14. Ibid. p. 4.
15. Ibid. p. 10.
16. Ibid. p. 7.
17. Louis Owens (1992), p. 194.
18. Erdrich (1994), pp. 7–8, 13, 29.
19. Ibid. pp. 51, 52, 57.
20. Ibid. p. 30.
21. Ibid. p. 41.
22. Ibid. pp. 41, 42.
23. Ibid. p. 43.
24. Ibid. p. 43.
25. Ibid. p. 46.
26. Ibid. p. 50.
27. Ibid. p. 54.
28. Ibid. p. 59.
29. Ibid. pp. 29–30.

30. Ibid. pp. 235–6.
31. Ibid. p. 241.
32. Ibid. p. 255.
33. Ibid. p. 367.
34. Owens (1992), p. 201.
35. Anna Lee Walters (1992), p. 43.
36. Ibid. pp. 51–2.
37. Ibid. p. 52.
38. Ibid. p. 11.
39. Ibid. p. 11.
40. Ibid. p. 17.
41. Walters et al. (1996), p. 141.
42. Ibid. p. 141.
43. Walters (1992), p. 222.
44. Jack F. Trope and Walter R. Echo-Hawk (2000), p. 136.
45. The Smithsonian collection was so vast that it was covered by separate legislation: the 1989 National Museum of the American Indian Act. Under NAGPRA, individual tribes can apply to have remains and artefacts returned to them, and museums are legally obliged to do so.
46. Devon A. Mihesuah (ed.) (2000), p. 101.
47. Gerald Vizenor (1990), p. 63.
48. In 1864, the US military massacred almost 200 Cheyenne and Arapaho in Colorado, whose bodies were mutilated and body parts displayed as war trophies. Three years after the massacre, army doctors returned to exhume Native bodies to study the effects of bullet wounds. The bodies were later transferred to the Smithsonian 'collection'.
49. Walters (1988), pp. 42, 43, 91.
50. Ibid. pp. 128–9.
51. Ibid. frontispiece.
52. James Clifford (1988), p. 221.
53. Thomas Biolsi and Larry Zimmerman (1997), p. 13.
54. Vizenor (1990), p. 86.
55. 'Benefits' include freedom from state law and taxation; the right to self-determination; access to funds for development and investment; provision of healthcare, housing and education; and positive preferment for federal employment. In practice, benefits are often subject to qualifications.
56. Walters (1988), pp. 91, 122.
57. Ibid. p. 91.
58. Ibid. p. 123.
59. Ibid. p. 125.
60. Ibid. p. 92.
61. Ibid. p. 93.
62. Ibid. pp. 226–7.
63. Ibid. p. 30.
64. Ibid. p. 78.
65. Ibid. pp. 224, 227.
66. Ibid. pp. 225, 27, 225.
67. Ibid. pp. 225, 228.

68. Ibid. p. 80.
69. Ibid. p. 93, emphasis added.
70. Rainwater (1999), p. 49.
71. Walters (1988), p. 81.
72. Ibid. p. 81.
73. Ibid. p. 144.
74. Ibid. pp. 45, 131.
75. Rainwater (1999), p. 162.
76. Walters (1988), p. 248.
77. Ibid. p. 207.
78. Luci Tapahonso (1993), p. x.
79. Ibid. p. x.
80. Ibid. pp. x–xi.
81. Ibid. p. xi.
82. Ibid. p. xi.
83. Ibid. p. xi.
84. Tapahonso (1997), p. xiii.
85. Tapahonso (1993), p. xii.
86. Ibid. p. xi.
87. Ibid. p. 7.
88. Ibid. pp. 9, 10.
89. Tapahonso (1997), p. xiv.
90. Ibid. p. xiv.
91. Susan Berry Brill de Ramirez (1999), p. 78.
92. Tapahonso (1997), p. 103.
93. de Ramirez (1999), p. 79.
94. Tapahonso (1997), pp. 103–4.
95. Ibid. p. 104.
96. Ibid. p. 104.
97. Ibid. p. 35.
98. Ibid. p. 35.
99. Ibid. p. 35.
100. Ibid. p. 35.
101. Ibid. p. 35.
102. Ibid. p. 35.
103. Ibid. p. 35.
104. Ibid. pp. 35–6.
105. Ibid. p. 36.
106. Ibid. p. 36.
107. Ibid. p. 36.
108. Tapahonso (1993), p. 8.
109. Tapahonso (1997), p. 36.
110. Ibid. pp. 36–7.
111. Ibid. p. 37.
112. Ibid. p. 37.
113. Ibid. p. 43.
114. Ibid. p. 43.
115. Ibid. p. 44.

116. Ibid. p. 44.
117. Ibid. p. 45.
118. Ibid. p. 46.
119. Ibid. p. 47.
120. Ibid. p. 47.
121. Ibid. p. 48.
122. Ibid. p. 19.
123. Ibid. p. 21.
124. Ibid. p. 21.
125. Ibid. p. 21.
126. Ibid. p. 22.
127. Ibid. p. 22.
128. Ibid. p. 22.
129. Ibid. p. 24.
130. Ibid. p. 24.
131. Ibid. p. 25.
132. Ibid. p. 26.
133. Ibid. p. 26.
134. Ibid. p. 26.
135. Ibid. p. 27.
136. Ibid. p. 28.
137. Ibid. p. 29.
138. Ibid. p. 32.
139. Ibid. p. 32.
140. de Ramirez (1999), p. 88.
141. Ibid. p. 88.

CHAPTER 5

Tricksters and Critics: Simon Ortiz, Louis Owens and Gerald Vizenor, 1980–2000

The publishing successes of writers such as Momaday and Welch clearly continue to influence a range of subsequent publications by both established and emerging Native American men. Like the Native women authors of the previous chapter, these writers engage with the complexities of male identity within Native cultures that has been deeply affected by Euro-American attempts at assimilation. This lengthy Euro-American drive for assimilation has eroded or eliminated many traditionally 'male' cultural pursuits, and so affected the social status and, more problematically, the actual social position or 'location' of many Native men. Euro-American attempts to eradicate traditional male cultural practices that were deemed an impediment to 'progress' and 'civilisation' included the wholesale slaughter of the buffalo as a means by which to subdue the Plains tribes by starvation, and a general opposition to hunting practices, because they encouraged tribal groups to migrate, was resolved by the imposition of the reservation system. Euro-America's subsequent emphasis upon land cultivation as part of its programme to civilise American Indians merely worsened matters as, for many tribal cultures, farming and agriculture were identified as female pursuits and seen as distinctly feminine, indeed feminised, activities. The enforced Indian education system contributed to this decline in social status for Native men, who were officially defined as 'masculine' only when they were 'civilised' and appeared 'white', with any adherence or desire to adhere to Native cultures identified as 'effeminate'. This effective emasculation of Native men's culture played a crucial and, for assimilation purposes, necessary role both in controlling Native tribal groups, and in breaking tribal spirit.

At the start of the twentieth century, there were few opportunities for Native men to reclaim their social status or even a remnant of their former warrior societies, and this provides some explanation for the attraction of popular 'entertainment' shows such as Buffalo Bill's Wild West, and the demographically disproportionate numbers of Native men who continue to enlist and serve in the US military forces. The loss of a comprehensive socio-cultural structure resulted in a deep sense of cultural and social dis-location for many Native men, evident in the behaviour of the male protagonists of texts from Mathews' *Sundown* to Welch's *Winter in the Blood*. Native men had been stripped not just of their social status, but of their ability to provide for their familial and tribal groups, as is evident in Erdrich's descriptions of gender relations in *Love Medicine*.

A clear distinction that can be made with the writings of Native women is the lack of any comparable Native men's rights movements: while Native women writers have gained a readership and a voice within developments in the feminist movement, Native men writers have had no such politically focused audience. Indeed, the effective breaking of Red Power and of the American Indian Movement, headed by high-profile Native men such as Dennis Banks, Clyde Bellecourt, Russell Means and John Trudell, after the 1973 Wounded Knee siege, plus the subsequent high-profile murder trials of Bob Robideau, Darelle Butler and Leonard Peltier, impacted negatively upon the development of further political movements for Native men. While Native women were able to tap into mainstream developments that acknowledged diverse female experiences based directly upon race and ethnicity, there were no corresponding acknowledgements outside tribal communities of Native men or their experiences. In this sense, patriarchy remains firmly in place, masculinity remains problematically defined as white, and male Native cultures continue to be excluded.

As a result, Native male writers have experimented with a range of literary forms and expressions that draw directly upon Native cultures yet make distinct references to and intersections with Euro-American literature and culture. While the writers analysed in this chapter – Simon Ortiz (Acoma Pueblo), Louis Owens (Choctaw-Cherokee) and Gerald Vizenor (Chippewa) – had published or were publishing alongside Momaday and Welch during the 1970s and 80s, their subsequent work (between 1980 and 2000) is nonetheless significant for its development of humour as a powerful and pointed form of cultural criticism. Indeed, Owens and Vizenor have also both worked within mainstream Euro-American education as academics, producing critical works on Euro-American and Native American literature and culture.

However, what is significant about the works of all three writers under discussion in this chapter is their employment, deployment and development of stories drawing upon the sacred Native figure of the trickster, as a means by which humour and the surreal can be used to challenge and subvert cultural stereotypes and preconceptions. While humour seems an unexpected medium through which to analyse some of the critical cultural issues at stake, it is, perhaps due to this very distinction, nonetheless a highly effective means through which to discuss the kinds of 'grave concerns' evident in the works of Ortiz, Owens and Vizenor.[1] Additionally, as Owens himself comments, the 'role of humor' has been 'crucial' to 'the long survival of Native American peoples'.[2] In this sense, trickster discourse engages directly with established Euro-American and European satirical traditions, to critique damaging Euro-American assumptions and – a key feature of satire – to give expression to Native men's anger. This discourse has been identified by Vizenor as a 'trickster hermeneutics',[3] the development of a deeply satirical form of interpretation that, like the tribal trickster, is essentially unpredictable, disruptive, revolutionary and highly active in its exposure and censure of damaging cultural practices. In this context, the trickster simultaneously represents both educator (the lessons that must be taught) and education (the learning that must be undertaken).

Humour is a deeply significant way in which powerful truths can be unexpectedly presented, especially to a wary or resistant audience; and Chris LaLonde comments that, in this context, trickster discourse is an 'economy that both free[s] us and compel[s] us to re-examine the world'.[4] This notion of compulsion with its fundamental yet paradoxical links to freedom is thus a highly pertinent concept: by employing a traditional sacred figure common to a range of Native cultures, Native male writers[5] therefore expose the intrinsically sacred basis not only of knowledge (especially self-knowledge) but of life itself. In most Native traditions, the trickster's actions are the basis of preventative stories due to his tendency to be 'sexually active, often violent, ravenous, impetuous, quick to play tricks on others, quick to deceive, and at times the unwitting sufferer of his own tricks'.[6] Traditionally, while audiences therefore empathise with the trickster, they want to avoid the results of his actions, and do so by learning the indispensable lessons and difficult truths embedded within the stories. It is these indispensable lessons and difficult truths that form the basis of the writings of Ortiz, Owens and Vizenor, all of whom adapt oral traditions and deploy humour and satire to make timely, necessary and effective critiques of Euro-American culture and federal–Indian relations.

Active and Activist Humour: Simon Ortiz (b. 1941)

Born in 1941 in Albuquerque, New Mexico, Simon Ortiz was raised in the Acoma village of McCarty's (Deetseyamah) within an Acoma-speaking family and close-knit community. Attending the BIA reservation day school, Ortiz was first exposed to the English language in which, much like other poets such as Momaday and Tapahonso, he developed a deep interest and was encouraged to write because he 'associated reading [and writing] with oral stories'.[7] Ortiz's academic achievements ensured that his subsequent education at St Catherine's Indian Boarding School and Grants High School was successful and, after working in the uranium mining industry, he went on to attend Fort Lewis College. Ortiz's academic career was interrupted by a brief period of military service, before he returned to the universities of New Mexico and Iowa to study creative writing. Ortiz's powerful and prolific works have ensured his critical acclaim both as a poet and as a fictional writer, and he has received a range of awards, including the National Endowment for the Arts Discovery Award (1969), the Pushcart Prize for Poetry (1981) and the Lifetime Achievement Award from the Native Writers Circle of the Americas (1993). Ortiz has taught at the universities of New Mexico, Toronto and San Diego State, and at the Institute of American Indian Arts and the Navajo Community College, and has served as consulting editor for the Pueblo of Acoma Press and as lieutenant governor of the Pueblo of Acoma. He continues to travel both nationally and internationally for lecture tours and poetry readings.

Much like Silko, Ortiz defines himself through his Acoma heritage and culture, which are 'the basis of who I was and how I came into being'.[8] Most importantly, the oral storytelling tradition is the medium through which both heritage and culture 'were expressed'.[9] Thus Ortiz had learnt the lessons of Acoma culture, identity and history through story, which became 'vitally important' to him as it 'tied me into the communal body of my people'.[10] In this context, Ortiz repeatedly identifies himself within the Acoma oral tradition, primarily as a storyteller. Acoma stories are, significantly, implicitly and often explicitly political:

> I had heard the oral history of the Spanish coming, the taking of land by them and later by the Mericano, the Treaty of Guadalupe Hidalgo

that was apocryphal to the native people, the coming of the railroad, the struggles to keep the land and a way of life and sovereignty as a people.[11]

This deep understanding of himself as 'a child of colonialism' whose community was constantly under threat from federal Indian policies, cultural assimilation, the Euro-American education system, plus the ongoing and destructive effects of alcohol on the Acoma that scarred Ortiz's own family with 'trauma', are all evident in prolific writings that remain above all highly politically aware.[12]

Ortiz published his first volume of poetry, *Naked in the Wind*, in 1971, which was soon followed by a range of other volumes, including *Going for the Rain* (1976), *A Good Journey* (1977) and *A Poem is a Journey* (1981). All convey not only a sense of Ortiz's own Acoma heritage but also the styles and structures of the spoken word and, through his inclusion of a variety of sacred stories, also a sense of the role and power of humour. This is evident in the many poems discussing Coyote, the Acoma trickster figure; and Coyote's intrinsically complex and duplicitous nature is illustrated through comments such as 'Coyote told me this,/and he was b.s.-ing probably'.[13] The complexity and dark humour of the trickster is perhaps best summarised in the poem 'How Much Coyote Remembered':

> O, not too much.
> And a whole lot.
>
> Enough.[14]

This undercurrent of humour runs throughout the majority of Ortiz's poems in these volumes, and serves to highlight and foreground the serious nature of his subject matter that is evident in poems such as 'To Insure Survival' that provides essential teachings on Acoma culture, 'Relocation' that discusses the effects of the policies that dis-located entire communities (*Going for the Rain* is full of dis-located Indians in transit), and the many poems considering the ongoing pain caused by colonisation and its consequences. These consequences include Ortiz's own hospitalisation for alcoholism after his military service, plus the culturally damaging imposition of 'Railroads', 'Electric Lines', 'Gas Lines', 'Highways', 'Phone Company', 'Cable TV' and 'Right of Way'.

This commitment to active political comment, and to political activism, is evident in three volumes of poetry: *Fight Back: For the Sake of the People, For the Sake of the Land* (1980), *From Sand Creek: Rising in this Heart which is Our America* (1981) and *After and Before the Lightning* (1994). The subject of the case study below, *Fight Back* is significant not only for the reasons behind its commission, but also for the subject matter and connections that Ortiz makes. Commissioned to commemorate the tercentenary of the Pueblo Revolt of 1680, which remains the only successful indigenous revolution in the world and marks the defeat of the Spanish colonisers, the volume of poetry and essays is important for its comparison of the neo-colonial practices of contemporary energy companies with the kinds of Spanish oppression that produced the original Pueblo rebellion. The Pushcart Prize-winning *From Sand Creek* makes similar connections between contemporary or recent events and historical abuses conducted against Indian peoples, in this case a comparison of the atrocities being committed by US troops in Vietnam and elsewhere with the similar atrocities committed against Native peoples in the nineteenth century such as the 1864 Sand Creek Massacre. In a similar vein, *After and Before the Lightning* details the year spent by Ortiz in South Dakota close to the site of both Wounded Knee confrontations, which outlines not only the ongoing legacy of such encounters but also the 'common trials: every day' endured by contemporary Native peoples.[15] In 1992, Ortiz republished three of his volumes of poetry in a single edition, *Woven Stone*. His most recent collection of poetry is *Out There Somewhere* (2002), which emphasises the profound Acoma 'connections' that he feels.[16]

Mindful of the role of story and storyteller in the learning process, Ortiz has also published children's literature, including *The People Shall Continue* (1988), *Blue and Red* (1982) and *The Good Rainbow Road* (2004); and he has edited numerous anthologies of Native writings. While perhaps best known for his poetry, Ortiz has also published a range of fiction and prose, including the three volumes of short stories *Howbah Indians* (1978), *Fightin': New and Collected Stories* (1983) and *Men on the Moon* (1999), plus the essay collection *Song, Poetry, Language* (1978). These embody his active and activist political and personal philosophy:

> Fightin' – we must. It's a struggle to live ... to maintain human integrity and dignity. We are faced constantly with small and large battles ... But we struggle in every case. Only by fightin', often fighting back, do we maintain a necessary vital life; this is our victory.[17]

Fight Back: For the Sake of the People, For the Sake of the Land (1980)

This active and activist political philosophy is evident in the title of Ortiz's 1980 multi-genre work, which openly calls his readers to action in the face of the increasingly environmentally damaging neo-colonial policies of contemporary multinational energy companies. As with Silko's concept of witchery in *Ceremony*, this includes the uranium industry and atomic and nuclear testing on or near to Native lands. Ortiz's call to action clearly contests Euro-American attempts to ideologically separate land (nature) and people (culture) by exposing the connections between the extreme environmental damage being caused in the American southwest and its direct human consequences. As readers, our fight is thus for both people and land, whose interests and welfare are interlinked and insepa-rable. In this context, *Fight Back* engages with a wide range of Native worldviews that, as Keith Basso comments, recognise that 'the landscape in which people dwell can be said to dwell in them'.[18] Ortiz explores this concept of relatedness, and the causality of relationships; exposing the connections between historical forms of oppression, such as the poor Spanish–Acoma relationship that precipitated the 1680 Pueblo Revolt, and the neo-colonialist attitudes of contemporary corporate enterprise that continue to oppress Pueblo peoples.

This idea of relatedness is enormously significant, since the 1680 Revolt reacted not only to exploitative and inhuman Spanish rule, but also to the unsuccessful Acoma rebellion of 1599. Disastrously unsuc-cessful, this rebellion resulted in the decisive defeat of the Pueblo and the introduction of punitive retaliatory measures: all children under the age of twelve were removed from their families; all those over the age of twelve were enslaved; and all men over the age of twenty were sentenced to lose one foot and one hand.[19] As a result, the Pueblos were united in an unprecedented manner in an alliance against the colonisers, resulting in the successful expulsion of Spanish forces from the region for twelve years.[20] It is with this legacy that Ortiz engages, connecting the exploitative practices of Euro-American corporate industry with seven-teenth-century colonial abuses, as the 'theft of land and resources, slave labor, religious persecution, and unjust tribute demands'[21] is repeated in federally guaranteed corporate leases, destructive mining processes, low wages and poor industrial safety, the illegal destruction of Native sacred sites, and federally-fixed low percentage tribal 'benefits' that protect the enormous profits of the corporate energy interests. The second section of *Fight Back*, 'No More Sacrifices', mixes and fuses the history of the Acoma Rebellion with the consequences of contemporary abuses of the Acoma environment and people.

Ortiz refuses to draw distinctions between varieties of European colonisation. Detailing the early Spanish forces' obsession with profit and loss, Ortiz exposes twentieth-century connections with the capitalist mentality of contemporary Euro-American corporate enterprise. The ongoing attraction of both 'the land and people' of Acoma therefore is their 'obviou[s] productiv[ity]' and 'the potential for colonization and profit'.[22] These connections are emphasised structurally: the Acoma history of Spanish colonisation is set between two framing poems that detail contemporary corporate colonisation. Spanish appropriation is therefore situated between the 'wail' of the 'freight train' that marks the beginning of Euro-American industrial appropriation of Native lands and their resources,[23] and the Rio de San Jose from which water is supplied to the railroad companies by the resourceful Irishman McCarty whose name is subsequently imposed on the Acoma village of Deetseyamah.

Tracing the establishment of the energy industry on Native lands through the transformation of Grants into 'the Uranium Capital of the World',[24] Ortiz indicates that the contemporary situation for the Acoma is far worse as the energy corporations threaten lives through unsafe industrial practices, and traditional ways of life through the pollution. Ortiz underlines the threat posed by these new types of assimilation in the poem 'Final Solution: Jobs, Leaving'. As the title indicates, Ortiz evokes Nazi ideology to suggest that the critical economic conditions that force many southwestern Native Americans to leave their lands and traditional ways of life are an economically expedient and publicly acceptable contemporary Euro-American 'final solution' to the persistent 'Indian problem'.

In his discussions of 'a ruthless, monopolistic U.S. empire',[25] Ortiz clearly agrees with Brian Jarvis's suggestion that 'the landscapes of capitalism are aggressive, parasitic, and predatory, engaged in a relentless process of creative destruction'.[26] The most pertinent symbol of creative destruction is the nuclear industry. In this context, Ortiz writes of his own experiences working in the Kerr-McGee uranium mine and mills. The underground mines 'were dusty' and the Navajo miners would later 'find themselves cancerous'; and almost equally dangerous was the preparation of uranium ore that Ortiz undertook, the 'crushing, leaching, and yellowcake' production.[27] Economically dependent upon Kerr-McGee for employment, Ortiz later 'got paranoid about my own health', and is 'angry' with the indifference of the energy corporations and federal government: 'there weren't any special precautions we were required or urged to take'.[28] In this context, Ortiz discusses the production methods, highlighting the disinterest the energy corporation showed for the health and safety of its employees:

> It was not the safety or health or lives of the miners there was concern for. In the national interest, mine operators, oil corporations, utility companies, international energy cartels, and investors sacrificed those men and women. In the Grants Uranium Belt area … there was a miner killed every month. At home in Aacqu, there are former miners who walk around crippled, as maimed as if they had been wounded in wartime.[29]

Radioactive poisoning is now so prevalent throughout the Four Corners region that the federal government has long been attempting to formally identify the location as a 'National Sacrifice Area'. However, the concept of a 'National Sacrifice Area' clearly exposes Native perceptions of the relationship between culture and nature: that geographical sacrifice is inseparable from its human costs.

Ortiz's recognition of the human costs of the US energy industry is informed by his understanding of relatedness, which is evident in his interpretation of his text both as an illustration of 'the reason for the Pueblo Revolt' and as an expression of his 'hope for the present and future'.[30] In this context, Ortiz articulates his hope through his understanding of continuation: of the connections he traces between contemporary industrial/economic colonialism and the Pueblo Revolt. Continuation suggests that the very fact that the people have endured thus far indicates that the people – all people – can, and will, continue to endure. It is this recognition of relatedness that calls the people to activism. Crucial to any activism is an understanding of the need for symbiotic and sustainable relationships that are the basis of any viable future, environmental and otherwise. Throughout *Fight Back*, Ortiz constantly presents Acoma ideas of relatedness:

> The land. The people.
> They are in relation to each other.
> We are in a family with each other.[31]

Here, relatedness is equated to kinship, and Ortiz comments that it is an understanding of kinship that ensures a reciprocal survival, '[t]he land had given us our life,/and we must give life back to it'.[32]

A significant example of relatedness is the poem 'To Change in a Good Way', which centres upon the friendship between two Kerr-McGee employees and their wives. All are clearly economic hostages of the corporate energy companies. Okies Bill and Ida have moved west to find employment and are white 'trailer trash', living in a 'mobile home park' and dreaming of saving enough to return home to buy 'some acreage in eastern Oklahoma'.[33] Through their friendship with the Laguna couple Pete and Mary, Bill and Ida are able to establish a reciprocal relationship with the land. Mary helps Ida to transform her 'kind of stunted and wilty looking' garden through the use of traditional Laguna methods and, as a result, Ida's relationship with the earth becomes productive, resulting in a crop of 'radishes and lettuce/and carrots and corn,/even tomatoes and chilli'.[34] Perhaps the most significant figure is Bill's younger brother, Slick. Fighting in Vietnam as a means of escaping his own poverty, Slick steps on a landmine and dies. Ironically, what kills Slick is 'an American mine –/isn't that the shits …?'[35] Through Slick's death, Bill realises what Pete has understood all along, that the state, and the corporate mining interests, are indifferent to the fate of the dispossessed and oppressed. As Joni Adamson comments, 'Bill realises that Slick did not die for democracy. He died because he was poor … and his economic need led him to a dangerous place'.[36] Ortiz thus expresses his central concern: the understanding that the powerful economic, social and political forces afflicting Native peoples will spread to afflict all peoples.

Most importantly, what Pete and Mary share with Bill and Ida is their understanding of death: Slick is physically translated into 'Indian corn' as a prayer stick, to indicate that his life 'will keep on' as he is transformed into a position from which he can offer protection to his family.[37] While Pete and Mary fully understand that the Okie couple 'are not Indian', and indicate that they themselves 'don't remember/much of what is done' in this Laguna ceremony, Bill and Ida – and, by extension, Slick also – nonetheless accept what is offered 'for all of us', in an attempt to 'change life in a good way'.[38] Having given much thought to the causal relationships that have led to Slick's death, and that have led to his own employment in an equally hazardous and exploitative industry, Bill decides to 'plant' Slick in the Kerr-McGee mine shaft to offer some protection to his co-workers:

> We need it, all the help we can get,
> even if it's just so much as holding up
> the roof of this mine that the damn company
> don't put enough timbers and bolts in ...[39]

As Bill's comments indicate, in the face of the disinterest in humanity shown by capitalist corporations, like Kerr-McGee, that are devoted to 'both profit and global nuclear domination', he is overwhelmingly aware of the sheer amount of 'help' that is required.[40] In this sense, Adamson argues that the juxtaposition of 'Bill and Ida's garden with a dangerous minefield in Vietnam and the dangerous Kerr-McGee mine shafts' allows Ortiz to 'confron[t] the abstract ethics that serve to explain and justify state and corporate oppression of nature and "Others"'.[41]

Through the pain of Slick's death, Bill gains an understanding of the causal nature of relationships. Moreover, Ortiz specifies that Bill and Ida have learnt how 'to change in a good way', as Bill confronts his own Euro-American culture with the awareness that 'we maybe/have been wrong sometimes'.[42] For Bill, the end result is a realisation of the value of Laguna understandings of relatedness, a belief that it is 'somehow ... more righter/than we've ever been', and the firm commitment that 'now I'm trying too'.[43] As a result, Bill and Ida's ideas are transformed into action: Ida's productivity in growing food to supplement Bill's low wages, and Bill's incorporation of Laguna ceremony into both his private and his working life. Above all, the poem seems to represent Ortiz's own sense of the growing need for political action and activism, on the part of both America and Native America.

Ortiz's awareness of relatedness is perhaps best illustrated by the structure of *Fight Back*. The text is divided into two complementary sections that recognise the reciprocity and symbiosis of culture–nature relationships. In 'Too Many Sacrifices', Ortiz insists that activism, 'the People's fightback', is 'critical' to the successful introduction and maintenance of a sustainable environmental future.[44] This activism is evident in the blunt refusal of the title of the second section, 'No More Sacrifices'. Ortiz's invitation is to activism, perhaps most evident in the juxtaposition of two autobiographical poems, located at the start and close of the text. The poem 'First Hard Core' shows the young Ortiz's first experiences of racism in his job within the uranium industry. Under a barrage of insensitive and often offensive Euro-American questions about his heritage, Ortiz finds himself literally robbed of his voice: 'I just felt powerless to

answer./I just said I didn't know.[45] Ortiz's inability to speak demonstrates his disempowerment, yet a further line suggests that this situation
can be overcome: 'I didn't know how to answer him *then*'.[46]

In the final poem, aptly entitled 'A New Story', Ortiz returns to this
theme of overcoming oppression. Also presented as autobiographical,
the poem outlines Ortiz's responses, as a recovering alcoholic 'at the VA
hospital/in Ft. Lyons, Colorado', to a persistent Euro-American woman
who is 'looking for an Indian' to include in her 'Frontier Day Parade'.[47]
The woman declares her aims:

> We want to make it real, you understand,
> put a real Indian on a float,
> not just a paper mache dummy
> or an Anglo dressed as an Indian
> but a real Indian with feathers and paint.
> Maybe even a medicine man.[48]

Indicating the ways in which powerful Euro-American stereotypes erase
actual Native Americans, the woman fails to appreciate the quiet irony of
Ortiz's reply: '"Yes", I said./"there are several of us here"'.[49] The poem
is notable in the division of the dialogue between the two characters: of
forty-eight lines of dialogue, Ortiz speaks only fourteen words. It is a
division that emphasises the inequality of the relationship between Euro-
America and Native America: apart from the line cited above, Ortiz's
replies consist almost entirely of the word 'yes'. The sole exception,
which is the culmination of the text, is his final response. In contrast to
his experiences in 'First Hard Core', Ortiz makes an emphatic stand in
the final line against the pervasive Euro-American perceptions that are
embodied by the woman in the poem:

> 'No', I said. No.[50]

In the final words of the text, Ortiz articulates his active opposition. The
reclamation of his voice, which overcomes the silence that denoted his
powerlessness, actively challenges his disempowerment. This emphatic
closing word embodies the invitation Ortiz extends to his reader: to recognise the reciprocal nature of the culture-nature relationship; to understand the unsustainable and short-sighted indifference of both corporate
industry and the state; and to join the active/activist response to environmental injustice that the text articulates. In its simplest sense, Ortiz's
invitation to his reader is exactly what it says, an invitation to say 'no'.

Comedy as Cultural Critique: Louis Owens (1948–2002)

Born in 1948 in Lompoc, California, Louis Owens was born into a highly mixed heritage that he defined as 'Choctaw-Cherokee-Welsh-Irish-Cajun mixed space in between',[51] and this conceptualisation of mixed blood is central not only to his deliberations on his life but to his fiction also. Owens' parents were migrant workers and he was raised both in rural Mississippi and California where his family endured the poverty of share-cropping, and environments like the 'small tent "city"' Owens recalls in his autobiographical writings.[52] Recognising his own life in the migrant workers camps within the descriptions of John Steinbeck's *The Grapes of Wrath*, an enduring interest in Steinbeck ensued and, after working as a forest ranger and a forest service firefighter, Owens entered academia to study Steinbeck's work. The only member of his family to go to college, Owens gained a BA, MA and PhD from the University of California. He subsequently became an academic, teaching at the universities of California, California State and New Mexico. Respected for both his academic and fictional writings, Owens won a range of awards, including the Roman Noir Award for the outstanding mystery novel (1995), the American Book Award (1997), the Wordcraft Circle Writer of the Year (1998) and a National Endowment of the Arts Creative Writing Fellow-ship (1989). Owens was Director of the Creative Writing Programme at the University of California, Davis, when he committed suicide in 2002.

Owens' own highly successful academic career can be divided between his love for Steinbeck's work and his interest in and promotion of American Indian writing. Owens' first publications were academic considerations of Steinbeck, upon whom he published extensively, including two respected monographs, *The Grapes of Wrath: Trouble in the Promised Land* (1989) and *John Steinbeck's Re-Vision of America* (1985). During his lifetime, Owens' dedication to Steinbeck's work ensured that he became one of America's leading Steinbeck experts. Owens also co-edited *American Indian Novelists: An Annotated Critical Bibliography* (co-edited 1985), and in 1992 published a widely acclaimed analysis of contemporary Native literature: *Other Destinies: Understanding the American Indian Novel* (1992). *Other Destinies* remains a highly significant work that continues to be widely recommended to students of Native American literature. Owens also published prolifically throughout his career in a range of journals and periodicals.

However, it is Owens' autobiographical and fictional work that is significant for its development and discussion of his own considerations of the complex and often problematic role of the mixed-blood Indian. Considerations of such a complicated identity are central to both of his collections of essays and memoirs, *Mixedblood Messages: Literature, Film, Family, Place* (1998) and *I Hear the Train: Reflections, Inventions, Refractions* (2001). In this context, Owens comments specifically that:

> I conceive of myself today not as an 'Indian,' but as a mixedblood, a person of complex roots and histories. Along with my parents and grandparents, brothers and sisters, I am the product of liminal space … [a] liminal existence and a tension in the blood and heart must be the inevitable result of such crossing. How could it be otherwise?[53]

This 'tension in the blood' is the theme of the majority of Owens' subsequent novels, all of which analyse what it means to be a mixed-blood Indian, and so engage with and continue the dialogues begun by writers such as Apess, Mourning Dove and Momaday, among others. In this context, Owens' novels are defined as 'mysteries', which is evident in his uncovering and detection of the paradoxes of the 'liminal existence'. Yet it is equally true that the 'crimes' within his texts are emblematic of the greater historical crimes committed both against Native peoples and against the earth itself. His first novel, *Wolfsong* (1991), was written during his employment in the forest service, and draws on related environmental concerns to analyse the impact of a copper mine on a small Indian community in Washington State. In spite of threats to their cultural traditions and identity by environmentally unsound practices, this Indian community is trapped by poverty into an unwilling acceptance of the mining activities. Additionally, the mixed-blood protagonist Tom Joseph's attempts to locate his dis-located identity are complicated by trickster discourse: by the acts of ecoterrorism and the campaign of guerrilla warfare waged against the mining company by his recently deceased uncle. It is through negotiations both with his own liminality and with his uncle's trickster hermeneutics that Joseph, significantly, 'brings together activism and identity'.[54]

Owens' next two novels, *The Sharpest Sight* (1992) and *Bone Game* (1994), have interlinked themes and characters, and continue his analysis of the 'tension in the blood'. *The Sharpest Sight* attempts to uncover the truth behind the murder of an Indian Vietnam veteran. Based heavily upon Owens himself and on his family, the 'mystery' that characters from both novels attempt to solve is that of identity. Like Walters' *Ghost Singer*, both texts are saturated with the presence of the dead who, like the living, must be carefully negotiated. In *The Sharpest Sight*, Owens makes careful reference to Rollin Ridge's early Californian novel *The Life and Adventures of Joaquín Murieta*, and this allusion to the history of Indian and Mexican resistance is further foregrounded by the dead, whose very presence indicates an ongoing cultural resistance and a call for active change. The dead are equally evident in the related novel *Bone Game*, which returns to the semi-autobiographical mixed-blood academic character Cole McCurtain. Switching between historical periods and figures against a contemporary mystery of serial killings, *Bone Game* calls into question the constructed nature of history and identity, and their relationships to location and locatedness. *Bone Game* is the subject of the case study below.

Owens' final two novels, *Nightland* (1996) and *Dark River* (1999), continue his analysis of mixed-blood liminality. *Nightland* is a crime thriller and also a study in the power of Euro-American cultural stereotypes and preconceptions. Here, significantly, Owens extends his consideration of liminality into a discussion of the Native American cultural identity since Euro-American settlement to argue that Native American communities have been marginalised without exception. Owens' final novel, *Dark River*, returns to the themes of the Vietnam veteran (as a popular symbol of contemporary cultural dis-location and individual fragmentation), and of powerful Indian stereotypes. Both provide a basis for his subsequent discussion of racism and political activism.

Owens has himself defined his own mixed blood as a form of 'radical displacement and fragmentation'.[55] In this sense, it is true to say that this kind of radical fragmentation marks lives irreparably. However, while Owens' subject matter is bleak and the projected outlook may often seem hopeless, his persistent deployment of humour provides not only a means by which such unpalatable truths can be better demonstrated, but also a deeply sardonic and ironic note through which some sense of hope can be generated. Indeed, part of the purpose of Owens' trickster characters is to refuse to allow closure through an insistence that such important topics remain exposed and open for discussion. All of Owens' novels therefore present both dis-location and location, detailing the ways in which individuals and communities can be (and have been) fragmented before offering, through a specifically Native worldview, the means by which they can be made whole again: the land itself. As Owens argued, 'there is no emptiness in this world unless we create it' and we are all, rather, integral parts of 'a richly interconnected web of life'.[56] In this context, Owens' commitment to Native understandings of cultural location and environment can therefore be read, as LaLonde argues, as 'literary activism'.[57]

Bone Game (1994)

Owens' 1994 novel *Bone Game* playfully presents his reader with a semi-autobiographical central character Cole McCurtain who, like Owens himself, is a mixed-blood academic. The text is set on campus at the University of Santa Cruz, with a wide-ranging Indian, mixed-blood and Euro-American cast, including the cross-dressing Navajo academic Alex Yazzie, and two Euro-American figures: the teaching assistant Robert Malin, and the ex-Special Forces veteran and mature student Paul Kantner. Additionally, Owens introduces a range of Indian extended family who arrive to offer spiritual/ceremonial help, and an alternative perspective, including Cole McCurtain's daughter Abby, father Hoey, great-uncle Luther and 'grandmother' Onatima. At its simplest level, the text is a murder mystery as the bodies of young female students are found either shot or brutally dismembered, suggesting the work of more than one killer. Indeed, the manner of the killings suggests also two very different motives: on the one hand, a calm and rational execution; and, on the other, murders provoked by rage and repressed sexuality. Both modes of killing relate directly to local historical influences of the early nineteenth century: to the cruelty of the Spanish priest Padre Andrés Quintana, whose barbaric and inhuman treatment of the local Indians derives both from a sense of Christian superiority and from his unsuccessful attempts to repress his own sexual desire for the Indian women; and to Quintana's own subsequent torture and murder by the Indians in 1812 as a result of his behaviour.

Deeply alienated and, like the protagonists of many other Native texts, increasingly dependent at the start of the text upon alcohol, McCurtain is besieged by dreams that are haunted by events and actual figures from local history. As in Walters' *Ghost Singer*, these ghosts break through the fragile barriers between the past and the present, the living and the dead, and the dream and waking worlds, to create an emphatic, deeply disturbing and undeniable presence. Owens places emphasis upon the undeniable to create a distinct dialogue with the historical acts of violence against Native peoples, ensuring that this history and its legacy are exposed and become a topic for debate. Engaging with concepts of Navajo witchcraft, and with Silko's analysis of the nature of witchery in

Ceremony,[58] Owens uses the actions and motivations of contemporary serial killers to discuss the ways in which 'evil' operates. 'Evil' can here be 'located' as the legacy of oppression, cruelty and sexual abuse evident within the Spanish settlement of the Santa Cruz region. Thus de Ramirez comments that the text demonstrates not only 'evil behaviours explicable in terms of particular sociohistorical and psychological factors' but also 'the very real struggles of individuals imposing their power over others (whom they attempt to disempower)'.[59] As a result, the text is peopled with a range of dangerous and powerful inter-tribal concepts such as witches, shapeshifters and 'souleaters'.[60] Perhaps most significantly, the concept of dangerous oppression is embodied in the mythic figure of the gambler, recognised by a range of diverse Native cultures, who invades the dreams and waking reality of the textual characters to persuade them to play the 'bone game' and so gamble both their lives and their souls.

The very real presence of actual historical events and persons provides the basis for Owens' analysis of Native understandings of cultural location and environment. This presence therefore allows an exploration of the ways in which location itself is a carrier of memory, history and, most importantly, cultural identity; and, concomitantly, of the ways in which many of the textual characters are culturally dis-located by the legacy of federal–Indian history, or by the basic biological fact of mixed heritage. In this context, the contemporary killings are themselves also inseparable from questions of identity, evident both in the reasoning of the killers, and in the manner in which the killings are executed. One murderer therefore kills to ensure that, in his own warped interpretation of a pan-tribal Native philosophy, he maintains the correct 'balance' between good and evil necessary for the earth's survival; while the other emulates yet perverts Indian ceremonies by producing ritual items from his victims' bodies, for example the 'prayer stick' complete with 'strips of flesh' from one of the victims.[61] While the text can be read as a simple murder mystery, it is nevertheless also an extended meditation on the 'mysteries' of identity and identity politics, and the pervasive and corrosive nature of both cultural assimilation and cultural appropriation. The mixed-blood Cole McCurtain's question, '"[h]ow come crazy white men want to be Indians?" is therefore answered within the text only by Alex Yazzie's own ironic question, '"[h]ow come crazy Indians want to be white men?"'[62]

Owens' exploration of cultural dis-location is perhaps most evident in his protagonist Cole McCurtain, and derives both from Cole's geographical displacement to California from his tribal homeland of Mississippi, and from an innate sense of alienation emerging from his mixed heritage. Regardless of his career successes, Cole quite clearly regards himself as liminal: '[s]omeday, he knew, the university would find him out, would recognize him as an imposter and have him removed ... Indians, even mixedbloods, or especially mixedbloods, did not belong'.[63] Like the mixed-blood protagonists of many other Native novels, Cole feels he fits nowhere. His dis-location is perhaps most evident when he attempts to participate in the Native ceremonies that have been arranged to help him: '[w]hen his turn [to pray] arrived, Cole opened his mouth and only silence was there. He tried to form the words of a prayer in his mind, but his thoughts remained shapeless, inarticulate'.[64] Significantly, this sense of dis-location extends even to incorporate the elderly Indian characters such as Luther and Onatima, exposing the impact of the colonial encounter. As Onatima argues, '[w]e have survived a five-hundred-year war in which millions of us were starved to death, burned in our homes, shot and killed with disease, and alcohol. It's a wonder any Indian is alive today'.[65] Engaging with the power of story within the oral tradition, Onatima also indicates the burden of such a history for contemporary Native Americans: 'It's not wrong to survive ... Survivor's guilt is a terrible burden and so we all feel guilty ...'[66]

Set alongside this Native alienation is an equal sense of Euro-American alienation, evident within the actions and explanations of the serial killers. Cole considers what attracts Euro-American students to his Native literature classes, and decides that it is the ongoing lure of 'ethnostalgia',[67] the attraction of the exotic cultural 'other' with which dis-located Euro-Americans attempt to fill the cultural voids that 'open before them like terrifying chasms'.[68] As a result, Cole finds that his students regularly indulge in cultural appropriation by 'imagin[ing] themselves reincarnations of Crazy Horse and descendents of Indian princesses' and paying a 'hundred bucks for a sweat ceremony or three hundred for a vision quest'.[69] This dis-location is clearly present in the serial killers, one of whom is the mature Euro-American student Paul Kantner. Kantner is ex-Special Forces, and he is clearly presented (alongside memories of Cole's own Vietnam veteran brother Attis) as a damaged warrior, desperately in need of healing and purification. His failure to achieve either is the direct cause of his killing spree, coupled with his own dis-location: 'I was trying to establish a relationship, that's all ... Is that so fucking much to ask?'[70] His killing spree derives in part, therefore, from his own alienation and inability to reconnect, which is represented textually by his identification only by surname by the other characters.

The second killer, Robert Malin, is identified at the start of the text as 'haunted' and is so similar to Vietnam veterans that Cole has known that he wonders 'what this young man could have in common with those others'.[71] What Robert has in common is not only his experience of killing repeatedly but, because of this repetition, also a growing acceptance of the normality of violent death. Like Kantner, Robert is culturally alienated, repeatedly reading his 'favourite book' *Black Elk Speaks* in an attempt to gain some sense of the sacred, *any* sacred.[72] In Robert's distorted vision, the sins of the past have to be atoned for as they are the cause of contemporary environmental disaster and 'somebody has to accept responsibility'.[73] In this context, his murders are sacrifices and he sincerely believes that '[i]f I had not sacrificed thirteen times, we all would have tumbled into the trenches of the molten sea'.[74] In accordance with the concepts of witchery, Robert's vision is thus a twisted version of pan-tribal Native philosophies and he believes his actions maintain the 'precariou[s] balance between good and evil'.[75] While Robert has, ironically, almost grasped the reality of the dangerous hold that the past continues to have over the present, he fails to see himself as part of the ongoing legacy of 'evil'.

In this context, Owens' text is a consideration of worlds out of balance, demonstrated by the ghosts that people the text. Significantly, these ghosts begin to permeate Cole's waking and physical world:

> The gambler from his dream stood beyond the window, the right half of the naked body painted a dull white, the left half black … The eyes, black with anger, locked on his own.[76]

While the dead thus walk among the living, the living also begin to emulate the dead, and a variety of characters repeatedly stress their own increasing transparency which begins to operate as physical evidence of the power not only of past events but also of established ways of thinking. Onatima in particular discusses the dangers of invisibility for Native peoples, which she links directly to the Euro-American education process that renders Native cultures absent through its assimilative goals. Recognising that she had 'learned too many stories in school', Onatima traces the direct outcome of the assimilation process: widespread Native alienation.[77] In this context Indians see themselves 'only through [Euro-American] … eyes' and 'become like ghosts', a truth that Onatima demonstrates at various points in the text by displaying her own increasing physical transparency: 'I'm disappearing once more'.[78] Onatima's use of the phrase 'once more' here emphasises the ongoing battles of Native peoples against the colonial legacy. Importantly, all of these historical and contemporary events also relate directly to the textual explorations of power, of disempowerment and of imbalances of power.

Imbalances of power and dis-located worldviews are the basis for the persistent intrusions of the dead into Cole's dreams, as they demand both recognition and some form of recompense. As Onatima comments, 'there's a great deal of pain in these mountains'.[79] To Alex Yazzie's mind, the reason for the enduring pain of the local Ohlone is the sheer conflict between their worldview and that of the invading Spanish, which ensured that their colonisation was accompanied by utter alienation within an incomprehensible universe:

> Just imagine it ... After ten thousand years, one morning they woke up and the world was unrecognizable. They must have felt like they were the dead and the Spanish were the living.[80]

In this context, the dead also demand some means by which their world can be put to rights. This concept of a world in balance is physically present throughout the text in the form of the gambler, whose body is divided in two with black and white paint. There are, in effect, three gambler figures within the text: the gambler proper, who represents a neutral manifestation of power that can be employed for either good or bad ends, yet who offers that power as a form of temptation; Robert, who disguises himself as the gambler when he makes his 'sacrifices'; and the Ohlone Indian Venancio Asisara, responsible for the death of the Spanish priest in 1812. The interpretation of the gambler as a neutral form of power whose use depends on the individual to which it is offered is therefore very interesting, and provides a counterpoint to the presence of the trickster. While the trickster can partially be identified with the dead, his energy is primarily embodied within the text by the humorous yet serious, cross-dressing yet recognisably masculine Alex, who employs comedy throughout to make serious points and expose historical oppression. Alex's purpose within the text is, as LaLonde comments, to keep Cole 'alert to danger' and to help him 'imagine alternatives to the existing state of things'.[81] In the context of the types of temptation offered by the gambler, Alex therefore provides the warning against being 'consumed by appetite'.[82]

Both Robert and Cole dream of the gambler and listen to the stories he tells of the events of 1812, and both react violently: Cole becomes effectively self-harming through his increased use of alcohol, while Robert chooses to harm others. The reader is left to wonder if Venancio Asisara's attack on the Spanish priest was the result of his own response to the temptations of the gambler. In this context, Cole's final realisation of the ways in which he can break the repetitive cycle of violence and oppression occurs at the close of the text, when he stops his daughter from playing the bone game:

> 'Venancio Asisara.' Cole spoke the name clearly, as he had heard it in his dream.
> A smile spread across the gambler's face. '*Eran muy crueles,*' he said. For a long moment he looked at Cole, and then he turned and walked slowly away towards the trees.[83]

Cole's acknowledgement of the gambler / Asisara through direct address makes clear the historical connections between varieties and forms of evil. The gambler / Asisara's response, 'they were very cruel', may therefore be read in numerous historically located ways, yet it ultimately should be read as a comment on evil and cruelty itself within the context of American / human history. Cole's ability to 'say no', which effectively breaks the cycle, is, as with Silko's *Ceremony*, presented as merely a respite. At the close of the text, the reader is reminded not only that evil has to be persistently fought and that the balance of the world needs constant attention, but also that history has an unfortunate habit of repeating itself. In this context, the text ends with the repeated warning: '*Eran muy crueles*'.[84]

Surreal Subversions: Gerald Vizenor (b. 1934)

Born in Minneapolis in 1934, Gerald Vizenor is of mixed Euro-American, French and Anishinaabe (Ojibwe or Chippewa) heritage, identifying himself as a 'crossblood'.[85] His parents separated before he was a year old, and his father was subsequently murdered (possibly in a racist attack) in 1936. Vizenor was raised by his mother (who kept abandoning him), in foster homes, and also periodically by his father's family at the White Earth reservation in Minnesota. After dropping out of high school, Vizenor joined the army and saw active service in Korea and later Japan, before returning to academic study to gain a BA from the University of Minnesota. Influenced by the emerging voice of the Red

Power movement, Vizenor began his writing career in journalism, where he developed his involvement with tribal politics. Vizenor eventually returned to academia to begin a distinguished career during which he taught at a variety of universities across the US, including Minnesota and Oklahoma (where he founded and edits the American Indian Literature and Critical Series). Awarded a range of prizes, including the American Book Award (1988), the Distinguished Achievement Award from the Western Literature Association (2005) and a Lifetime Achievement Award from the Native Writers Circle of the Americas (2001), Vizenor currently teaches at the University of California, Berkeley.

One of Native America's most prolific contemporary writers, Vizenor began his publishing career in the early 1960s with the self-published haiku volume *Two Wings the Butterfly* and a subsequent five volumes of haiku. The connections that Vizenor saw between haiku and traditional Ojibwe forms are evident in the other texts that he published during this early era, which were all focused on Chippewa literature and traditions: *Summer in the Spring: Ojibwe Lyric Poems and Tribal Stories* (1965) was followed by *The Everlasting Sky: New Voices from the People Named the Chippewa* (1972) and *The People Named the Chippewa: Narrative Histories* (1984). This tribal focus ensured that, in the late 1960s, Vizenor became involved in tribal politics, and political analysis and sharp political comment is at the forefront of all of his fiction and non-fiction writings.

Vizenor's work is characterised by his linguistic experimentations: the use of neologisms to better describe the experiences of Native peoples and the attitudes of Euro-America. In this sense, Vizenor's writing employs rhetorical strategies to disempower the colonisers and re-empower the colonised. For example, Vizenor's term 'survivance'[86] describes contemporary Indian existence as a complex combination of both survival and endurance/resistance. Vizenor's work is therefore infused with elaborate and highly political wordplay, through which he disrupts distinctly drawn boundaries to present a range of alternatives to accepted realities. Significantly, the boundaries that Vizenor erodes are not only between the real and the imagined, but also between genres: his work is often simultaneously fictional and autobiographical, and incorporates a range of 'real' figures as characters. This breaking of boundaries of all kinds signifies Vizenor's emulation of the trickster tradition, primarily as a means by which hidden truths can be exposed and dialogues enforced, and relates directly to the kinds of word and story power persistently emphasised by a range of Native writers. This is perhaps most immediately evident in the range of essays and socio-political comments that Vizenor has published. The 1978 volume *Wordarrows: Indians and Whites in the New Fur Trade* (reprinted in 2003 with the subtitle *Native States of Literary Sovereignty*) is a blend of memoir, essay and fiction that analyses the economies of exchange between Euro-American and Indian communities and cultures which Vizenor identifies as 'the new fur trade'. In this context, Vizenor clearly flags the unequal power relations within the exchange, illustrated at the close of the text through his reconsideration of the murder trial of Thomas White Hawk, and suggests that one means of resistance is through the 'wordarrow', by the staging of strategic word wars.

These political considerations are also evident in two volumes from 1990: *Crossbloods: Bone Courts, Bingo, and Other Reports* and *Interior Landscapes: Autobiographical Myths and Metaphors*. In *Crossbloods*, Vizenor engages with a range of contemporary problems besetting Native cultures, including the proliferation of casinos and other forms of gambling as the new basis for Indian economies, and – continuing the discussion begun by Walters' *Ghost Singer* – the increasingly problematic treatment of Native human remains by American museums and anthropologists. Central to *Crossbloods* is Vizenor's analysis of the growing complexities of identity and mixed blood, and mixed blood becomes a trope through which Vizenor explores the figure of the trickster, notions of possibility and, perhaps most importantly, the power of subversion and subversive action. Further consideration of the relationship between power imbalances and American law is evident in *Interior Landscapes*. A series of memoirs, *Interior Landscapes* begins with an analysis not just of Vizenor's own father's murder, but also of the investigations or lack of investigations of that murder.

Vizenor's more recent essays have become even more political, as his experimentation with language has become more complex to illustrate the connections between language and power. *Manifest Manners: Postindian Warriors of Survivance* (1994) explores the ways in which terminology simultaneously glosses over yet also incorporates ideologies. The 'manifest manners' to which Vizenor refers represent, therefore, the survival of the doctrine of Manifest Destiny as a key Euro-American ideology, and the ways in which these 'manifest manners' are at the heart of the majority of contemporary federal–Indian interactions. To Vizenor's mind, these inequalities are based, at least in part, upon enduring cultural stereotypes and he is highly critical of several

American Indian Movement (AIM) leaders whose subsequent actions he interprets as having reinforced Euro-American prejudices. Vizenor's examination of Andy Warhol's iconic representation of Russell Means as a 'traditional' Indian warrior complete with feathers and breastplate is therefore condemned in a parody of European art: 'This portrait is not an Indian'.[87]

Manifest Manners explores one of Vizenor's most significant ideas, the oppositional forces of 'survivance' and 'victimry'. While survivance embodies Native survival and endurance, victimry is identified as an Indian acceptance of the role of the tragic victim which is, notably, the only role offered to them by Euro-American society. Pitting tragedy against comedy, Vizenor argues that this *'indian'* (signalled by lower-case italics) is a tragic Euro-American stereotypical creation, whereas the 'postindian' represents a subversive use of humour to ensure and maintain the survival of Native cultures. Vizenor's critique of a range of contemporary Native ideologies makes him a contentious and controversial figure. These ideas are discussed further in the 1998 volume *Fugitive Poses: Native American Indian Scenes of Absence and Presence*, where Vizenor argues that Native American reality has been subsumed and made absent by the emphatic presence of imposed Euro-American ideas of the *indian*. Indian reality is, therefore, conveniently ignored while stereotypes endure and proliferate. Vizenor's key critical ideas are reiterated in two further texts: the collected volume *Shadow Distance: a Gerald Vizenor Reader* (1994) and a series of interviews with A. Robert Lee, *Postindian Conversations* (1999).

Vizenor's firm focus on wordplay and his commitment both to political commentary and to subversive humour is evident in all of his fictional works, which are deeply satirical. In this context his work is, as Owens argues, 'radically imaginative',[88] and he engages with postmodern theories to expose the instability of concepts and ideologies. Vizenor's approach acts to defy terminal creeds: the damaging and deadly beliefs that he identifies within the tragic poses of *indian* victimry. As a result, his fictional works subvert a range of Euro-American assumptions regarding Native writings, philosophies and humour. Significantly, for Vizenor the '[t]ribal tricksters' not only 'arise in the imagination' but act specifically to 'liberate the mind'.[89] As Krupat and Elliott note, this sense of 'comic utopianism', the 'imagining [of] a truly decolonized or postcolonial world', sets Vizenor's work apart.[90] Vizenor's first novel, *Darkness in St Louis Bearheart* (1978), embodies these concepts. Later reprinted as *Bearheart: the Heirship Chronicles* (1990), the text outlines the importance of community as an assorted group of Indians and Euro-Americans attempt to right a world gone horribly wrong through greed, racism and environmental destruction which are embodied, as in Owens' *Bone Game*, within the figure of the gambler. Moving beyond the alien-ation normally associated with the mixed-blood, Vizenor emphasises the potential of those with the ability to adapt. This emphasis upon adapt-ability is equally evident within Vizenor's second novel, *Griever: An American Monkey King in China* (1987), in which the protagonist, Griever de Hocus, connects with Chinese trickster traditions to subvert not only Euro-American literary conventions but also the powerful restrictions of the Chinese communist state, at which the text is 'aimed like an explo-sive mine'.[91] This explosively liberating satire is also evident in the 1988 novel *The Trickster of Liberty: Tribal Heirs to a Wild Baronage*, which employs 'socio-acupuncture' to celebrate the subversion of ineffective or damaging traditions in favour of productive inter-cultural negotiations.

These productive inter-cultural negotiations are evident in Vizenor's more recent novels. In *The Heirs of Columbus* (1991), Vizenor's claim that Columbus was a Mayan mixed-blood resulting from Mayan explorations of Europe inverts accepted histories of New World conquest to challenge unequal power hierarchies. In *Hotline Healers* (1997), the appropriately named mixed-blood Almost Browne indulges in a range of ambiguous cultural 'performances' that subvert established perceptions of Native American cultures. Vizenor's most recent novel, *Chancers* (2000), is a deeply satirical engagement with the debate over Native human remains, and the subject of the case study below. These subversive inter-cultural explorations are equally evident within Vizenor's three volumes of short stories: *Earthdivers: Tribal Narratives on Mixed Descent* (1981) combines autobiography with fiction; *Landfill Meditation: Crossblood Stories* (1991) uses refuse meditations to expose the connotations of the term 'refuse' both as rubbish and as denial; and *Dead Voices: Natural Agonies in the New World* (1992) challenges Vizenor's readers to hear the real Indian stories rather than the tragic words uttered by 'dead voices'.

A truly prolific writer, Vizenor has also edited two volumes on Native literature, *Narrative Chance: Postmodern Discourse on Native American Indian Literatures* (1993) and *Native American Literature: a Brief Introduc-tion and Anthology* (1995), and produced both a screenplay (*Harold of Orange*, which was produced as a film) and a drama (*Ishi and the Wood Ducks*). Vizenor's most recent publication is a volume of poetry, *Bear*

Island: The War at Sugar Point (2006). Here Vizenor employs traditional Ojibwe oral storytelling techniques to create an epic poem that
analyses the 1898 conflict between the traditional Ojibwe Pillager family
(who also feature heavily in Erdrich's fiction) and the US military. In this
context, Vizenor extends his engagement with the trickster tradition as
he exposes the Native stories and histories that continue to be elided and
made absent by the hegemonic national narrative.

Chancers (2000)

Vizenor's engagement with the trickster tradition is evident in the title
of his novel *Chancers*. Like the majority of his other novels, *Chancers* is
highly self-referential and intertextual, presenting the first-person narrative of the mixed-blood academic Cedarbird, who teaches at the University of California and identifies himself as 'a trickster with a computer ...
in the best tradition of transformation'.[92] The text also incorporates and
comments upon a range of critics and critical texts, including Momaday,
Roland Barthes's *Mythologies* and Vizenor's own earlier text *Bearheart*. In
this context, *Chancers* continues Vizenor's ongoing 'word wars' as it struggles, as Kimberly Blaeser argues, with 'both the underlying philosophies
and structures of language use in contemporary society, and the particular appropriations and misrepresentations of the Native American which
have resulted'.[93] In this context, Vizenor's specific (and ongoing) engagements with the Ojibwe trickster figure Naanabozho can be interpreted
as highly political and expressly transformative inter-cultural interventions. Through an 'overturn[ing of] all laws, governments, [and] social
conventions',[94] Vizenor's tricksters therefore create distinct and often
un-settling dialogues with both Native and Euro-American cultures.

The text is divided into five sections – 'Solar Dancers', 'Wetland
Sovereignty', 'Round Dancers', 'Chicken Pluck' and 'Holy Decadence'
– which, structurally, emulates traditional European drama even while
it imposes an overwhelming sense of the comedic through its analysis of
a range of complex and deeply ironic cultural worldviews and attitudes.
Cedarbird's narrative is initially presented as a novel within the novel,
and the first section we read is Cedarbird's reconstruction of events so
far that is being prepared for publication by 'Random Nation Books'.[95]
Here, Cedarbird introduces the reader to the main focus of the text: the
murder or 'sacrifice' on campus of a range of academics, such as the
provost Pontius Booker, who are beheaded and whose skulls subsequently replace the Native remains in the Phoebe Hurst Museum of

Anthropology. However, Cedarbird's highly self-conscious narrative is almost immediately interrupted: 'I had written that much, line for line as you read it now' when he is 'cornered' by the 'Solar Dancers'.[96] As students who are 'possessed by the ideologies of victimry', Cedarbird defines the Solar Dancers as 'terminal creeders' whose embracing of victimry also embraces the Euro-American stereotypes that ensure a Native 'absence'.[97] As tragic *indian* victims, the Solar Dancers are satirically identified as 'Touch Tone' ('Lakota and Hindustani'[98]), 'Fast Food' ('Athabaskan and Russian'[99]), 'Bad Mouth' and her brother 'Knee High' ('Miwok and Bedouin'[100]), 'Injun Time' ('Lumbee and others'[101]), 'Fine Print' (Cherokee and Chinese[102]), 'Cloud Burst' ('the maniacal ... veteran of the Second World War' with 'no evidence ... that he was native'[103]) and 'Token White' (the 'German and Norwegian' who is 'a fierce native by adoption'[104]). Their actions throughout the text therefore emphasise highly negative cultural and personal traits such as an advocation of 'racial separatis[m]'.[105] As a result, Bad Mouth practises the 'vile curses' of tragic victimry that attracts the *wiindigoo*, the 'cannibal monster'[106] of traditional Ojibwe stories, to the Solar Dancers and enables their subsequent possession and transformation into murderers. The *wiindigoo* are, ironically, attracted specifically by the 'thick, incredible consonance of cultural torments, dangerous visions, resentments, and low grades in required courses'.[107]

In this context, the text presents a range of Native and non-Native cultural essentialists whose adherence to terminal creeds marks them either for annihilation by the Solar Dancers, or as potential victims for the *wiindigoo*. For example, the 'poseur' Pardone de Cozener who 'always wore feathers' and is incurably flatulent;[108] and the 'Creek and Seminole crossblood' Ruby Blue Welcome who, accompanied by her 'trusty hand puppet' Four Skins, persistently imposes herself upon Native student protests as an 'uninvited' and highly unwelcome speaker.[109] By contrast, what is celebrated within the text is the ability to subvert and transcend the dangerous limitations of cultural essentialism, be it Euro-American or Native American. Alongside Cedarbird, the text therefore celebrates individuals such as Cedarbird's 'mentor' Peter Roses, the director of Native Studies known as 'Round Dance',[110] who 'would not stand for even the slightest pout or plea of victimry' from Native students.[111] And, in a deeply ironic move, Vizenor also celebrates the 'Round Dancers', the 'blondes' with whom Round Dance is sexually 'very active' and who are identified as 'the natural enemies of the poseurs'.[112] In this context,

Vizenor plays not only upon the Ojibwe traditions that link 'survivance stories with carnal play',[113] but also parodies the links between 'dumb blondes' and sexual availability within Euro-American popular culture. A further crucial figure is Conk Browne, a relation of Almost Browne from *Hotline Healers*. Conk is, significantly, identified as 'forever in motion'[114] due to her tendency to have visions in elevators, and in this sense she embodies Vizenor's concept of 'transmotion',[115] the creative motion that allows us to evade stasis of all kinds. As a result, Conk creates 'an original native sense of presence'[116] that comments directly on a Euro-American erasure of Native America: perhaps inevitably, the academic faculty exhibit a distinct disregard for her stories to which they 'only preten[d] to listen'.[117]

Significantly, at the centre of the text is Round Dance's lecture on Native literature that creates a dialogue with the Solar Dancers – and so therefore also with extra-textual Native and Euro-American proponents of similar terminal creeds – to explore Vizenor's own notions of Indian and *indian* identity. Quoting subversively from Vizenor's own novel *Bearheart*, Round Dance therefore outlines Vizenor's own argument regarding the pervasive power of imposed linguistic and ideological definitions of 'indianness' to expose the ways in which the Solar Dancers themselves embrace *indian* victimry and so 'lose th[e] sense of humor and irony' that is essential to cultural, communal and individual survivance.[118] This sense of irony is perhaps most evident in Vizenor's satire on cultural 'trash',[119] which is foregrounded by his introduction of the 'survivance shaman' Martin Bear Charme and the subsequent focus on his creation of 'a million dollar mountain out of waste' that the BIA have 'recognized … as the Waste Mountain Reservation'.[120] Claiming ironically that 'we cannot refuse our own refuse',[121] Bear Charme plans to build a casino to complement Old Darkhorse's 'Half Moon Bay Skin Dip' where mixed-blood Indians could 'darke[n]' their 'light skin' in order to look more authentically Indian and so 'find work in native services'.[122] It is this highly ambiguous and identity challenging skin dip that is later used to ensure that the bones of the university faculty can 'pass' for those they replace in the museum: the 'native chancers' who are 'resurrect[ed]' as a result.[123]

While *Chancers* is, like Owens' *Bone Game*, ostensibly a murder mystery, with intended victims marked in advance by strange and unidentified blue characters on their clothing, the reader is nonetheless ironically aware from the start of the identities of the murderers. Indeed, the story of the provost's murder is told by Token White to Cedarbird, and we read her interpretation of events: Pontius's concern that he is stripped naked is because 'he had such a tiny penis that he lost his fear of death'.[124] As a result, the text is an exploration of the motivations of a range of characters, both murderers and murder victims. Significantly, these motivations are linked directly to the legacy of a specific period of federal–Indian history, both through the location of the text at the Berkeley campus, and through the figure of Token White. In this context, Token White claims her archery skills as an inheritance from the historical Indian Ishi, the focus of her childhood obsession, which acts to expose Berkeley as the site of one of the most shameful episodes of federal–Indian and anthropological history. A key figure in many of Vizenor's texts, Ishi was a Yahi Indian who was hailed as the 'last of his tribe' when he emerged from the Californian mountains in 1911. Handed over to the anthropologist Alfred Kroeber at the University of California, Ishi subsequently lived in a diorama 'performing' for Euro-American visitors by crafting traditional bows and arrows. Ishi's story has become symbolic of the deceitful nature of the federal–Indian relationship: on his death in 1918 from tuberculosis, his body was subject to post-mortem and, against his expressed wishes, his brain was removed. It is only in recent years that the Smithsonian has admitted 'stewardship' of Ishi's brain, and repatriated it for reburial under the NAGPRA legislation. Within the text, the Phoebe Hurst Museum is implicated in this history, both through the artefacts that are held, and through the implicit cultural values that inform the collections that effectively hold Native peoples in what Vizenor defines as 'osteological bondage'.[125]

In this context, Vizenor analyses Ishi's re-creation as an emblem for both Native and Euro-American culture, as part of his wider consideration of the attraction that Native bodies and body parts continues to hold for Euro-American scientists: identified within the text as 'erotic osteology'.[126] While Vizenor satirises this erotic attraction through the 'crania and pelves ... mounted on [the] ... laboratory bench in the most suggestive [of] positions', the humour of the discussion nonetheless exposes Euro-American reverence of bones (and so of the past) as a means by which to ensure a continued 'absence of [contemporary] natives'.[127] The osteologist in question, Dr Paul Snow, has an erotic obsession for 'unrestrained sex with a primitive native woman in a circle of crania'.[128] Significantly, Snow's obsession with Native bones as 'aphrodisiac' is matched by the appropriately named Blue Welcome's own 'rather desperate' desire to be 'the source of his erotic pleasure', and her 'excite[ment]' at the idea of a Native presence in the form of 'bone voyeurs'.[129] Snow and Blue Welcome's sexual activities among the bones, which incorporates the penetration of 'orbital bones',[130] results in a 'terminal orgas[m]'[131] as the concomitant sexual arousal of the Solar Dancers voyeurs ensures a 'double sacrifice'.[132] Significantly, Blue Welcome's death is preceded by the dismemberment of her beloved puppet Four Skins, the only part of whom survives is his erect over-sized penis, ironically mis-identified and discarded by the museum director as 'another anthropology dildo joke'.[133]

Events culminate with the election of the new provost, Hildie Harridan, who, unsurprisingly given her name, is exposed as 'an ethnic faker and feminist by measured scorn'.[134] To Vizenor's mind, there is little difference between the racial essentialism of the Solar Dancers and the gendered essentialism of individuals such as Hildie. Hildie's decision to order an investigation of Round Dance and the Native Studies department seals her fate and she becomes the second provost to fall victim to the Solar Dancers. Harridan's investigation is headed by the private eye Tulip Browne (Conk's aunt), who has previously found professional success investigating Griever (of *Griever: An American Monkey King in China*) for the Chinese government. This further inter-textual reference emphasises the connections that Vizenor sees between the repressions of the communist state and the repressions of academic freedom (i.e. the strict policing of academic disciplines) within the contemporary US university system. Since Vizenor has worked within both US and Chinese education systems, he is therefore more qualified than most to make such judgements, even if he does so tongue in cheek. The results of Tulip's investigation provoke the final showdown between the opposing ideologies of the Solar and Round Dancers, through a series of audio and video tapes of Round Dance's sexual encounters, 'the teases, sex chatter, moans, and the round dash rush' with 'seventeen blondes, one solar dancer, and the provost', during his aptly entitled 'orifice hours'.[135] Hildie is only exposed by a public broadcast of the tapes in 'a masterly act of vengeance' by the Solar Dancers.[136] Significantly, the real showdown occurs due to the Solar Dancers' identification of Token White as one of Round Dance's blondes, and their subsequent 'outrag[e]'.[137]

As Token White 'never forgave the solar dancers', she plans revenge through 'silent rage and savage jealousy'.[138] The 'dance off' between the opposing cultural viewpoints of the Solar and Round Dancers occurs, perhaps appropriately, at graduation. With Hildie already sacrificed due to her 'betray[al] of the remains and memory of Ishi'[139] through her refusal to petition the Smithsonian for the return of his remains, the Solar Dancers turn, somewhat ironically, on the last proponent of *indian* victimry, Pardone de Cozener. Identified by Vizenor as a 'simulation' of indianness,[140] the aptly named Cozzie White Mouth has found that he can 'pass' as Indian if he 'mention[s] native names at strategic moments' and 'stain[s] his skin a burnt cinnamon brown at the Half Moon Bay Skin Dip'.[141] Significantly, it is Cozzie's ambition to 'take control of native studies'[142] and his stance on the repatriation of the remains in the Phoebe Hurst Museum that ensures the enmity of the Solar Dancers. Exposed as a fake in an extended exchange of insults with the Solar Dancers, Cozzie is further exposed as a convicted 'sexual molester' of chickens and a purveyor of sexual favours with poultry at the 'Paraday Chicken Pluck Center' where he keeps 'the book of chicken pluck confessions'.[143] However, it is the acting provost Ransom Greene's reaction that ensures the subsequent bloodletting. Due to 'bloodline resentments and irreconcilable administrative problems', the native studies department is to be 'terminate[d]'.[144] In the final showdown, the Solar Dancers are first refused graduation then, after they attack the resurrected Four Skins hand puppet, they are themselves executed by Token White's archery skills. The last words of the text go to Ishi and emulate the accent that linguists documented. Perhaps appropriately, the text ends with a deeply ironic question: 'Evelybody hoppy?'[145]

Vizenor's ambiguous ending emphasises his persistent focus on trickster discourse, which evades cultural stereotyping and frees the mind to a range of creative cultural possibilities. This transformative potential is crucial to Vizenor's own inter-cultural interventions as an example of alternative forms of cultural understanding. As Blaeser comments, Vizenor's concept of 'mixedblood trickster marginality is a type of existence … it is a state of being as well as a way of being'.[146] In this context, Vizenor's satirical and surreal writings subvert our interpretations of 'reality' to suggest the possibility of a less fixed, more fluid, and therefore more promising, worldview. In his 'insist[ance] upon ethics beyond aesthetics' Vizenor has, as Owens rightly argues, 'loosen[ed] the shrouds of [cultural] identity' for all.[147]

Recent texts by Native men have highlighted an interesting development in Native writing more generally: an increased gendering not only of expression, but also of experience. While early writers such as William Apess did not gender Indian civil rights nor distinguish them from the wider racial debate on African American rights, this is obviously no longer the case in the early twenty-first century. Such developments clearly illustrate the impact of Euro-American patriarchal cultural values, which demand the creation and maintenance of distinct gender boundaries. In contrast to the experiences of Native women, Native male writers continue to be excluded, yet literary strategies have been developed to enable a male Native literary voice and presence. A 'trickster hermeneutics' is one distinctive feature of contemporary Native men's writings, allowing not only men's concerns and experiences to be discussed, but also the expression of ongoing anger. The impact of these developments upon more recent Native literature has resulted in a range of more recent Native writers 'extending the can(n)on' in complex and diverse ways.

Notes

1. See Chris LaLonde (2002).
2. Louis Owens (1998), pp. 159–60.
3. Gerald Vizenor (1994), p. 15.
4. LaLonde (2002), p. 22.
5. While women writers such as Silko and Erdrich also engage with the trickster tradition, the discourse is markedly more developed within the writings of Native American men.
6. LaLonde (2002), p. 36.
7. Simon Ortiz (1992), p. 9.
8. Ibid. p. 18.
9. Ibid. p. 18.
10. Ibid. p. 9.
11. Ibid. p. 17.
12. Ibid. p. 11.
13. Ibid. p. 41.
14. Ibid. p. 224.
15. Ortiz (1998), p. 31.
16. Ortiz (2002), p. 133.
17. Ortiz (1983), p. 6.
18. Keith H. Basso (1996), p. 102.
19. Joe S. Sando (1998), p. 248.
20. Ibid. pp. 59–60.
21. Ortiz (1992), p. 31.
22. Ibid. p. 342.
23. Ibid. p. 340.
24. Ibid. p. 342.
25. Ibid. p. 348.

26. Ibid. p. 153.
27. Ibid. pp. 356–7.
28. Ibid. p. 358.
29. Ibid. p. 358.
30. Ibid. p. 31.
31. Ibid. p. 324.
32. Ibid. p. 325.
33. Ibid. pp. 308, 309.
34. Ibid. pp. 309, 311.
35. Ibid. p. 312.
36. Joni Adamson (2001), p. 65.
37. Ortiz (1992), p. 313.
38. Ibid. pp. 313, 314.
39. Ibid. p. 317.
40. Adamson (2001), p. 65.
41. Ibid. p. 65.
42. Ortiz (1992), p. 317.
43. Ibid. p. 316.
44. Ibid. p. 293.
45. Ibid. p. 308.
46. Ibid. p. 308, emphasis added.
47. Ibid. pp. 363–4.
48. Ibid. p. 364.
49. Ibid. p. 365.
50. Ibid. p. 365.
51. Owens (1998), p. 176.
52. Ibid. p. 172.
53. Ibid. p. 176.
54. LaLonde (2002), p. 58.
55. Owens (1998), p. 147.
56. Ibid. p. 236.
57. LaLonde (2002), p. 190.
58. In a direct reference to *Ceremony*, one of Owens' 'witches' (who abduct a drunken Navajo woman to 'sell' for undisclosed reasons in California) is also called Emo.
59. de Ramirez (1999), p. 164.
60. Owens (1994), p. 132.
61. Ibid. p. 133.
62. Ibid. p. 50.
63. Ibid. p. 22.
64. Ibid. p. 163.
65. Ibid. p. 165.
66. Ibid. p. 165.
67. Ibid. p. 43.
68. Ibid. p. 22.
69. Ibid. p. 21.
70. Ibid. p. 220.
71. Ibid. p. 16.
72. Ibid. p. 19.

73. Ibid. p. 235.
74. Ibid. p. 237.
75. Ibid. p. 238.
76. Ibid. p. 12.
77. Ibid. p. 140.
78. Ibid. pp. 140, 139.
79. Ibid. p. 140.
80. Ibid. p. 54.
81. LaLonde (2002), pp. 141–2.
82. Ibid. p. 142.
83. Owens (1994), p. 241.
84. Ibid. p. 243.
85. Vizenor (1990a).
86. Vizenor (1994).
87. Ibid. p. 18.
88. Owens (1992), p. 225.
89. Vizenor (1990b), p. 73.
90. Arnold Krupat and Michael A. Elliott (2006), p. 142.
91. Owens (1992), p. 242.
92. Vizenor (2000), p. 11.
93. Kimberly M. Blaeser (1996), pp. 72–3.
94. Owens (1992), p. 227.
95. Vizenor (2000), p. 9.
96. Ibid. p. 9.
97. Ibid. p. 9.
98. Ibid. p. 30.
99. Ibid. p. 30.
100. Ibid. p. 26.
101. Ibid. p. 30.
102. Ibid. p. 30.
103. Ibid. pp. 26, 42.
104. Ibid. pp. 30, 33.
105. Ibid. p. 28.
106. Ibid. p. 26.
107. Ibid. p. 26.
108. Ibid. p. 7.
109. Ibid. pp. 17–18.
110. Ibid. p. 31.
111. Ibid. p. 7.
112. Ibid. p. 7.
113. Ibid. p. 8.
114. Ibid. p. 101.
115. Ibid. p. 101.
116. Ibid. p. 100.
117. Ibid. p. 101.
118. Ibid. p. 95.
119. Ibid. p. 70.
120. Ibid. p. 70.

121. Ibid. p. 71.
122. Ibid. p. 71.
123. Ibid. p. 79.
124. Ibid. p. 49.
125. Ibid. p. 56.
126. Ibid. p. 55.
127. Ibid. p. 55.
128. Ibid. p. 56.
129. Ibid. pp. 56, 57.
130. Ibid. p. 66.
131. Ibid. p. 64.
132. Ibid. p. 67.
133. Ibid. p. 55.
134. Ibid. pp. 83–4.
135. Ibid. pp. 110, 80.
136. Ibid. p. 109.
137. Ibid. p. 111.
138. Ibid. p. 111.
139. Ibid. p. 113.
140. Ibid. p. 116.
141. Ibid. p. 117.
142. Ibid. p. 117.
143. Ibid. pp. 129, 133.
144. Ibid. pp. 134, 136.
145. Ibid. p. 159.
146. Blaeser (1996), p. 157.
147. Owens (1992), p. 254.

CHAPTER 6

Extending the Canon: Recent Native Writing

New Blood: Current Developments in Native Literature

More recently, new and emerging Native writers have begun building upon the successes of writers such as Momaday, Silko, Erdrich and Vizenor to produce a range of writings that continue to engage with Native cultures, histories and politics, and with the literary heritages evident within oral storytelling traditions. As with previous Native writings, gender concerns and gender roles continue to be a focus. These writings, like their authors, are highly diverse and range from engagements with the Euro-American horror or thriller genre to considerations of what it means to be an 'urban Indian', and from analyses of the ongoing connections between the old world and the new through the many faces of colonialism to attempts to re-locate the dis-located. A clear and ongoing focus for many Native writers is the complex relationship between Native cultures and the land, and the impact this has upon concepts of Indian identity. While many writers publish with small independent presses, others have taken advantage of the range of Native literature series developed by American university presses to showcase the continuing developments of the 'Native American literary renaissance'.

Significantly, some recent writers such as Sherman Alexie and David Treuer are, like Erdrich, producing powerful discussions of contemporary Native political realities that are nonetheless aimed at, and well received by, a popular Euro-American market. Given the sheer numbers of emerging Native writers, the following discussion is necessarily restricted, but the writers who are discussed are those who have been recognised by literary awards, who have produced highly unusual texts, or who have gained popular acclaim and a wide and diverse audience. Due to his popularity, his high profile and his increasing diversification into other media, the Spokane–Coeur-d'Alene writer Sherman Alexie has proved to be as popular as Erdrich (possibly more popular), with an equally powerful appeal to mainstream Euro-American readers. As a result, this chapter will focus initially on Alexie and a case study of his novel *Indian Killer* (1996), before giving an overview of a further range of important recent works and authors.

The Indian *Enfant Terrible*: Sherman Alexie (b. 1966)

One of the most exciting and prolific Native writers to emerge in recent years has been Sherman Alexie (Spokane-Coeur d'Alene), who has produced an astounding ten volumes of poetry, three collections of short stories, two novels and three screenplays since 1991, while also venturing into film direction. Alexie has exhibited not only a well-developed sense of his market and readership, but a desire and ability to move beyond the realm of literature to diversify into a range of other significant and far-reaching media such as music and film. In this context, Alexie's work is significant for its conscious attempts to reach wider audiences, and its simultaneous highly political presentation of the often bleak realities of contemporary Native American life. Crucially, what Alexie is most keen to demonstrate to this wider audience is that these realities are the direct legacy of Euro-American settlement, and of subsequent federal–Indian relationships and policies. However, Alexie's work and perhaps especially his approach are not without criticism, even from other Native writers and critics. Alexie's own tendency at times towards racial essentialism, especially in his critiques of the approaches of mixed-blood Native writers such as Momaday, Owens, Silko and Vizenor, his problematic reproduction (and so reinforcement) of long-standing Indian stereotypes, and his deliberate pursuit of a 'trickster' status has ensured a controversial reputation as the self-styled *enfant terrible* of contemporary Native literature.

Alexie's forceful public persona and his often aggressive forms of expression therefore ensure that he frequently indulges in what Arnold Krupat aptly identifies as 'smart-ass, bad-boy cracks'.[1] Ironically, this confrontational attitude is exactly what ensures Alexie's high visibility as a Native writer: his work is frequently characterised as both '"angry" and "funny"'.[2] In this context, his writings can be directly linked with the kind of gendered trickster discourse developed by Ortiz, Owens and Vizenor. Significantly, Alexie's combination of anger and humour also exposes his very well-developed understanding both of Euro-American popular culture and of the media, and his enthusiastic engagement with contemporary popular culture has been one reason for his success. The

1995 novel *Reservation Blues* is, as its title suggests, based around an Indian rock and roll band attempting to penetrate the American music industry; and Alexie has more recently exploited his high profile and skill as a public performer through stand-up comedy and, during the 1998 Initiative on Race, through a televised political dialogue with President Clinton. In promoting the Museum of Tolerance project with which he was involved in 2003, Alexie also moved briefly into popular light entertainment, appearing on the *Oprah Winfrey Show*. As a result, it can be argued that Alexie 'extends the can(n)on' in more ways than one.

Alexie's fighting spirit is perhaps the product of his own quite specific personal experience. Born in 1966 with hydrocephalus, he was not expected to survive childhood and, in spite of surgery at six months old, his best prognosis was severe mental impairment. However, Alexie successfully battled the severe seizures from which he continued to suffer throughout his childhood, and his less than active early life was compensated for by his avid reading habits, which meant that he began to achieve exceptionally well in his education. Recognising the limits of education at the local reservation school that most of his own family had attended in Spokane, Washington State, Alexie relocated to a nearby Euro-American high school in Wellpinit. Although the only Indian student, Alexie later graduated with honours and went on to attend both Gorganza and Washington State universities. It was at Washington State that Alexie began attending poetry workshops, and shortly after graduation he won two poetry fellowships, including the National Endowment for the Arts fellowship in 1992. Alexie has since proved a prolific writer, winning a range of literary awards, including the 1996 American Book Award, the 1998 Sundance Film Festival Audience Award (for his screenplay *Smoke Signals*) and, most recently, the 2005 Pushcart Prize for poetry. Significantly, Alexie proved his mainstream appeal in 1999, when he was named by *The New Yorker* as one of the top twenty American writers of the twenty-first century.

Like Ortiz, Owens and Vizenor, Alexie skilfully blends humour with anger, and his tendency for confrontation is evident throughout his work. In this context, his own definition of Native American cultural endurance is significant: 'Survival = Anger × Imagination'.[3] Indeed, the term 'Native American' is deeply problematic for Alexie, and he insists on using the term 'Indian', even though he himself often tends towards a homogenisation of Indian peoples through his failure to differentiate between the vast diversity (cultural, linguistic, geographical to name but a few) of many tribal groups. Similarly, his textual Indians are often culturally alienated and even stereotypical (John Smith in *Indian Killer* is both tragically noble and appropriately savage), yet these characters are also angrily vocal about Euro-American appropriations of Native cultures: as Owens comments, all these characters 'know how to do is to protest the existence of white people'.[4] In this context, what links Alexie's Indians together is their shared experience of colonialism, which is the direct source of his verbally aggressive textual anger that sometimes transforms into physical violence. In this context, Alexie engages clearly with Frantz Fanon's assertions that colonialism – the brutal imposition of one people's will upon another – is 'violence in its natural state' and so 'will only yield when confronted with greater violence'.[5] This is especially true of Alexie's 1996 novel *Indian Killer*, which engages both with the horror genre and with the ever-popular topic of the serial killer, and which, because of its highly political and sometimes troubling representations of both Euro-Americans and Indians, is the subject of the case study below. Significantly, Alexie's engagement, consciously or unconsciously, with the ideas expressed by postcolonial theorists such as Fanon suggests that, while he traces the effects of colonialism, his work also foregrounds a consideration of the possibilities and, more importantly, the means of de-colonisation within the United States.

Alexie first came to public attention as a poet, and his first two volumes of poetry, *The Business of Fancydancing* (1991) and *I Would Steal Horses* (1993), were published soon after his first poetry fellowships and followed by a further eight volumes: *Old Shirts and New Skins* (1993), *First Indian on the Moon* (1993), *Seven Mourning Songs for the Cedar Flute I Have Yet to Learn How to Play* (1993), *Water Flowing Home* (1996), *The Summer of Black Widows* (1996), *The Man Who Loves Salmon* (1998), *One Stick Song* (2000) and, most recently, *Dangerous Astronomy* (2005). *The Business of Fancydancing* which, in 2003, Alexie adapted and directed as a film, provides the perfect introduction to Alexie's poetic style, and is a skilful blend of poetry and short story that employs the kind of idiosyncratic visual images and concisely mocking comments for which Alexie has subsequently become well known. His consideration of the blood quantum, for example, is pertinent. Used by both federal and tribal governments to regulate tribal enrolment (i.e. the legal identification *as* Indians, which is then demonstrated through a 'certificate of degree of Indian blood'), the blood quantum is intrinsically racist in its measurement of the amount of 'Indian blood' an individual has:

the current requirements for tribal enrolment vary from tribe to tribe, from as little as one thirty-second to as much as five-eighths. The blood quantum is, as a result, an issue that deeply divides Native communities, and which Vizenor for one identifies as 'perverse arithmetics'.[6] Alexie's satirical comments in *The Business of Fancydancing* are therefore highly pertinent:

> I cut myself into sixteen equal pieces
> keep thirteen and feed the other three
> to the dogs ...
>
> It is done by blood, reservation, mathematics, fractions:
> father (full blood) + mother (5/8) = son (13/16).[7]

This early volume acts as an introduction not only to the style of Alexie's satirical anger, but also to a range of important characters, such as the traditional storyteller Thomas Builds-the-Fire, who persistently re-appears in Alexie's subsequent works.

Significantly, Alexie's poetry frequently outlines his political opinions and concerns as, for example, in the poem 'The Unauthorized Biography of Me' in *One Stick Song*, which presents his analysis of contemporary Native American literature:

> Everytime I venture into the bookstore, I find another book about Indians. There are hundreds of books about Indians published every year, yet so few are written by Indians. I gather all the books written by Indians. I discover:
> A book written by a person who identifies as mixed-blood will sell more copies than a book written by a person who identifies as strictly Indian.
> A book written by a non-Indian will sell more copies than a book written by either a mixed-blood or an Indian writer.
> Reservation Indian writers are rarely published in any form.[8]

Here, Alexie raises a range of valid points: as Vine Deloria Jnr argued succinctly in his seminal text *Custer Died For Your Sins* (1969), Indians have long been classified and discussed only by non-Indian 'experts' such as those identified by Alexie. However, Alexie's comments about Native writers are more problematic, since he appears to be imposing an alternative racial hierarchy, where 'Reservation Indians' are presented as more authentic than 'mixed blood' writers, and identified as such through their lack of popular appeal: 'they are rarely published'. Such a suggestion thus ironically comments on Alexie's own highly popular status: alongside Erdrich, he is one of very few Native writers to be published in the United Kingdom in a British imprint. Perhaps most problematic is Alexie's emphasis upon identification as solely or 'strictly Indian', which imposes essentialist ideas of racial exclusivity upon those Native writers who are a product of both their Indian *and* their Euro-American ancestry: evident, for example, in the works of writers such as Silko, Owens, Vizenor and Erdrich. This is clearly not a viewpoint that Alexie promotes in all of his works – for instance, many of his poems and stories speak of inter-racial relationships and the internal conflicts of a mixed heritage – and it can be argued, as Krupat and Elliott suggest, that Alexie is thus engaging, albeit in 'contradictory ways', with 'the legacy of racism in the United States'.[9] Alexie's complicated racial dialogues are therefore significant both for the controversy and for the debate they generate, and, in this context, they have proven significant for raising popular Euro-American awareness of ongoing racial issues.

Regardless of these internal contradictions and external controversies, Alexie's work is nonetheless notable for its sheer passion, which emerges both in the lyricism of his language that is often hauntingly beautiful, and in his outspoken and pointed critiques of Euro-America. Indeed, the power of Alexie's writing often derives from the simultaneous presence and unusual combination of poetic lyricism and satirical, often deeply comical, anger. In this context, Alexie clearly enters into a dialogue with ongoing literary strategies evident in Native men's writing. Alexie's style is highly effective for drawing attention to the contemporary socio-cultural and political situation for Native American peoples, and for publicising that situation to an ever-increasing audience. This is evident in all three of his short story collections: *The Lone Ranger and Tonto Fistfight in Heaven* (1993), *The Toughest Indian in the World* (2000) and *Ten Little Indians* (2003). As its title suggests, *The Lone Ranger and Tonto Fistfight in Heaven* is an analysis of the Euro-American and Indian relationship, especially within the context of popular culture. The text, therefore, contests a range of popular Indian stereotypes through representations of a range of Indians on the Spokane Reservation. From this specific geo-cultural location, Alexie points to the distinct tensions between traditional Native worldviews and the incursions being made by contemporary Euro-American culture, and it is pertinent that the traditional storyteller, Thomas Builds-the-Fire, is persistently ignored by his fellow Spokane. Yet the story of Thomas's 'trial' is the focal point of the text, where Alexie traces the connections between historical events and contemporary Indian lives, and reiterates the power of story and story-telling within a fiercely funny tale. Opening with an inter-textual reference to Franz Kafka's Joseph K., Thomas is on trial for his 'extreme need to tell the truth' and his threats to 'make significant changes' to 'the tribal vision'.[10] Charged in the late twentieth century with a murder committed in 1858, Thomas's testimony both traces the legacy of federal–Indian relations, and re-creates nineteenth-century tribal (hi)story. This finally ensures he has an Indian audience who repeatedly emphasise that '"we're all listening"'.[11] In this way, Alexie demonstrates the ongoing efficacy of the oral tradition, and the power that stories, and histories, continue to hold. This analysis is extended in both *The Toughest Indian in the World* and *Ten Little Indians* to consider a range of 'indiannesses', from the reservation to urban relocation, and from the unemployed to the professional, to paint often painfully honest pictures of contemporary Native lives through a combination of sharp socio-political commentary and wry humour.

This wry humour is equally evident in Alexie's novels and, perhaps especially, in his film work, which has ensured that his ideas and satirical approach have been broadcast to as wide an audience as possible. The 1995 novel *Reservation Blues* is significant not only for the irrepressible comedy that runs throughout, but for its eclectic blend of diverse elements from popular Euro-American culture. Like Vizenor, Alexie confuses the boundaries between reality and fiction through his incorporation of actual historical figures, and the text begins with the arrival of the Blues musician Robert Johnson on the Spokane Reservation. Playing on the long-standing legend that Johnson sold his soul to the devil to gain his power to play guitar, Alexie depicts Johnson passing both guitar and devilish debt over to Coyote Springs, a group of Spokane musicians headed by Thomas Builds-the-Fire. Alexie's subsequent representation of the ways in which Coyote Springs are fêted and then abandoned by Euro-American record producers provides an analysis not only of the ongoing commodification and appropriation of Native culture within America, but also of the myriad ways in which contemporary Indians can sell their souls. Ironically, this very Indian commodification is, nonetheless, what Alexie himself has tapped into in his more recent extra-textual experiments, for example in music (Alexie has since released a music soundtrack for *Reservation Blues* and for a number of his films) and in film, where he has identified his biggest audience. Given the history of Native American representations by Hollywood, and the range of powerful images that have perpetuated long-standing Indian stereotypes for generations of Euro-Americans, film is perhaps the most far-reaching medium through which to challenge formulaic, limited and limiting representations.

Alexie's venture into screenwriting and film direction demonstrates his understanding both of his audience and of his potential audience: film is by far the best medium through which to reach the largest possible numbers, and to challenge their assumptions. In a country such as the US, which has film and the film industry at its cultural centre, the move is highly astute. Alexie's venture into film is especially significant, as his collaboration with the Cheyenne-Arapaho director Chris Eyre on *Smoke Signals* marks the first solely Native film production: with Indian writers, producers and directors, and an almost entirely Indian cast. Adapted from the short story 'This is What it Means to Say Phoenix, Arizona' in *The Lone Ranger and Tonto Fistfight in Heaven*, *Smoke Signals* was made on a tiny budget financed by an independent production company. Premiering at the Sundance Film Festival in 1998, *Smoke Signals* won not only the Audience Award but also the Filmmakers Trophy, attracting the wider attention of the film industry. This resulted in another first: a national distribution deal with Miramax Films, and *Smoke Signals* has since been screened internationally. The film is also significant for the sheer buoyancy of its humour, even when dealing with reservation poverty, alcoholism, broken families, domestic violence and death. In this sense Alexie was, as Jacqueline Kilpatrick comments, not only 'candid about the mass audience' he aimed to attract, but also concerned with '[m]aking it real' in the context of contemporary Indian experiences.[12]

Re-creating yet subverting the typical American road trip movie, Alexie's screenplay depicts reservation cars that are stuck in reverse, Indians taking the bus for their road trip because they have no car, and songs devoted to 'John Wayne's teeth', which are deeply suspicious to the Indians because Wayne never smiles and so his teeth are never seen. Significantly, given its subsequent national distribution, *Smoke Signals* makes comic yet pointed attacks on Indian stereotypes, allowing the 'real' Indian characters to shine through in all of their idiosyncratic or even tarnished glory. Key to this is Alexie's representation of Thomas Builds-the-Fire as a traditional storyteller, where his non-acceptance by the contemporary Indians around him is understandable for a Euro-

American audience, as is his eventual cultural re-integration as his story-telling power is gradually proven. The film is thus a major achievement, with a warmth and humour that is engaging and poignant. Following on from this success, and perhaps engaging with some criticisms that *Smoke Signals* could have been a less popular and more overtly Indian product, Alexie has subsequently written two further screenplays: *The Business of Fancydancing* (2002), which was adapted from the collection of the same name and which Alexie also directed, and *49?* (2003). Both films have a much clearer focus on Indian culture. *The Business of Fancydancing* provides a detailed analysis of identity through Alexie's semi-autobiographical focus on a successful Indian writer within an urban location who must negotiate not only his own cultural identity but accusations that he has sold out. Emphatically non-linear and poetic, the film is vastly different to the media-savvy *Smoke Signals*, and the action is punctuated by traditional dance performances that allow a constant refocus not just upon cultural meaning but upon cultural performance. Alexie's most recent film, *49?*, is a documentary that analyses the Indian music style of the '49'. Given this lesser focus on a mainstream Euro-American audience, both films have had less commercial success. However, both have ironically attracted wider critical attention and acclaim. Alexie is currently working on screenplays for both *Reservation Blues* and *Indian Killer*.

Indian Killer (1996)

Alexie's second novel, *Indian Killer* is both complex and problematic in its analysis of the ongoing legacy of racism in the US. While attempting to challenge Euro-American preconceptions, the text also manages to reinforce a range of damaging Indian stereotypes. As its title suggests, the story revolves around a serial killer (the killer remains both nameless and genderless) on the loose in Seattle, who scalps 'his' randomly chosen white male victims and leaves two owl feathers on the bodies. Yet even within the title ambiguity is immediately evident: is this a killer of Indians, or a killer who *is* Indian? Indeed, this ambiguity is commented on within the text by the Spokane student Marie Polatkin: '"calling him the Indian Killer doesn't make any sense, does it? If it was an Indian doing the killing, then wouldn't he be called the Killer Indian? I mean, Custer was an Indian killer, not a killer Indian."'.[13] While a 'killer of Indians' might aptly reflect numerous events of American history that demonstrate powerful forms of ongoing racism, a 'killer who is Indian' is, significantly, a better reflection of what is, within the text, a growing Indian fury at both this history and its legacies. Indeed, the text explores an entire spectrum of rage and racism, deriving from both Euro-Americans and Indians. In part, both rage and racism emerge from the deep sense of alienation within the text. A diverse number of Indians have relocated to the city and appear either as struggling university students or, due to an inability to return home that is often financial or emotional, end up homeless on the city streets. By contrast, a range of Euro-Americans are interpreted, by the Indian characters and by the killer, as self-alienated either through an arrogant individualism and inflated sense of self worth, or through a sense of guilt over ongoing white–Indian relations or a fascination that manifests itself through cultural appropriation. Significantly, this alienation is exposed as the direct result of colonisation with, as Fanon has suggested, both rage and racism identified as a normal, perhaps even necessary, product of any struggle for decolonisation.

The killer is very carefully anonymised and de-gendered within the text, and this androgynous anonymity is evident within the testimony of the young kidnap victim Mark Jones, whom the killer unexpectedly returns alive to his parents. Mark, to the bewilderment of those questioning him, persistently refers to the killer as 'it', noting that '"It was a bird that was there ... It could fly, I bet"'.[14] Connected within the text to a range of Native beliefs that identify owls as harbingers of death, the killer is persistently surrounded by owls and leaves two crossed owl feathers on his victims' chests. In this context, the narrative is framed by opening and closing chapters entitled 'Mythology' and 'A Creation Story', where Alexie very carefully emphasises not only the subsequent Indian cultural dis-location within the text, but also the wide applicability of this dis-location to unspecified numbers of Native peoples. Clearly refusing geo-cultural specificities in an attempt to present the scale of colonialism's impact, the opening and closing action is set '[o]n this reservation or that reservation. Any reservation, a particular reservation'.[15] In both these opening and closing chapters, Alexie engages with the kinds of evil that is discussed in Silko's *Ceremony* and Owens' *Bone Game*. Much like the characters within *Bone Game*, those of *Indian Killer* have some clear choices to make, yet in contrast to the other writings discussed so far, Alexie's urban characters are perhaps too alienated and dis-located for such choices to sufficiently overcome the rage and racism that saturates the text. With little sense of cultural identity or wider community within the text, evil is thus exposed as exceptionally resilient.

In this context, the killings are merely a catalyst for powerful and long-standing racial tensions between Indian and white communities and individuals to re-emerge, and profound racial hatred is fed not only by cultural alienation but also by ongoing persistent failures in inter-cultural negotiation and mediation. There is, in this sense, little if any useful or significant interaction between Indian and white characters, who are almost entirely racially and culturally segregated within the text. While this is clearly a product of federal–Indian relations, it is also a clear choice made by the textual characters. In this context, Alexie's text is somewhat problematic due to its apparent complicity with the widespread racial essentialism that is exhibited. This racial essentialism can be partially traced to the cultural hybridity of the majority of the principal textual characters, which is the primary cause of their personal alienation and by which they are all deeply disturbed and discomfited. This is especially evident in the three Native characters, John Smith, Marie Polatkin and Reggie Polatkin (Marie's cousin), all of whom express not only deep hostility towards Euro-Americans at various points within the text, but also very real desires 'to kill a white man'.[16]

John Smith's alienation is embodied within his extremely inappropriate name, which is paradoxically both highly specific (in its referencing of the historical figure 'saved' by Pocahontas) and profoundly indistinct (it is an amalgam of two of the most unexceptional names in the English language). In this context John is, even at the simplest level of his name, almost completely undefined. Adopted at birth by white parents, Olivia and Daniel Smith, John's subsequent schizophrenia as an adult is linked by Alexie to his cultural dis-location: he has no knowledge of his Indian background. Although Olivia and Daniel attempt to expose John to elements of a Native heritage, spending 'hours in the library' on 'research', taking him to powwows, and even finding an Indian Jesuit priest (Father Duncan) to baptise him,[17] John emerges nonetheless with a real sense of cultural fracture. In accord with critiques of the nineteenth-century 'friends of the Indian' who did more harm than good, the text suggests that this is partially due to the Smiths' own good intentions that merely serve to compound John's sense of cultural loss.

In this context, Alexie's text engages with federal Indian policies to provide a highly pertinent analysis of the ways in which Euro-American adoption of Indian children have worked alongside education programmes to play a key role in the assimilation process. The imposition of Euro-American Christian values upon Native communities meant that, until the late 1970s, large numbers of Native children were removed from their parents. This was especially true, as in John's case, for unmarried teenage mothers whose children were often forcibly removed. In spite of the numbers affected, matters remained unresolved until the 1978 Indian Child Welfare Act, which outlawed the previously common practice of enforced adoption without parental consent or knowledge, and recognised the widespread problem of cultural dis-location. In spite of changes to the law, the Act has been undermined since 1996 by attempts to make it easier for Euro-American families to adopt Native children (largely for the reasons that Alexie cites in the text: 'there were simply not enough white babies to go around'[18]), and a key problem seems to be the continued pressurisation of Indian communities by Euro-American authorities (i.e. social workers, doctors, missionaries, priests), who remain convinced of the superiority of Euro-American cultural concepts.

Alexie's text clearly engages with this unpleasant history through John, who is quite literally caught between cultures, knowing that he belongs to neither. His desire for some kind of cultural heritage is compounded by his desire as an adoptee to know the circumstances of his birth and the identity of his parents. His inability to know either – the 'adoption agency refused to divulge John's tribal affiliation and sealed all of his birth records' – ensures that he is perpetually angry and 'confused'.[19] As a result, John persistently and painstakingly re-creates an Indian life and family for himself, even while he spends his childhood 'rubb[ing] at his face, wanting to rub the brown away' so he can 'look like his parents'.[20] Indeed, John's alienation is intensified by his associations with Father Duncan who, even as a child, he recognises as equally culturally dis-located. Asked questions by John about the murder of Jesuits by Indians, 'Duncan was afraid to answer the question. As a Jesuit, he knew those priests were martyred just like Jesus. As a Spokane, he knew those Jesuits deserved to die for their crimes against Indians'.[21] Even to the child John, it is palpably clear that Duncan cannot reconcile his identity as a Spokane priest with his knowledge of brutal Catholic oppression of Native Americans. Once Duncan 'los[es] his faith in God', his removal 'from active duty' to a retreat in Arizona ends with his unsolved disappearance 'into the desert'.[22] John's close identification with Father Duncan as another cultural hybrid guarantees that this episode has a profound impact on John's life, and his inability to decipher the motives for Duncan's apparent suicide proves crucial to John's own eventual suicide, as he continues to search both for Duncan and for answers to his disappearance.

As a result both of Euro-American misconceptions of Indians and of this misguided connection with the damaged Father Duncan, John's life is full of increasing anger and rage which he battles to control. As an adult, John's 'anger [had] increased in intensity and frequency'[23] to such an extent that he has become mentally ill, experiencing his rage as an all-encompassing physical sensation:

> He felt the heat build in his stomach, rise through his back, and fill his head. It started that way. The heat came first, followed quickly by the music. A slow hum. A quiet drum. Then a symphony crashing through his spinal column.[24]

John's problems are magnified by his physical appearance: he is so emphatically Indian that 'he looked like some cinematic warrior, and constantly intimidated people with his presence'.[25] Given that John is only 'Indian in the most generic sense',[26] the attention that he attracts both from other Indians and from Euro-Americans deeply discomfits him. His growing identification with Father Duncan throughout the text indicates the extent of John's own increasing cultural dis-location. John's eventual identification as the Indian Killer, following his abduction of the thriller writer and wannabe Indian Jack Wilson and John's subsequent suicide, is perhaps inevitable given his increasing mental disintegration and dis-connection throughout the text. As a character, therefore, John somewhat problematically tends to re-create and reinforce established Euro-American Indian stereotypes.

Yet John's cultural dis-location is also experienced to varying degrees by Reggie and Marie Polatkin. As a mixed blood, Reggie is the most culturally alienated of the two, having been raised by an Indian-hating Euro-American father, Bird Lawrence. Persistently beaten by Bird, who 'hated hostile Indians',[27] Reggie is taught a specifically Euro-American version of federal Indian history where loyalty to the nation is paramount and any disloyalty justifiably punished with violence. As a result, Reggie's belief that he can clearly separate and differentiate between his dual identities – the anachronistic concept 'that he was successful because of his father's white blood, and that his Indian mother's blood was to blame for all his failures'[28] – is disastrously alienating and ultimately self-defeating, while also illustrating the alarming longevity of nineteenth-century racial understandings. The outcome of this cultural alienation is evident: having refused to learn anything about Spokane culture, '[h]e'd buried his Indian identity so successfully that he'd become invisible'.[29] Reggie's successful attempts to 'play Indian' for his university tutor Dr Clarence Mather are significant as a means by which he can 'earn the respect of white men'.[30] While Reggie 'for the first time in his life ... felt as if being Indian meant something', Mather uses Reggie's cultural identity as 'means of entry' into the local Indian community.[31] Reggie's subsequent falling out with Mather (a dispute over cultural interpretations of anthropological attitudes to Native data) and his expulsion from the university directly feeds Reggie's own rage and increasing racism. However, the reasons for Reggie's expulsion – his attempts to ensure that recordings of Spokane oral stories are erased – sit uneasily alongside his persistent characterisation as dis-located from, and even uncaring about, his Spokane community.

Unlike her cousin, Marie Polatkin comes from a traditional Indian home, yet is equally dis-located due to her parents' refusal to teach her the Spokane language or about Spokane culture because 'it would be of no use to her in the world outside the reservation'.[32] Marie is, therefore, equally culturally dis-located, achieving a university scholarship as a means of 'escape', and rarely visiting the home where 'she felt like a stranger'.[33] Due to perceived differences from other Native children, Marie was also bullied at the reservation school, and as a child she 'wanted to be white' so much that she had 'rubbed her face with a piece of her dad's sandpaper, trying to get rid of her colour'.[34] Given this personal context, Marie's subsequent representation at university as a defender (often self-represented as the *sole* defender) of authentic indianness – through her desire to 'challenge [the white] Mather's role as the official dispenser of "Indian education" at the University',[35] and her critique of mixed-blood Native writers as 'pretend Indians' who 'never admitted that their pale skin was a luxury'[36] – is both deeply ironic and somewhat contradictory.

This tendency towards an essentialised representation of racial/ cultural identity is equally evident within the Euro-American textual characters, to the extent that they often appear as two dimensional caricatures. Nonetheless, what is significant about the majority of the Euro-American characters – Jack Wilson, Dr Clarence Mather, David Rogers – is their equal sense of cultural alienation. The ex-cop and wannabe Indian Jack Wilson[37] is a clear example. Orphaned and raised in a series of brutal foster homes, Wilson, much like John Smith, creates a family background for himself: he claims to be Shilshomish and descended from the tribal leader Red Fox. While this is a not unusual form of romantic escapism during childhood, Wilson's continuation of these claims into adulthood ensures that he is a figure of fun for Indians and colleagues alike. More problematically, this cultural appropriation moves into the realm of fraud when Wilson begins to profit financially from his claims through his role as a mystery writer and his creation of the Indian private eye Aristotle Little Hawk. Wilson's romantic view of Aristotle as a noble savage, mystically communing with nature and his ancestors to solve his cases as the 'the very last Shilshomish Indian',[38] reproduces static and long-established Euro-American stereotypes. Alexie's demonstration of this within the text, through Wilson's recognition of the deeply alienated John as a startlingly accurate physical representation of Aristotle, also paradoxically emphasises John's own static and stereotypical representation within the text.

Based on the kinds of Euro-American anthropologists critiqued by Vine Deloria in the late 1960s, Dr Clarence Mather[39] is a 'supposed lover of Indians, or perhaps his idea of Indians', whose reading list for his class on Native American literature is, to Marie's mind, so flawed that 'Marie knew that Dr Mather was full of shit'.[40] With the figure of Mather, a self-important and self-serving individual devoted to damaging cultural appropriations, Alexie engages with the kinds of critiques of academia evident within Walters' *Ghost Singer*, to raise a range of highly pertinent issues demanding further debate. Indeed, Mather's condescending attitude towards Marie mockingly apes the entrenched attitudes within the federal Indian education programmes: 'I'm trying to present a positive portrait of Indian peoples, of your people. Of you. ... Don't you understand I'm on your side?'[41] And Marie's challenges make some significant points, including the fact that Mather's 'Native' literature course includes a range of disputed texts written by Euro-Americans masquerading as Indians which, while they appropriate Native cultures, more damagingly also appropriate the economic benefits that would otherwise go to actual Indian writers. However, Alexie's less than sympathetic portrayal of Marie's motives and motivations undermines and complicates this interpretation: according to her own admission, Marie 'felt compelled to challenge' Mather to the point of 'harass[ment]' because her own survival depends on 'conflict'.[42]

This complex and paradoxical representation is equally evident in the depiction of the quiet and bookish student David Rogers, who falls victim to robbers who kill him for his casino winnings. Failing to fit in with his ultra-macho father and elder brother Aaron, David's fear of guns is accompanied by his discomfort at shooting at an Indian family digging for camus roots on the family farm and his active prevention of Aaron's attempt to fire at the Indians rather than over their heads; and is compounded by his refusal to acknowledge his father's assertion that 'Indian is Indian' through his recognition that 'they were kids ... [a]nd an old woman'.[43] In this context, David only takes Mather's Native American literature class out of 'a specific sense of guilt and a vague curiosity' with a culture that he defines as 'exotic'.[44] All three characters tend to the two-dimensional, which undermines their efficacy in the roles that Alexie creates for them. Most problematically, David's abduction from a tribal casino and subsequent death (suspected to be Indian-related but actually committed by two Euro-Americans) is presented in part as a result of his own general good will and naivety.

In this context, the only characters to survive are those who have little good will, Euro-American and Indian alike. David's death is used both by his brother Aaron and by the right-wing radio host Truck Schultz to promote inter-racial hatred and violence. In this sense, Truck Schultz is such a dangerously influential figure that, within the textual power hierarchy, he is comparable to the figure of the Indian Killer. Schultz's broadcasts represent incitements to racial hatred: having denounced the killing of white men who were 'guilty [only] of the crime of being white', Schultz vilifies Indians because 'despite all th[e] special advantages [guaranteed by treaty rights], Indians still live ... in filth' due, apparently, to the fact that they 'cannot take care of themselves'.[45] Ignoring the role played by enforced assimilation, Schultz declares that Indian separatism is the cause of Indian poverty and alienation, and his conclusion is especially pertinent in its reflection of the paternalism of the federal government: 'what happens to a child that is given everything he wants? That child becomes an aggressive, domineering brat'.[46] Alexie's portrayal of Schultz is particularly powerful, with his power emerging from his ability to provoke rage and racism in others. This rage and racism manifests itself as brutal racial violence, and is remarkably wide-ranging as gangs of Euro-Americans and Indians make random attacks on a range of unlucky individuals.

In revenge for David's death – ('payback, motherfucker, payback!'[47]) – and to assuage his own feelings of guilt, Aaron Rogers and two white accomplices engage in a series of attacks on a range of helpless and

sometimes elderly homeless Indians, whose viciousness is matched only
by the attack that Reggie Polatkin and his Indian accomplices launch on
a randomly chosen white man. Reggie's violence is especially extreme,
as he reproduces the violence he experienced as a child from his father
(complete with history lessons) and tapes his attempt to rip out his
victim's eyes: '[he] forced his thumbs into the white man's eyes. The
white man screamed as Reggie dug into his eyes, searching for whatever
existed behind them. The white man fainted from shock and pain'.[48]
While Reggie's violence emulates that of the Indian Killer who eats one
of his victim's hearts, it also evolves into something more when Reggie's
own cultural dis-location ensures that his racial hatred is effectively
indiscriminate and he launches an attack on another Indian: John. The
textual hatred becomes palpable, and John himself acts as a barometer to
identify its growing presence:

> All the anger in the world had come to my house. It's there in my
> closet. In my refrigerator. In the water. In the sheets. It's in my clothes.
> Can you smell it? I can never run away from it. It's in my hair. I can
> feel it between my teeth. Can you taste it? I hear it all the time.[49]

Alexie's text is a powerful snapshot of a deeply alienated urban Indian
culture, and a pertinent analysis of rage and racism in the contemporary
United States: at the close of the text, the Indian Killer remains both at
large and unidentified. Alexie's vigorous depictions of the types of Euro-
American attitudes that continue to inflict harm on Indian communities
provide concise, if controversial, starting points for reader debate, and
work well to expose his reader's own inbuilt assumptions and preconceptions. Indeed, Alexie's instinctive understanding of Euro-American
markets has ensured his choice of genre is both highly popular and likely
to reach the widest possible market. However, it is in this final context
that Alexie's text becomes problematic, as his attempts to deconstruct
established Indian stereotypes paradoxically result in their reiteration
and reinforcement. In this context, Euro-American readers emerge
'with a sense ... that no one is really to blame but the Indians, no matter
how loudly the author shouts his anger'.[50] Indeed, Alexie's text is most
problematic in its refusal or inability to present actual Indian communities or political groups as offering any kind of practical resistance.
Krupat's conclusion is therefore perhaps the most pertinent: although
Alexie raises numerous highly relevant political points, the text fails to
provide 'even a tentative resolution of the important issues it raises'.[51]

As a result, Alexie's vision is, ultimately, unremittingly bleak for both Native American and Euro-America.

New Directions in Native Writing

Alexie's profound popular success builds upon that of Erdrich, and both have been highly influential in encouraging further Indian writers to publish. While Alexie and Erdrich's success has ensured the continuance of dedicated Indian literature series with university presses due to a wider popularity of Native writing, it has also been responsible for attracting the attention and interest of mainstream publishers interested in the demands of the popular market. Recent Native writers have therefore been presented with a range of choices regarding where to publish which, in turn, has influenced the kinds of literary strategies that are adopted. My subsequent discussion provides a brief overview of these choices, examining one mainstream popular approach, before turning to the gender interests, approaches and strategies evident in a range of recent Native writings.

One of the most significant writers to emerge in recent times, certainly in terms of gaining a popular audience and widespread critical attention, has been David Treuer (Ojibwe). Born in 1971, Treuer was raised on the Leech Lake Reservation in northern Minnesota, and is the son of a Holocaust survivor and a tribal judge. Graduating from Princeton in anthropology and creative writing, Treuer currently teaches English at the University of Minnesota and is active in work to maintain the Ojibwe language. Treuer has published two novels, with a third novel (*The Translation of Dr Apelles*) plus a 'users manual' for Native American fiction published in 2006, and his work has won a range of prizes including, in 1996, the Minnesota Book award and the Pushcart Prize. Treuer's work is significant in part for its wide distribution: like Erdrich and Alexie, Treuer has published with a mainstream publisher and so attracts a wide Euro-American audience. However, Treuer's work is equally important for the complex socio-cultural and political issues that he discusses. For instance, his first novel, *Little* (1995), opens in a small reservation community called Poverty where '[t]he grave we dug for my brother Little remained empty even after we filled it back in'.[52] Tracing the mystery of Little's death, Treuer's novel ensures that the re-creation of Little's story is also the re-creation of the history of Poverty and its inhabitants, thus presenting a detailed and terse picture of Indian life across three generations. Treuer's second novel, *The Hiawatha* (1999), focuses on an urban setting, commenting on the federal relocation initiatives of the 1960s. Textual events revolve around a family attempting to come to terms with one son killing another under the influence of alcohol and so, significantly, comment not only on the devastating effects of alcohol within Native communities but the often concomitant familial violence. Treuer's third novel will explore Native translations of Native texts, and so looks set to provide a timely consideration of the power of language.

Treuer's strategy continues a long tradition within Native writing that taps into the ongoing popular appeal of Native cultures for a Euro-American readership. Significantly, by making a clear intervention into the Euro-American literary market, it is also Treuer's aim (as a professor of English literature) to emphasise the literary 'value' of contemporary Native writing, the subject both of his recent critical work and of some heated debate within Euro-American literary criticism.[53] While concepts of literary value are clearly highly significant, and represent one means by which Native literature can be excluded from mainstream literary study, it is of less importance in other recent Native writings which emphasise the ongoing political debates and current realities of Native lives. While many recent writers discuss very similar topics – for example, the links between land and Native identity is a constant presence in all of the subsequent texts that I analyse – there seems, as with the previous writers under discussion, to be a distinct gender divide with regard to literary strategy. As a result, a range of recent Native texts have adopted gendered approaches in their negotiations with Euro-American perceptions and in their translations of Native cultures, which can be interpreted in light of the kinds of popular Euro-American audiences that Native writers attract. The following discussion, therefore, emphasises gender and gendered strategies.

Recent Writing by Native Men

Like Ortiz, Owens, Vizenor and Alexie, many recent Native men writers have turned to specific literary genres or strategies to locate their work, both within Native cultures and for a more mainstream Euro-American readership. Continuing Native interventions into popular horror and thriller genres, one unusual recent writer has been Aaron Carr (Navajo-Laguna Pueblo), whose first novel, *Eye Killers* (1995), is a fascinating intervention into the European gothic tradition. Born in 1963, Carr is primarily a film-maker, having made a range of documentaries about contemporary Native life, including *A Laguna Woman* (1987) detailing the life of his grandmother, and *States of Being* (1995), which discussed the role of identity in the work of Native writers including Louis Owens. In 1995, Carr also produced the documentary *War Code: Navajo*, an analysis of the Navajo code talkers of World War Two, directed by his film-maker mother Lena. This cinematic background not only influences Carr's subject material (for example, his interest in vampire films), but also suffuses his novel with highly cinematic visual imagery, additionally linking him directly with the kinds of extra-textual interventions being very successfully made by Alexie. What makes Carr's text significant is his skill in blending European gothic with Native cultural traditions, and in exposing a range of ongoing oppressions – for example, resource exploitation in the American southwest – through the deployment of the vampire figure, who makes clear connections between the 'Stench of petroleum waste. And the timorous scent of blood'.[54] Carr's European and Euro-American vampires are truly monstrous, with 'long teeth like steel spikes' and a 'putrified stink' of decomposition.[55] Carr's comparison of the vampire with the Navajo 'skinwalker' prefigures the textual climax where, significantly, the vampires can only be overcome by a necessarily hybrid community, Native and Euro-American, who through diverse cultural traditions can fully identify and thus eliminate the vampiric threat. Thus Navajo ritual prayer sticks become most effective when used within a European tradition, as stakes. In this sense, Carr's text is interesting for the ways in which he demonstrates the power of a collective and pan-ethnic memory as an effective form of re-integration and healing.

This emphasis upon corporate industry in the southwest clearly draws upon Ortiz's earlier ecocritical discussions of culture–nature interactions, and makes specific links between industrial and corporate practices and their profound human results. This is also a key feature of the works of two recent Navajo writers, Irvin Morris and Sherwin Bitsui, who empha-sise the damaging and inter-related activities of science, technology and industry, all of which are significant for their identification within mainstream Euro-American society primarily as male concerns or entities. Like Tapahonso, Morris and Bitsui both derive from a very traditional Navajo background which ensures that their texts present Navajo cultural ideas both through cultural translation and through their textual form, which echoes oral storytelling traditions.

Morris's semi-autobiographical multi-genre volume *From the Glittering World: a Navajo Story* was published in 1997. Born in 1958, little is publicly known about Morris biographically except for his recent academic career. Having completed an MFA in creative writing at Cornell, Morris subsequently taught at the State University of New York (where he completed his PhD) and, more recently, at the University of Arizona. Morris currently teaches at the Diné College in Shiprock, New Mexico. *From the Glittering World* is interesting for its combination of autobiographical material with a wider consideration of communal story and history, and for Morris's clear juxtaposition of his experiences living both within the Navajo Nation and in the emphatically Euro-American world of Los Angeles. Significantly, Morris's comparisons expose Euro-America's tendency to use technology to 'conque[r]' the land, through an inability to see the earth as 'a living, sacred entity'.[56] Morris's considerations of environmental abuse within the southwest, of the 'oil refineries, abandoned uranium mines, natural gas wells' that litter the landscape,[57] are subsequently identified as potentially fleeting through a comparison with long-established Navajo cultural interactions with the land. Thus the landscape 'is ripe with the stories of my people',[58] whose lives, joys, sufferings and deaths are firmly located within the very soil. As a result, Morris's text is a fascinating analysis of Navajo identity in the late twentieth century, which is clearly in constant negotiation both with the historical forces of events such as the Navajo Long Walk of 1864 (where Morris's nineteenth-century narrator is emphatic that 'I shall tell my children about the horror, and they shall tell their children. We cannot ever forget what happened ... we must remember every detail'[59]), and with contemporary recolonisation by the energy multinationals.

This concern with the connections between culture and nature, and with the damaging activities of the industry, is also the focus of Sherwin Bitsui's work. Born in 1975 in Fort Defiance, Arizona, Bitsui is a graduate of the Institute of American Indian Arts in Santa Fe and has already won awards including the 1999 Truman Capote Creative Writing Fellowship and the 2002 University of Arizona Academy of American Poets Student Poetry Award. In 2003, Bitsui published his first volume of poetry, *Shapeshift*, which juxtaposes often conflicting Euro-American and Native understandings of human and natural worlds. Bitsui's focus is evident in his opening lines: '[f]ourteen ninety-something,/ *something* happened'.[60] Here, Bitsui traces the 'something' that happened through the 'needle' that silences individuals by 'writ[ing] over their lips with thread', and the '[p]ioneers [that] wanted in'.[61] Ultimately, Bitsui connects this directly to the contemporary situation in the American southwest, and his consideration of colonisation is illustrated by 'the ends of our feet [that] are yellowed to uranium at the edge of fear'.[62] In 'The Northern Sun', his response to the 'white anthropologist' who asks why 'your people speak like weeping Mongolians' is both beautifully constructed and highly telling: 'Perhaps it is because we have been staring at airplanes too long ... that our throats have been turned into hollowed out spider-legs extending over the rough wings of a salivating mouth'.[63] The following verses offer stark juxtapositions of modern American and traditional Navajo worldviews: '[t]he cab driver asked if I was American Indian. I said, *No, I'm of the Bitter Water People'*.[64] The final poem, 'Chrysalis', explores the ways in which the 'ash' of modern American and Native American existence is transformed as 'we finally become mountains'.[65] Significantly, this 'is not about sadness', nor 'about the rejection of our skin', but a celebration of Native voice: that the 'linguist' who 'runs his hands up the length of our tongues' is 'perplexed that we even have a tongue at all'.[66] Indeed, Bitsui's imagery can be interpreted as an illustration of the profound political and physical silencing of Native men's voices in recent years.

Recent Writing by Native Women

By comparison, Native women have very successfully entered into a dialogue with a range of external markets, especially the wide feminist debates that ensure a buoyant market for discussions of ethnicity, gender and sexuality. As a result, recent writings by Native women are marked by their emphatic political discussions, and their assertions not only of Indian presence but of Indian agency. In this context, one significant recent voice is Deborah Miranda, whose work is marked by her analysis of mixed blood, of lesbian or 'two spirit' sexuality, and avowed refusal to indulge in racial essentialism. Born c. 1961 in Los Angeles, Miranda's cultural background is a blend of Esselen, Chumash, French and Jewish, and she has worked extensively with her parents to re-establish their shared tribal heritages. Miranda was nominated for the Pushcart Prize in 1994, and won the First Book Award in 1997 from the Native Writers Circle of the Americas for her poetry collection, *Indian Cartography*. Miranda currently teaches at the Washington and Lee University, Virginia, and recently published another poetry volume, *The Zen of La Llorona* (2005). As her title *Indian Cartography* suggests, Miranda's volume provides an effective remapping of America's west coast to emphasise an ongoing Native presence in California where, to cite

Miranda's own experience, the majority of Americans, both Native and non-Native, assume 'all those Indians died'.[67] For Miranda, to reiterate the survival of Californian Indians means that 'the air becomes electric' as '[w]e disturb the façade of conquest' within which '[o]ur demise was legally and officially planned [and] executed'.[68] Miranda's volume thus demonstrates an emphatic presence, through poems such as 'The Territory of Love', which reconsiders the conquest of the Americas in terms of desire: 'the secret passage to/cities of gold' populated by 'natives/ sauntering along naked' and 'voices full of longing' that reflect 'your own fierce desire to/enter this land'.[69] Significantly, the Territory of Love engages directly with the kinds of debates on relationships and relatedness evident in Erdrich's *Love Medicine*. In this context, the Territory of Love 'does not take kindly to being/colonized'.[70] Through repeated reiterations of Native presence in poems such as 'Without History', 'Indian Cartography' and 'After Colonization', Miranda produces valuable dialogues that, as she aptly comments, 'testify to a miracle: *Here we are, here we are, here we are*'.[71]

This emphasis upon Native presence is equally evident in the work of Janet McAdams. Of mixed Creek, Scottish and Irish ancestry, McAdams was born in Alabama, and gained an MFA in creative writing from the University of Alabama and a PhD in comparative literature from Emory College. McAdams has taught at the universities of Alabama and Oklahoma, and currently teaches at Kenyon College, Ohio, where she is the Robert P. Hubbard Professor of Poetry. McAdams' work has been well received, and she was awarded the 1999 First Book Award from the Native Writers Circle of the Americas for her poetry collection *The Island of Lost Luggage*, for which she also won the 2001 American Book Award. With subtitles such as 'The Thousand-Year War' and 'A Map of the Twentieth Century', *The Island of Lost Luggage* makes clear connections between various forms of imperial aggression as McAdams charts 'the disappeared, the lost children, the Earharts/of modern life' whose 'bad luck' it is 'to die in the cold/wars of certain nations'.[72] Blending highly personal poetry with deeply political commentary, McAdams' verse 'lick[s] the salt from the long wound of history'.[73] The scope of the subject matter is vast, ranging from an engagement with destructive forms of modern warfare to a consideration of the ways in which contemporary societies engage with and dominate the natural world. Throughout, our own individual and collective complicity with war, violence and environmental disaster is exposed in our refusal to take responsibility: in this context, McAdams clearly enters into dialogue with recent ecofeminist discussions on human–nature relatedness and concepts of responsibility. This is most evident within the poem 'The Thousand-Year War', where we are asked to '[i]magine how, when the weather changed/we shrugged/and went about our leisure', only to find a 'world pared down to Winter'.[74] McAdams' parting question is highly pertinent: '[w]ill we ever speak of it?'[75]

While an emphasis upon vocalising Native experiences and concerns is evident within the work of Karenne Wood (Monacan), it is notable that her writing also focuses on women's political issues. Born c. 1960, Wood has long been an activist for Monacan tribal concerns, campaigning for Native women's rights and environmental issues, and against domestic violence. More recently, Wood has been active politically as a member of the Tribal Council, and through her work to ensure the repatriation of Native human remains and sacred goods to the Monacan. Wood was awarded the First Book Award from the Native Writers Circle of the Americas in 2001 for her poetry collection *Markings on Earth*. Opening with a ceremonial-style poem to the 'Directions', *Markings on Earth* traces the ways in which Native stories and histories are deeply embedded within specific landscapes. This is especially evident in the poem 'Site of a Massacre', where the soil holds the pain of past atrocities: the 'thuds of/the children collapsing/limp spattered dolls'.[76] Demonstrating the 'lingering grief' that is palpably present, Wood's question to her reader is thus highly pertinent: '[c]an you say you see/only a field or hear/nothing but the breeze[?]'.[77] This painful legacy is also evident in 'In Memory of Shame', where the guilt felt by the colonised is both for a failure to resist enough and for concomitant feelings of complicity. Thus the poem balances deeply contradictory emotions: 'because it was our fault and because we did nothing wrong' and equally 'because we were children or women or not/white or just not enough'.[78] Above all, like many other Native writers, Wood emphasises the deep connections between her Monacan culture and their ancestral landscape, where 'my bones turn with knowings' that 'our songs [are] buried under dry riverbeds' and that 'the true circle of voices' of 'my relative[s]' 'call to us over this ground'.[79] Most importantly, these 'voices of mothers and fathers … ask us/to hear the earth/singing',[80] reiterating the calls within recent Native women's writing for a recognition of the profound nature and ramifications of relationships and relatedness of all forms.

There are, of course, many other emerging Native voices that deserve equal attention. Winners of recent First Books Awards from the Native Writers Circle of the Americas include, for prose, Kimberley Roppolo (*Back to the Blanket* 2004), Mia Heavener (*Tundra Berries* 2005), Judy R. Smith (*Yellow Bird* 2006) and Frederick White (*Welcome to the City of Rainbows* 2006). Recent winners of the poetry awards include Christina M. Castro (*Silence on the Rez* 2004), Cathy Ruiz (*Stirring up the Water* 2004), Kim Shuck (*Smuggling Cherokee* 2005) and Rebecca Hatcher Travis (*Picked Apart the Bones* 2006). In addition, many influential established writers have necessarily, but very regrettably, been excluded, and the interested reader is therefore recommended to look at the writings of Diane Glancy, Joy Harjo, Linda Hogan, LeAnne Howe, Thomas King, Carter Revard, Wendy Rose, Greg Sarris and Ofelia Zepeda, to name but a few.

Such a proliferation of Native writers and texts suggests an increased burgeoning of contemporary Native literature, with the continued availability of established markets drawing upon entrenched Euro-American fascinations with, and conceptualisations of, Native cultures. Additionally, recent writers – such as Erdrich, Alexie and Treuer – have created new readers and markets through the popular appeal of their literary strategies. Nonetheless, clear gender distinctions seem to be emerging in recent Native writings with regard to both literary strategies or topics and Euro-American markets. While recent writings by Native women have successfully tapped into the markets established by Third World feminism, ecofeminism and women writers of colour more generally, Native men writers have been forced to rely upon the appeal of genres and topics conventionally defined as 'male' by the dominant discourse. While the erasure of a wider notion of Native men's politics could have been highly detrimental, recent writings by Native men have, nonetheless, very successfully engaged with popular horror, thrillers and notions of ecocriticism. This form of cultural translation has ensured not only a Native male presence in more mainstream American literature, but also an awareness and discussion of important social, cultural and political issues that are of concern to Native men.

Most significantly, the titles of recent Native texts give ample evidence of Native writers' continued foci upon issues originally raised to the public attention more than two centuries ago by Indian writers such as Samson Occom and William Apess. In this sense, contemporary Native literature offers ongoing resistance to continued colonialism in order to assert a powerful and political Native voice and agency. Like the post-colonial critic Gayatri Spivak, Native writers have always demanded not just to speak but 'to be listened to seriously' without 'benevolent imperialism': Spivak's subsequent question, which she leaves unanswered, is '[w]ho will listen?'.[81] In its creation of an active reader, Native literature provides one answer. Vizenor has suggested that Native writing introduces a critical strategy of 'active listening' on the part of its readers; de Ramirez likewise has argued for a 'conversive' approach to Native writing that, in its allusions to both conversion and conversation, exposes the role of active dialogue and exchange within Native textual strategies. One potential answer to Spivak's question, '[w]ho will listen?', is thus the active, and potentially activist, reader of Native literature. It is, therefore, through Native writers' abilities in cultural translation, and through the direct engagement of readers with the politics of Native texts, that the relationship between Native writers and their readers becomes one of active exchange. In this context, both Native writers and their readers can, according to David Moore, attain the power to 'effect a different reality'.[82]

Notes

1. Arnold Krupat (2002), p. 142.
2. Arnold Krupat and Michael A. Elliott (2006), p. 166.
3. Sherman Alexie (1997), p. 150.
4. Louis Owens (1998), p. 79.
5. Frantz Fanon (1967), p. 48. Fanon's comments are based on his observations of Algeria's battle for independence, 1954–62, and on his findings as a psychiatrist analysing the mental state/attitudes of both colonisers and colonised.
6. Vizenor (1990a), p. 12.
7. Alexie (1991), p. 16.
8. Alexie (2000), pp. 20–1.
9. Krupat and Elliott (2006), p. 168.
10. Alexie (1997), p. 93.
11. Ibid. p. 99.
12. Jacqueline Kilpatrick (1999), pp. 230, 232.
13. Alexie (1998), p. 247.
14. Ibid. p. 324.
15. Ibid. p. 3.
16. Ibid. p. 25.
17. Ibid. p. 12.
18. Ibid. p. 9.
19. Ibid. pp. 12, 14.
20. Ibid. p. 306.
21. Ibid. p. 15.

22. Ibid. p. 16.
23. Ibid. p. 19.
24. Ibid. p. 24.
25. Ibid. p. 32.
26. Ibid. p. 31.
27. Ibid. p. 92.
28. Ibid. p. 94.
29. Ibid. p. 94.
30. Ibid. p. 136.
31. Ibid. p. 136.
32. Ibid. p. 33.
33. Ibid. p. 34.
34. Ibid. p. 232.
35. Ibid. p. 58.
36. Ibid. p. 232.
37. Jack Wilson was the Euro-American name of the Pauite prophet Wovoka, who was adopted by a white family and converted to Christianity, and subsequently introduced the ill-fated Ghost Dance that precipitated the Wounded Knee massacre and the end of the Indian Wars.
38. Alexie (1998), p. 162.
39. The ironic reference is to the seventeenth-century Puritan preacher Cotton Mather, infamous for the damaging nature of his attitude towards Native Americans.
40. Alexie (1998), pp. 58–9.
41. Ibid. pp. 84–5.
42. Ibid. p. 61.
43. Ibid. p. 65.
44. Ibid. p. 61.
45. Ibid. pp. 208–9.
46. Ibid. p. 208.
47. Ibid. p. 215.
48. Ibid. p. 259.
49. Ibid. p. 200.
50. Owens (1998), p. 80.
51. Krupat (2002), p. 117.
52. David Treuer (1997), p. 3.
53. See, for example, Robert Franklin Gish's discussion of his identification by academic colleagues 'as a professor of "buffalo chip lit"' accused of 'corrupting the "Great Tradition"' of English literature due to his introduction of Native literary texts within university literature courses. Gish (1999), p. ix.
54. Aaron A. Carr (1995), p. 4.
55. Ibid. p. 125.
56. Irvin Morris (1997), p. 33.
57. Ibid. p. 37.
58. Ibid. p. 34.
59. Ibid. p. 23.
60. Sherwin Bitsui (2003), p. 3.
61. Ibid. pp. 3–4.
62. Ibid. p. 4.

63. Ibid. p. 17.
64. Ibid. p. 18.
65. Ibid. pp. 63–4.
66. Ibid. p. 64.
67. Deborah Miranda (1997) p. ix.
68. Ibid. p. ix.
69. Ibid. p. 48.
70. Ibid. p. 48.
71. Ibid. p. xiii.
72. Janet McAdams (2000), p. 13.
73. Ibid. p. 16.
74. Ibid. pp. 29–30.
75. Ibid. p. 30.
76. Karenne Wood (2001), p. 20.
77. Ibid. p. 20.
78. Ibid. p. 44.
79. Ibid. p. 51.
80. Ibid. p. 51.
81. Gayatri Spivak (1990), pp. 59–60.
82. David L. Moore (1999), p. 151.

Bibliography and Further Reading

Achebe, Chinua (1993), 'The African Writer and the English Language', in Patrick Williams and Laura Chrisman (eds), *Colonial Discourse and Post-Colonial Theory: a Reader*, London: Harvester Wheatsheaf, pp. 428–34.

Adamson, Joni (2001), *American Indian Literature, Environmental Justice, and Ecocriticism: The Middle Place*, Tucson: University of Arizona Press.

Alexie, Sherman (1997), *The Lone Ranger and Tonto Fistfight in Heaven*, London: Vintage.

Alexie, Sherman (1998), *Indian Killer*, London: Vintage.

Alexie, Sherman (2000), *One Stick Song*, New York: Hanging Loose Press.

Allen, Paula Gunn (1992), *The Sacred Hoop: Recovering the Feminine in American Indian Traditions*, Boston: Beacon Press.

Apess, William (1992), *A Son of the Forest and Other Writings*, Amherst: University of Massachusetts Press.

Ashcroft, Bill, Gareth Griffiths and Helen Tiffin (eds) (1989), *The Empire Writes Back: Theory and Practice in Post-Colonial Literatures*, London: Routledge.

Ashwill, Gary (1994), 'Savagism and Its Discontents: James Fenimore Cooper and his Native American Contemporaries', *American Transcendental Quarterly*, 8:3, 211–27.

Barnett, Louise K. and James L. Thorson (eds) (1999), *Leslie Marmon Silko: A Collection of Critical Essays*, Albuquerque: University of New Mexico Press.

Barth, Gunther (ed.) (1998), *The Lewis and Clark Expedition: Selections from the Journals*, New York: Bedford/St. Martin's Press.

Basso, Keith H. (1996), *Wisdom Sits in Places: Landscape and Language Among the Western Apache*, Albuquerque: University of New Mexico Press.

Beidler, Peter G. (1995), 'Literary Criticism in *Cogewea:* Mourning Dove's Protagonist Reads *The Brand*', *American Indian Culture and Research Journal*, 19:2, 45–65.

Bernardin, Susan (2001), 'On the Meeting Grounds of Sentiment: S. Alice Callahan's *Wynema, a Child of the Forest*', *American Transcendental Quarterly*, 15:3, 209–24.

Bevis, William (1987), 'Native American Novels: Homing In', in Brian Swann and Arnold Krupat (eds), *Recovering the Word: Essays on Native American Literature*, Berkeley: University of California Press, pp. 580–620.

Bhabha, Homi (1994), *The Location of Culture*, London: Routledge.

Biolsi, Thomas and Larry Zimmerman (eds) (1997), *Indians and Anthropologists: Vine Deloria Jr. and the Critique of Anthropology*, Tucson: University of Arizona Press.

Bitsui, Sherwin (2003), *Shapeshift*, Tucson: University of Arizona Press.

Black Elk (1979), *Black Elk Speaks: Being the Life Story of a Holy Man of the Oglala Sioux*, ed. John G. Neihardt, Lincoln: University of Nebraska Press.

Blaeser, Kimberly M. (1996), *Gerald Vizenor: Writing in the Oral Tradition*, Norman: University of Oklahoma Press.

Bradford, William (2003), 'Of Plymouth Plantation', in Nina Baym (ed.), *The Norton Anthology of American Literature* 6th edn, New York: W. W. Norton & Co., vol. 1: pp. 157–95.

Callahan, S. Alice (1997), *Wynema, A Child of the Forest*, ed. A. LaVonne Brown Ruoff, Lincoln: University of Nebraska Press.

Caputi, Jane (1992), 'The Heart of Knowledge: Nuclear Themes in Native American Thought and Literature', *American Indian Culture and Research Journal*, 16:4, 1–27.

Carr, Aaron A. (1995), *Eye Killers*, Norman: University of Oklahoma Press.

Cheyfitz, Eric (2002), 'The (Post)Colonial Predicament of Native American Studies', *Interventions: International Journal of Postcolonial Studies*, 4:3, 405–27.

Christensen, Laird (1999), 'Not Exactly Like Heaven: Theological Imperialism in *The Surrounded*', *Studies in American Indian Literatures*, 11:1, 2–16.

Clifford, James (1988), *The Predicament of Culture: Twentieth Century Ethnography, Literature, and Art*, Cambridge, MA: Harvard University Press.

Dannenberg, Anne Marie (1996), '"Where, then, shall we place the hero of the Wilderness?": William Apess's *Eulogy on King Philip* and Doctrines of Racial Destiny', in Helen Jaskoski (ed.), *Early Native American Writing: New Critical Essays*, Cambridge: Cambridge University Press: pp. 66–82.

de Ramirez, Susan Berry Brill (1999), *Contemporary American Indian Literatures and the Oral Tradition*, Tucson: University of Arizona Press.

Durham, Jimmie (1993), *A Certain Lack of Coherence: Writings on Art and Cultural Politics*, London: Kala Press.

Eastman, Charles A. (1971), *Indian Boyhood*, New York: Dover Publications.

Eastman, Charles A. (2001), *From the Deep Woods to Civilization: Chapters in the Autobiography of an Indian*, Chicago: Lakeside Classics.

Emberley, Julia V. (1993), *Thresholds of Difference: Feminist Critique, Native Women's Writings, Postcolonial Theory*, Toronto: University of Toronto Press.

Erdrich, Louise (1994), *Love Medicine*, London: Flamingo.

Fanon, Frantz (1967), *The Wretched of the Earth*, London: Penguin.

Fisher, Dexter (ed.) (1980), *The Third Woman: Minority Women Writers in the United States*, Boston: Houghton Mifflin.

Fisher, Dexter (1981), 'Introduction', *Cogewea the Half-Blood*, Lincoln: University of Nebraska Press.

Fleck, Richard F. (1994), *'Black Elk Speaks:* A Native American View of Nineteenth-Century American History', *Journal of American Culture*, 17:1, 67–9.

Frischkorn, Craig (1999), 'The Shadow of Tsoai: Autobiographical Bear Power in N. Scott Momaday's *The Ancient Child*', *Journal of Popular Culture*, 33:2, 23–9.

Gish, Robert Franklin (1999), 'Preface: Silko's Power of Story', in Louise K. Barnett and James L. Thorson (eds), *Leslie Marmon Silko: A Collection of Critical Essays*, Albuquerque: University of New Mexico Press, pp. vii–xi.

Hale, Frederick (1993), 'Acceptance and Rejection of Assimilation in the Works of Luther Standing Bear', *Studies in American Indian Literatures*, 5:4, 25–41.

Hans, Birgit (1996), 'Rethinking History: A Context for *The Surrounded*', in John L. Purdy (ed.), *The Legacy of D'Arcy McNickle: Writer, Historian, Activist*, Norman: University of Oklahoma Press, pp. 33–52.

Harriot, Thomas (2003), 'A Brief and True Report of the New Found Land of Virginia', in Nina Baym (ed.), *The Norton Anthology of American Literature* 6th edn, New York: W. W. Norton & Co., vol. 1: pp. 80–5.

Hunter, Carol (1982), 'The Historical Context in John Joseph Mathews' *Sundown*', *MELUS*, 9:1, 61–72.

Jarvis, Brian (1998), *Postmodern Cartographies: The Geographical Imagination in Contemporary American Culture*, London: Macmillan.

Jaskoski, Helen (1990), 'Thinking Woman's Children and the Bomb', *Explorations in Ethnic Studies*, 13:2, 1–22.

Jaskoski, Helen (1992), 'Mightier than the Sword? An Introduction', *Studies in American Indian Literatures*, 4:2/3, 1–14.

Jaskoski, Helen (ed.) (1996), *Early Native American Writing: New Critical Essays*, Cambridge: Cambridge University Press.

Jehlen, Myra and Michael Warner (1977), *The English Literatures of America 1500–1800*, New York: Routledge.

Kelsey, Penelope Myrtle (2003), 'A "Real Indian" to the Boy Scouts: Charles Eastman as a Resistance Writer', *Western American Literature*, 38:1, 30–48.

Kent, Alicia (1999), 'Mourning Dove's *Cogewea*: Writing Her Way into Modernity', *MELUS*, 24:3, 39–66.

Kilpatrick, Jacqueline (1999), *Celluloid Indians: Native Americans and Film*, Lincoln: University of Nebraska Press.

Krupat, Arnold (1999), 'From "Half-Blood" to "Mixedblood": Cogewea and the "Discourse of Indian Blood"', *Modern Fiction Studies*, 45:1, 120–45.

Krupat, Arnold (2002), *Red Matters: Native American Studies*, Philadelphia: University of Pennsylvania Press.

Krupat, Arnold and Michael A. Elliott (2006), 'American Indian Fiction and Anticolonial Resistance', in Eric Cheyfitz (ed.), *The Columbia Guide to American Indian Literatures of the United States Since 1945*, New York: Columbia University Press, pp. 127–82.

LaLonde, Chris (2002), *Grave Concerns, Trickster Turns: the Novels of Louis Owens*, Norman: University of Oklahoma Press.

Larson, Sidner (2005), 'Colonization as Subtext in James Welch's *Winter in the Blood*', *American Indian Quarterly*, 29:1/2, 274–80.

Limerick, Patricia Nelson (1988), *The Legacy of Conquest: the Unbroken Past of the American West*, New York: W. W. Norton & Co.

Lincoln, Kenneth (1983), *Native American Renaissance*, Berkeley: University of California Press.

Lowe, John (1992), 'Space and Freedom in the Golden Republic: Yellow Bird's *The Life and Adventures of Joaquín Murieta, the Celebrated California Bandit*', *Studies in American Indian Literatures*, 4:2/3, 106–22.

McAdams, Janet (2000), *The Island of Lost Luggage*, Tucson: University of Arizona Press.

McClure, Andrew S. (1999), 'Sarah Winnemucca: [Post]Indian Princess and Voice of the Paiutes', *MELUS*, 24:2, 29–51.

McFarland, Ron (2000), *Understanding James Welch*, Columbia: University of South Carolina Press.

McNickle, D'Arcy (1994), *The Surrounded*, Albuquerque: University of New Mexico Press.

Mann, Barbara Alice (2005), *George Washington's War on Native America*, Westport, CT: Praeger.

Mathews, John Joseph (1988), *Sundown*, Norman: University of Oklahoma Press.

Mihesuah, Devon A. (2000), 'American Indians, Anthropologists, Pothunters, and Repatriation: Ethical, Religious, and Political Differences', in Devon A. Mihesuah (ed.), *The Repatriation Reader: Who Owns American Indian Remains?*, Lincoln: University of Nebraska Press, pp. 95–105.

Miranda, Deborah A. (1999), *Indian Cartography*, New York: Greenfield Review Press.

Mohante, Chandra Talpade (2003), *Feminism Without Borders: Decolonizing Theory, Practicing Solidarity*, Durham, NC: Duke University Press.

Momaday, N. Scott (1976), *The Names: A Memoir*, Tucson: University of Arizona Press.

Momaday, N. Scott (1989), *House Made of Dawn*, New York: Harper and Row.

Momaday, N. Scott (1992), *In the Presence of the Sun*, New York: St. Martin's Press.

Momaday, N. Scott (1999), *In the Bear's House*, New York: St. Martin's Press.

Moore, David L. (1999), 'Silko's Blood Sacrifice: The Circulating Witness in *Almanac of the Dead*', in Louise K. Barnett and James L. Thorson (eds), *Leslie Marmon Silko: A Collection of Critical Essays*, Albuquerque: University of New Mexico Press, pp. 149–83.

Morris, Irvin (1997), *From the Glittering World: A Navajo Story*, Norman: University of Oklahoma Press.

Mourning Dove (1981), *Cogewea, the Half-Blood*, Lincoln: University of Nebraska Press.

Murray, David (1991), *Forked Tongues: Speech, Writing and Representation in North American Indian Texts*, Bloomington: Indiana University Press.

Nelson, Robert M. (1993), *Place and Vision: the Function of Landscape in Native American Fiction*, New York: Peter Lang.

Occom, Samson (1997), '*Sermon Preached by Samson Occom ... at the Execution of Moses Paul, an Indian*', in Myra Jehlen and Michael Warner (eds), *The English Literatures of America, 1500–1800*, New York: Routledge, pp. 643–59.

Ortiz, Simon (1983), *Fightin': New and Collected Storries*, Chicago: Thunder's Mouth Press.

Ortiz, Simon (1992), *Woven Stone*, Tucson: University of Arizona Press.

Ortiz, Simon (1998), *After and Before the Lightning*, Tucson: University of Arizona Press.

Ortiz, Simon (2002), *Out There Somewhere*, Tucson: University of Arizona Press.

Owens, Louis (1992), *Other Destinies: Understanding the American Indian Novel*, Norman: University of Oklahoma Press.

Owens, Louis (1994), *Bone Game*, Norman: University of Oklahoma Press.

Owens, Louis (1998), *Mixedblood Messages: Literature, Film, Family, Place*, Norman: University of Oklahoma Press.

Owens, Louis (2001), *I Hear the Train: Reflections, Inventions, Refractions*, Norman: University of Oklahoma Press.

Powell, Malea (2002), 'Rhetorics of Survivance: How American Indians *Use* Writing', *College Composition and Communication*, 53:3, 396–434.

Powell, Timothy B. (1999), 'Historical Multiculturalism: Cultural Complexity in the First Native American Novel', in Timothy B. Powell (ed.), *Beyond the Binary: Reconstructing Cultural Identity in a Multicultural Context*, New Brunswick: Rutgers University Press, pp. 185–204.

Rainwater, Catherine (1990), 'Reading Between Worlds: Narrativity in the Fiction of Louise Erdrich', *American Literature*, 62:3, 405–22.

Rainwater, Catherine (1999), *Dreams of Fiery Stars: the Transformation of Native American Fiction*, Philadelphia: University of Pennsylvania Press.

Reid, E. Shelley (2000), 'The Stories We Tell: Louise Erdrich's Identity Narratives', *MELUS*, 25:3/4, 65–86.

Ridge, John Rollin (2003), *The Life and Adventures of Joaquín Murieta, the Celebrated California Bandit*, ed. Paul Reilly, Grass Valley: Poitin Press.

Ridge, John Rollin (2004), *The Poems of John Rollin Ridge: A Reproduction of the 1868 Publication*, eds James W. Parins and Jeff Ward, The Electronic Text Center, University of Virginia Library. http://etext.virginia.edu/toc/modeng/public/RidThep.html.

Rowe, John Carlos (1998), 'Highway Robbery: "Indian Removal", the Mexican-American War, and American Identity in *The Life and Adventures of Joaquín Murieta*', *Novel: A Forum on Fiction*, 31:2, 149–73.

Rowlandson, Mary (2003), 'A Narrative of the Captivity and Restoration of Mrs Mary Rowlandson', in Nina Baym (ed.), *The Norton Anthology of American Literature* 6th edn, New York: W. W. Norton & Co., vol. 1: pp. 309–40.

Ruoff, A. LaVonne Brown (1992), 'Introduction: Samson Occom's *Sermon Preached by Samson Occom ... at the Execution of Moses Paul, an Indian*', *Studies in American Indian Literatures*, 4:2/3, 76–81.

Ruoff, A. LaVonne Brown (1997), 'Editor's Introduction', in S. Alice Callahan, *Wynema, A Child of the Forest*, Lincoln: University of Nebraska Press, pp. xiii–xlviii.

Sando, Joe S. (1998), *Pueblo Nations: Eight Centuries of Pueblo Indian History*, Santa Fe: Clear Light Publishers.

Schubnell, Matthias (1985), *N. Scott Momaday: The Cultural and Literary Background*, Norman: University of Oklahoma Press.

Sequoya, Jana (1993), 'How (!) is an Indian?', in Arnold Krupat (ed.), *New Voices in Native American Literary Criticism*, Washington: Smithsonian Institution Press, pp. 453–73.

Silko, Leslie Marmon (1981), *Storyteller*, New York: Arcade Publishing.

Silko, Leslie Marmon (1986), *Ceremony*, New York: Penguin.

Silko, Leslie Marmon (1991), *Almanac of the Dead*, New York: Penguin.

Silko, Leslie Marmon (1996), *Yellow Woman and a Beauty of the Spirit*, New York: Simon and Schuster.

Spivak, Gayatri (1990), *The Post-Colonial Critic: Interviews, Strategies, Dialogues*, ed. S. Harasayam, New York: Routledge.

Standing Bear, Luther (1975), *My People, the Sioux*, Lincoln: University of Nebraska Press.

Standing Bear, Luther (1978), *Land of the Spotted Eagle*, Lincoln: University of Nebraska Press.

Swann, Brian and Arnold Krupat (eds) (1987), *Recovering the Word: Essays on Native American Literature*, Berkeley: University of California Press.

Szasz, Margaret Connell (1994), *Between White and Indian Worlds: The Cultural Broker*, Norman: University of Oklahoma Press.

Tapahonso, Luci (1993), *Sáani Dahataal: The Women are Singing*, Tucson: University of Arizona Press.

Tapahonso, Luci (1997), *Blue Horses Rush In*, Tucson: University of Arizona Press.

Tatonetti, Lisa (2004), 'Behind the Shadows of Wounded Knee: The Slippage of Imagination in *Wynema, A Child of the Forest*', *Studies in American Indian Literatures*, 16:1, 1–31.

Treuer, David (1997), *Little*, London: Granta.

Trope, Jack F. and Walter R. Echo-Hawk (2000), 'The Native American Graves Protection and Repatriation Act, Background and Legislative History', in Devon A. Mihesuah (ed.), *The Repatriation Reader: Who Owns American Indian Remains?*, Lincoln: University of Nebraska Press, pp. 123–68.

Van Dyke, Annette (1992), 'An Introduction to *Wynema, A Child of the Forest*, by Sophia Alice Callahan', *Studies in American Indian Literatures*, 4:2/3, 123–8.

Vizenor, Gerald (1990a), *Crossbloods: Bone Courts, Bingo, and Other Reports*, Minneapolis: University of Minnesota Press.

Vizenor, Gerald (1990b), *Interior Landscapes*, Minneapolis: University of Minnesota Press.

Vizenor, Gerald (1994), *Manifest Manners: Postindian Warriors of Survivance*, Hanover, NH: Wesleyan University Press.

Vizenor, Gerald (2000), *Chancers*, Norman: University of Oklahoma Press.

Walters, Anna Lee (1988), *Ghost Singer*, Albuquerque: University of New Mexico Press.

Walters, Anna Lee (1992), *Talking Indian: Reflections on Survival and Writing*, New York: Firebrand Books.

Walters, Anna Lee, Peggy Beck and Nia Francisco (1996), *The Sacred: Ways of Knowledge, Sources of Life*, Tsaile: Navajo Community College Press.

Warrior, Robert (2004), 'Eulogy on William Apess: Speculations on His New York Death', *Studies in American Indian Literatures*, 16:2, 1–13.

Welch, James (1986), *Winter in the Blood*, New York: Penguin.

Welch, James (1995), *Killing Custer: The Battle of the Little Bighorn and the Fate of the Plains Indians*, New York: Penguin.

Welch, James (1997), 'Introduction' to the *Third Catalogue of Native American Literature*, Ken Lopez. http://www.lopezbooks.com/articles/welch.html.

Williams, Roger (2003), 'A Key into the Language of America', in Nina Baym (ed.), *The Norton Anthology of American Literature* 6th edn, New York and London: W. W. Norton & Co., vol. 1: pp. 227–34.

Winnemucca, Sarah (1994), *Life Among the Piutes: Their Wrongs and Claims*, Reno: University of Nevada Press.

Wood, Karenne (2001), *Markings on Earth*, Tucson: University of Arizona Press.

Index

The British Association for American Studies (BAAS)

The British Association for American Studies was founded in 1955 to promote the study of the United States of America. It welcomes applications for membership from anyone interested in the history, society, government and politics, economics, geography, literature, creative arts, culture and thought of the USA.

The Association publishes a newsletter twice yearly, holds an annual national conference, supports regional branches and provides other membership services, including preferential subscription rates to the *Journal of American Studies*.

Membership enquiries may be addressed to the BAAS Secretary. For contact details visit our website: www.baas.ac.uk.